By Kenneth Atchity

Homer's Iliad: The Shield of Memory
Italian Literature: Roots and Branches
Homer: Critical Essays
A Writer's Time
The Mercury Transition
Cajun Household Wisdom
The Renaissance Reader
The Classical Greek Reader
The Classical Roman Reader

WRITING
TREATMENTS
THAT SELL

KENNETH ATCHITY · CHI-LI WONG

WRITING
TREATMENTS
THAT SELL

· · · · ·

How to Create and Market
Your Story Ideas to the
Motion Picture and TV Industry

SECOND EDITION

A Holt Paperback
Henry Holt and Company · New York

Holt Paperbacks
Henry Holt and Company, LLC
Publishers since 1866
175 Fifth Avenue
New York, New York 10010
www.henryholt.com

A Holt Paperback® and ® are registered trademarks of
Henry Holt and Company, LLC.

Library of Congress Cataloging-in-Publication Data
Atchity, Kenneth John.
    Writing treatments that sell : how to create and market
your story ideas to the motion picture and TV industry /
Kenneth Atchity & Chi-Li Wong.—Rev. Holt Paperbacks ed.
        p.   cm.
"A Holt Paperback."
Includes bibliographical references and index.
ISBN-13: 978-0-8050-7278-5
ISBN-10: 0-8050-7278-0
    1. Motion picture authorship.   2. Television authorship.
3. Treatments   (Motion pictures, television, etc.)
I. Wong, Chi-Li.   II. Title.
    PN1996.A84 2003
    808.2'3—dc21   2002027556

Second Holt Paperbacks Edition 2003

Printed in the United States of America
13   15   14   12

Contents

. . .

Acknowledgments to the First Edition

■ ■ ■

We're grateful to our friends, clients, and associates in the entertainment world for doing their best to keep us on track with what we say here about the treatment. In particular we want to credit, alphabetically:

Steve Alten, novelist and client, for his hard work and inspiration.

David Angsten, AEI development VP, for his comments on and off the court.

Theresa Burns, our editor at Owl Books, for her dogged persistence in making the text clearer and more useful.

Joel Carlins, for his legal wisdom and limo wanderings.

Moira Coyne, for her excellent and detailed notes.

Monica Faulkner, Writers' Lifeline senior editor, for her conscientious notes.

Rosemary McKenna, for her careful proofreading and incisive comments.

Joel McKuin, *Jeff Frankl*, and *David Colden* of Colden-McKuin, for legal counsel and service beyond the call of duty.

Paul D. Nawrocki, of the Writers Guild of America, for his contributions to chapter 8.

Sandy Watt, our loyal and indefatigable agent, who insisted that we do this book.

Norton Wright, friend, mentor, and heroic protagonist, for clarifying and correcting.

And to the authors of all the books we cannibalized to paint a picture of the working entertainment industry and of the writer's struggle, especially William Safire and Leonard Safir for their *Good Advice on Writing*. We list our sources as recommended reading at the end of this book.

The authors take full credit for errors and omissions and blame discrepancies on a volatile and challenging industry that changes its way of operating not only yearly, but daily.

A Note on the Revised Edition

So many events, so many people have come into our lives since the first edition, that it's impossible to thank everyone strongly enough here. We're deeply appreciative to the industry and our stars for our good fortune in both television and film. And we appreciate our many readers who called for repeated printings of this book, and for this revised and expanded second edition, which we hope will be even more helpful for the extra and updated information it includes.

Thanks to Craig Perry at Zide-Perry Entertainment; Teddy Zee at Overbrook; Matt Gross; Terrence Myers at Laurence Mark Productions; Wendy Japhets and Donald De Line at De Line Pictures; Scott Aversano at Scott Rudin Productions; Stuart Cornfeld at Red Hour; Kara Francis and Peter Cramer at New Regency; Carla Hacken and Peter Kang at Fox 2000; Susanna Jolly and Jennifer Moyer at Alphaville; Kristin Harms and Tracy Underwood at John Wells Productions; Richard Brener at New Line; Bryan Hickel at Adam Schroeder Productions; Valarie Phillips, Debbie Klein, Matt Bedrosian, Lucy Stille, and Pat Quinn at Paradigm; Jon Levin at Creative Artists; Clair Belcher and Jason Burns at United Talent Agency; Victoria Wisdom at BWK; Steve Weiss at William Morris Agency; Margo Hamilton; and to then-client, now partner John Scott Shepherd.

For help in putting this revision together, we're particularly grateful to our editors at Holt, Elizabeth Stein, Rebecca Lindenberg, and Deborah Brody; to Andrea McKeown, of the writerslifeline.com; AEI client and Nicholls multifinalist John Robert Marlow; Brenna Lui, AEI Executive VP; and producer Judy Cairo, of Cairo-Simpson Entertainment. For his generous consultation on all matters regarding television, we're especially indebted to Russell Schwartz, Executive VP, Creative Affairs, Business and Planning, HBO Independent Productions; and to Kayoko Mitsumatsu for sharing her prodigious research on copyright.

Los Angeles and New York
2002

Introduction

● ● ●

Hollywood is one place in the world
where you can die of encouragement.
                                    —Dorothy Parker

This book answers the two questions we're asked most often by aspiring screenwriters at film and television workshops, lectures, and writers' conferences:

> What's a treatment?
> How do I write a treatment?

The answers provided in *Writing Treatments That Sell* are based on our own practical experience as screenwriters, literary managers, and producers (for TV and film)—as well as what we've learned from our development and editorial associates and clients at Atchity Editorial/Entertainment International, Inc., and AEI's Writers' Lifeline, Inc.

Our advice is descriptive rather than prescriptive, based on observations of industry practices rather than on philosophical principles. This means you should use what works for you and ignore the rest—because everyone who knows anything about show business knows that there are no hard-and-fast rules. Success comes through individual effort combined with access and luck (luck being just another word for timing). If you're serious about your writing career, you'll figure out everything we say here on your own. We're just hoping to expedite your learning curve so you get where you want to go sooner rather than later—and with fewer painful detours.

The third frequently asked question that inspired us to write this book is "Why do I need a treatment?" The honest answer is "If you have already written a screenplay, or if you're very lucky, or both, you may not." But sooner or later, if you want to sell a story idea without writing the entire script, you'll need to know about treatments. If you're having story problems *now*, a treatment will help solve those problems. The two primary functions served by the treatment in today's entertainment business are *selling* and *diagnosing a story*.

Every storyteller dreams of seeing the characters in his story come alive each week on television or up on the silver screen. There's nothing more exciting! We've shared this happy experience with the writers we manage. A project called *Sign of the Watcher*, by Brett Bartlett, was rejected (under the title *Walk into My Parlor*) fourteen times in its first submission to buyers. AEI's Writers' Lifeline reevaluated Brett's story, used the treatment form to focus plot and characters, changed the title, and sent the treatment of the retooled story back out through Brett's manager-producer, Warren Zide. Several studios were intrigued enough by the treatment to request the full manuscript, which eventually sold to Propaganda Films for $750,000. Was refocusing the story easy for the writer? No. It took months of reworking the characters and action line and rewriting—dozens of times—the treatment we used as our selling tool. It was the roller-coaster ride of Brett's life. Brett's journey began with the excitement of a great story idea, the dream of seeing his story become a film, then passed through the fright of the dips and sudden turns of rejection and rewriting, to the exhilaration of having hung on to the end, a little out of breath, a bit bruised but, damn, what a ride! And Brett's not the only one who's taken this ride.

With the proliferation of channels and new cinematic

distribution media, new writers are in demand now more than ever before. The Writers Guild reported that between 1985 and 1994, screenwriting accounted for 393 millionaires. The highest-paid 25 percent of employed writers earned more than $575,000 each in 2000. "Writers' odds have never been better," according to Thom Taylor, writing in *ScreenWriter Quarterly*. But because an estimated 10,000 scripts are submitted to Hollywood every year, in those same nine years 90,000 scripts were read to produce those 393 big winners—and only 10 percent of the scripts submitted even get read. Those odds are 229 to 1. Still, we've always believed, and advise our writers to believe, that "the odds don't apply to us." We've written this book to help you stack the cards in your favor with inside industry information about the buying and selling of stories, and advice on how to use the treatment to accelerate your break into Hollywood.

Most people we know in the industry take their work very seriously. We certainly do. The game of creating images for the big and small screens is the most exciting one we know, and its players are intense. But though writing and selling your writing is a serious business with serious upside potential, don't get so serious that you forget the fun of creating. Creation, after all, is an adult form of play. Don't be so married to your way of playing that you can't consider making a change: a change that might sell your story, or that might sell it for more money. Keep yourself inspired by continuing to write while you market what you've already written; if one story doesn't sell today, it might tomorrow. And when you sell the first one for big bucks, all the others you've written suddenly become valuable commodities.

TREATMENTS AS CLIFFHANGERS

Treatments should feel like pictures rushing together to form a story in which you can see the characters and hear them speak. A treatment should never read like a synopsis, like dull beats of a plot moving forward, trudging toward a predictable outcome. When you're reading the pages, however simple, the thrill of the story must be captured. And how do you do that? You forget that you're writing a treatment and tell the story like a classic around-the-campfire cliffhanger—as if every event happened before your very eyes and you can't wait to share it.

The structure should reveal itself like the design of the master architect crossed with a clever composer. The beginning immediately captivates. Why? Because you know exactly where to start the story because you have thought about it very carefully. And you know exactly whose face has just appeared on the screen. The character's journey should feel random and spontaneous, as if rolling down a hill, not a step-by-step contrivance of events.

The energy of the beginning should carry us into the middle—and now you're in trouble. The subplot has to subtly kick in here, and its momentum carries us through to the end.

An architect's blueprint or a sheet of music is dull only to those who do not have the passion to appreciate its execution. These "treatments" of a breathtaking building or a moving symphony should be just as exciting as seeing the Pantheon or hearing the Ninth Symphony for the first time. And this is your job. When you tell your story, you'll be like the projectionist alone in the dark booth, until the lights come back on again and then everyone understands—finally—exactly what you wanted to say.

—Victoria Wisdom, agent and partner,
Becsey-Wisdom-Kaledjian

We start, in chapter 1, by examining exactly what a treatment is and how it's used in the industry to make a sale and/or to lay out a story. Here we also differentiate the treatment from its cousins the synopsis, the outline, the beat sheet, and the coverage. Chapter 2 discusses original treatments for motion pictures, emphasizing the dramatic elements that effective treatments contain: hooks, climaxes, protagonist, conflict, action, scenes, theme, and character. We offer a summary outline of the motion picture's three-act structure that reminds you to ask yourself: Who's my protagonist? What's her problem? How does she overcome it?

Treatments for television, following their own special rules and with their distinctive seven-act structure, are the subject of chapter 3, in which we also consider television's need for subject matter to fit demographically specialized audiences. Chapter 3 also shows you how a television movie deal works, and how to get from treatment to deal. In chapter 4, we present the *bible*, as the treatment for a dramatic television series is known in the industry. Chapter 5 scrutinizes the writing of treatments "based on" true stories, "inspired by" true stories, and "from" true stories, and also tells you how to find and secure the rights to a true story. Adapting a novel to film is the subject of chapter 6, which offers, as an example of the adaptation treatment, *Shadow of the Cypress*, a modern retelling of *Jane Eyre*.

Once you know what a treatment is and how to write one for every occasion, *Writing Treatments* moves in chapter 7 to the crucial questions, Who are the buyers? and What are they buying? We deal here with both the complex and unpredictable television markets and the more stable feature film market. In presenting the latter, we tell you how to distinguish between *in-house production companies* and *independent producers*, and what to ask of each as you approach them with your story.

This leads naturally to a question we hear repeatedly: "How do I protect myself?" Chapter 8 answers the question both technically—by outlining copyright law and Writers Guild of America registration procedures—and practically, by letting you know what the actual industry practice is when a story is submitted for consideration. Our industry glossary will help you interpret terms such as *turnaround*, *buzz*, and *right of first refusal*; and understand exactly what *option* and *high concept* mean. *Writing Treatments* concludes with a list of recommended further reading, which includes the sources we've drawn on in preparing this book.

Two final pieces of introductory advice: In learning about all the trees in the entertainment industry woods, don't lose sight of the woods themselves. As several coaches before us have pointed out, assuming timing is on your side, there are only two important considerations in making a solid sale: *concept* and *castability*. You have to have a great idea, with a "wow factor" of 7 to 10 (on a scale of 10), if you want to break into show business in a big way. *High concept* means an idea so clearly focused that it can be expressed in few words, like "Jurassic shark," the pitch we used to sell Steve Alten's *Meg* to Walt Disney Pictures and Doubleday-Bantam. The second element is *castability*, which simply means creating a protagonist that every top star in the business will want to play. Focus on those two, and, with the help of the practical techniques presented in this book, you will find your way into the fold.

Our second piece of final advice is *Maintain your optimism*. According to Jack Valenti, entertainment copyrights—which begin with you, the writer—were worth $89 billion in 2001. Optimism is the only faith capable of sustaining the daily ups and downs of the screenwriter's life; besides that, it's the attitude your successful entertainment industry colleagues will recognize as their own, and for which they'll respect you the most. You'll succeed in this business if you believe you'll succeed, and after you make an irrevocable commitment to continue writing and marketing your stories until your success is acknowledged by both buyers and audience. See yourself receiving that first Emmy or Oscar. And don't forget to send us our commission!

1

The Nature and Role
of the Treatment

. . .

I read part of it all the way through.
—Samuel Goldwyn

The key to closing a deal in Hollywood is getting a *player* (as deal makers are called) to read your work. Since the entertainment industry is so personal and depends on access to buyers—like a vice president at a network, a development executive at a star's or director's production company, or the president of a studio—the sequence of events by which a seller convinces a buyer generally begins with a chance encounter or a telephone conversation that conveys urgency. Ideally, the buyer responds by saying, "Okay, send it over."

"Promise me you'll read it yourself."

"I promise," the buyer lies, or maybe even means it at the time. "How long is it?"

"Three hundred pages."

"Do you have a treatment?"

"Yes."

"Good. Why don't you send that along, too?"

Because the buyer rarely has time to read a screenplay or a novel without knowing what he's about to read, the treatment very often becomes the most important tool in the selling sequence.

When community education courses advertise "Sell your ideas to TV," they mislead inexperienced writers who don't understand that the word *ideas* is being used loosely. The inexperienced writer doesn't sell an idea. Instead, he must write his idea *at least* into a treatment and try to get it into the hands of an active film-maker. Second only to writing an entire screenplay or teleplay "on spec" (the industry term for "speculative work done without a contract"), your treatment may be the best tool for getting a foot in the door of moviemaking.

But the treatment is a strange animal, quite unlike any other kind of writing. If a screenplay focuses the story for a film, the treatment does the same thing for a screenplay. Yet there are as many kinds of treatments as there are writers. None of this confusion helps the new writer trying to break into the business, but for the outsider's purposes, what distinguishes one treatment from another is simply its effectiveness in making the sale, and/or laying out the story.

With the proliferation of cable programming, the expansion of video rentals, and the industry's acutely competitive need for films and programs to fill home and theatrical screens, the function of the treatment in today's motion picture and television industries has expanded. The usefulness of the treatment is behind the scenes, in developing a story; and/or in pitching it efficiently to filmmakers who might be sold on making the writer's story into a film.

> A script is a selling tool; it's not a blueprint for a movie, in spite of what they tell you. Screenplays ought to be sold as prose. It's entirely about storytelling, explaining that story to the reader.
>
> —Kurt Wimmer

Treatments can help the writer acquire an overview of his story, presenting the profile of the woods in contrast to the varied texture of the trees. By the same token, for a story editor or development executive the treatment is a useful diagnostic tool for getting the story straight. By reading a short treatment, the editor obtains a perspective that may be lost when reading a faulty script.

Nothing can take the place of a live pitch, where the writer dramatizes his story for an attentive audience. But a written pitch is still needed to assist in the next stage of the filmmaking process, where the story is "repitched" to the next person higher up along the chain of production. When an oral pitch is impossible, a written pitch can do the job. (The treatment is a written pitch.) Everything we say in this book is intended to assist you, the writer, in understanding and creating the treatment to serve one or the other, or both, of these two crucial purposes.

For our purposes then, a treatment is a relatively brief, loosely narrative written pitch of a story intended for production as a film for theatrical exhibition or television broadcast. Written in user-friendly, dramatic, but straightforward and highly visual prose, in the present tense, the treatment highlights in broad strokes your story's hook, primary characters, acts and action line, setting, point of view, and most dramatic scenes and turning points.

The Key Elements of a Treatment

Let's take a closer look at the key elements that make a good treatment:

"relatively brief": A treatment's brevity or length is relative to the writer's purpose at hand. A top network executive, such as the Vice President of Motion Pictures for Television, may request a one-page treatment; his boss, the Senior Vice President of Motion Pictures for Television, may need only one paragraph. The writer may have started with a twenty-page treatment, which he used to clarify the story elements as he was thinking them through.

"loosely narrative": A treatment both *tells* and *shows* a story, moving from one to the other as the writer sees fit in his overall aim of helping his audience—whether an individual buyer from a network or studio, or the ultimate consumer in front of the tube or in the theater—visualize the story and become involved with its emotional content. It's "loose," because the rules for writing a treatment aren't hard and fast. The closest analogy we can think of is a vivid and intense letter to your best friend relating a series of amazing events that you've just experienced.

"pitch": This word describes the act of relaying a story for the purpose of selling it to the person listening to you. You spontaneously pitch the movie *Joe Somebody* to your best friend if you enjoyed it and are urging her to go see it. The director or producer at a friendly business lunch with the studio president pitches the story he's most excited about in answer to the question, "What are you working on these days?"

"user-friendly": The best treatments are easy on the eye. A treatment looks much like a short story because it's written in paragraph form, uses quotation marks for dialogue, and omits the technicalities of screenplay format. Use wide margins, a standard typeface, and short paragraphs rather than long ones. Leave a line of space between each paragraph, instead of indenting them.

"dramatic": A treatment is not an essay or a school composition filled with rhetorical and syntactical niceties. It's more closely comparable to an advertising campaign. The prose must be dramatic, or the treatment fails. Dramatic qualities include focus, intensity, dialogue, concrete characterization, and, most of all, *action*. Phrases like "the story starts with" or "in this act we see" serve no purpose in a well-written treatment. Instead, a treatment might open with:

> The black limousine hurtles around the corner and slams to a stop at the front steps of the courthouse.

It's not "a" limousine or "a" corner, but "the" limousine and "the" corner because your intention is to make your reader believe that this story, with all its concrete details, is coming to life before his eyes as he reads.

"straightforward": The treatment's language is simple and unpretentious; its sentences forceful and declarative. The language draws no attention to itself, intent upon presenting only what will push the action forward.

"highly visual prose": Remember, your purpose in a treatment is to show us the pictures or scenes by which this story can be brought to life. Use your skill to evoke these pictures in as few words as possible.

"present tense": Writing in the present tense places your audience immediately in the action rather than distancing them. In the example given, note that the limousine "hurtles" and "slams to a stop."

"highlights": The treatment needn't include every single detail that the screenplay will spell out. It must include all the highlights, the *necessary* details (often called "obligatory scenes") without which the story makes no sense to the audience or reader. Highlighting must be positive. The treatment is not a critique and should contain no qualifiers or uncertainties.

"broad strokes": Please don't kill us with detail. The human mind can only absorb so much new information at a time. Stay focused on the most important elements of the story, remembering that your purpose is to tease your reader into asking for more detail—or for the screenplay.

"hook": What makes this story's approach to its subject matter different from other stories on the same subject? That difference or angle is what will hook your audience and, for that reason, your buyer.

"primary characters, acts and action line, setting, and point of view": By the time your prospective buyer has finished reading your treatment, he should clearly understand the main character or characters, the general shape of your story's action line, the impact of its setting on its development, and the attitude toward its subject matter. The treatment generally indicates, implicitly or overtly, the act breaks for a feature film (three acts) or movie for television (seven acts).

"most dramatic scenes": Skip the transitions and skim over the background scenes or "back story." Just give us the obligatory scenes required to imagine the overall shape of the story.

"turning points": Turning points or "twists" are moments in the story when the characters move into some kind of jeopardy under the impulse of previous events and their character makeup. A twist is an unexpected turning point that surprises the audience. Turning points include *cliffhangers*, used to propel the audience from one act to another.

"intended for production": Never forget that the intention of the treatment is to initiate the process of filmmaking. In filmmaking, as screenwriter William Goldman (*Butch Cassidy and the Sundance Kid, Marathon Man*) put it, "Nobody knows anything." This means that there are no true rights or wrongs in creating effective treatments. The best treatments are great because their writers are expert dramatists.

"theater or television": A treatment for each medium should follow rules prescribed by that medium. A film treatment, with its three acts, may perplex television executives worried about TV's traditional seven-act structure. A television treatment will trouble theatrical developers until it has been restructured for their audience.

A treatment generally varies in length from one to twenty-five or more pages, depending on the kind of treatment it is and its purpose. The treatment of the motion picture *One-Night Stand* with Wesley Snipes and Nastassia Kinski that garnered writer Joe Eszterhas (*Basic Instinct*) $2.5 million from New Line Cinema (with another $1.5 million to be paid on production) was four and a half pages long. AEI (with Zide Films) sold Steve Alten's *Meg* to Walt Disney Pictures for $700,000 based on a hundred sample pages of the novel and a fifteen-page treatment of the rest of the story by screenwriter Tom Wheeler.

The typical treatment for a television movie is seven to fifteen pages; for a feature film ten to twenty pages.

The Brief, Happy Life of the Treatment

Although there are as many scenarios for a Hollywood script sale as there are personalities in Hollywood, a typical sequence involving a "spec" script—one that you've written on your own, without being paid—goes like this:

1. The development executive, whose job is "acquisitions" of new "material," reads the treatment you sent over with your script (as described in the conversation on page 7).
   - *YES*. He likes the subject matter and the writing and decides to read the script himself. Or he asks the assistant whose taste most closely mirrors his own to give it a "quick read."
   - *NO*. He can tell from the subject matter or from the writing (or both) that it's "not for us." He sends the script back with a note to that effect.
2. The reader's report, known as *coverage*, comes back.
   - *YES*. The coverage is positive. So the development executive reads the script himself. Or he proceeds to the next step immediately.
   - *NO*. The reader's report is negative. Depending on how negative it is and why, the executive either gets another reader's opinion, or he sends the script back with a polite note. Since no one in Hollywood wants to close doors, he most likely "passes" on the script rather than rejecting it.
3. The development executive, using your treatment as a crib sheet, pitches the story idea to his boss, who is either the

head of development, the head of production, or the owner of the company.

- *NO.* The boss isn't interested ("We have another one too similar already in development"; "The networks aren't doing any more drug-related stories"; "Sorry, it doesn't grab me"). The development executive sends the script back to you.
- *MAYBE.* The boss is intrigued. "Is there a treatment?" she says. The development executive hands her your treatment. "I'll get back to you."
- *YES.* The boss likes it. If she has the power to say yes, she asks the development executive to set up a meeting with you.

4. The development executive calls you (or your agent or manager) to say, "We like the story very much and would like to meet."

5. At the meeting you are praised for your story and given "notes" from the development executive and/or from his boss. Your willingness to accommodate these notes in a subsequent rewrite influences their decision to move forward or not.

- *YES.* You seem like a fun person to work with and are flexible enough to understand and address their story concerns. It's obvious from hearing you talk about the story that you've considered it from every angle, and they're eager to work with you.
- *NO.* You seem to be bent on an "authorial" stance, reluctant to change anything in your masterpiece. You or your agent/manager calls for a "follow up," and you receive a call back a week later saying, "We've decided to move in another direction."

6. A day or two after the meeting, the executive calls you or your agent and says, "We'd like to move forward with this. Who do we talk to?" You have a deal! The next step is business. You put the executive in touch with your attorney or your agent/manager to negotiate their offer.

- *NO.* The negotiations go badly. You can't come to terms. The deal falls apart, usually because of the new writer's unrealistic expectations or his agent/manager's lack of experience.
- *YES.* The deal is done. Even before you sign it, you may very well move to the next step.

7. Your executive (now you refer to him as "my executive at . . .") calls for a development meeting. At this meeting, you discuss modifications to the story. You agree to undertake the modifications. The executive asks you, first, to write a new treatment that reflects the changes so he can see them in the context of the whole story before you go through the painstaking work of revising the script itself. The treatment, in one form or another, continues to be used as a diagnostic tool until the final, or shooting, script is accepted.

Kinds of Treatments

In both television and major motion picture filmmaking, the three most common kinds of treatments are:

1. **Original dramatic treatments:** These are treatments of dramatic stories invented by writers. (Chapter 2 deals at length with these.)
2. **Treatments of true stories:** These show how the writer would turn fact into drama, organizing actual events and characters to create a compelling story line. Think about Mel Gibson's *Braveheart* and how he made a visually exciting movie based on the exploits of the thirteenth-century Scottish hero William Wallace. Or the heartwarming *Fly Away Home* with Anna Paquin and Jeff Daniels, which dramatized the true story of a man who taught endangered geese their migratory route. (Chapter 5 deals at length with these treatments.)

3. **Adaptation treatments:** These show how a writer would dramatize an existing story by another writer. A treatment for adapting *Little Women* by Louisa May Alcott might convince a studio to develop a script for a remake. Producer Denise DiNovi did indeed produce a very successful screen version of *Little Women* starring Winona Ryder and Susan Sarandon. Emma Thompson won an Academy Award for her first attempt at screenwriting, an adaptation of Jane Austen's *Sense and Sensibility*. And Alicia Silverstone's catapult to stardom, *Clueless*, was an innovative, hip, '90s version of Austen's *Emma*. (We deal with adaptations in chapter 6.)

Confusing Terms

As we mentioned earlier, the term *treatment* is thrown around loosely in the film and TV world and has been used from time to time by development or creative executives, writers, and business affairs persons to mean variously a one-pager, a synopsis, an outline or "beat sheet," or a coverage. But there are some differences in these forms, as follows:

Treatment *v.* Synopsis

Synopsis is the term used by those in the entertainment industry to indicate a matter-of-fact summation of a story's plotline, a shorter version of a longer work, whether that work is a novel, a nonfiction book, a screenplay, or even a treatment. Think of the synopsis as a more or less complete and detailed recitation of all the scenes and events in a story, a condensed version of the plot. The purpose of the synopsis is to describe, not to sell. The treatment's purpose is to sell, and that's why it's written with an intensity and urgency the synopsis characteristically lacks.

Treatment *v.* Coverage

Coverage is the industry term used to describe the diagnostic document provided by the story department readers for executives making acquisition decisions in theatrical film and television. The typical coverage document consists of:

- identifying information (name of story, name of writer, name of person doing the coverage, type of story, etc.);
- a synopsis, as previously defined;
- a set of comments giving the reader's opinion of the cinematic worthiness of the piece covered;
- a rating chart, allowing the reader to rate the piece on characterization, dialogue, action, setting, and commercial appeal.

A script may be covered by:

- a talent agency for casting purposes;
- a talent agency, for *packaging* (the term for attaching talent—an actor, actress, or director);
- a director, actor, or actress's company to assess its suitability for involvement;
- a production company, to assess a film's viability;
- an agent or manager, to help determine whether the writer should be represented or the work produced.

The coverage's purpose is to report the strong and weak points of a story as objectively and comprehensively as possible. But a treatment, drawing its energy from its writer's personal enthusiasm, is *not* objective.

The Beat Sheet

A beat sheet is a writing tool used to identify the sequence of events, turning points, and action in your story. It's an abbreviated way (no longer than three pages, please) to break down the structure of your story, making it easier to organize and change.

The beat sheet charts the sequence of events that cause your main character to do something and maps how your main character changes from the beginning to the end of your story.

Create a beat sheet by using bullet points that illustrate in one or two lines the order of your plot's progression. Remember, plot takes place when a character does something or acts upon another character.

Here is an example of a beat sheet for AEI:

JUDAS SILVER

by Jon Hargrove

- A tight-knit group of six graduate students, all best friends, are conducting a historical excavation of a colonial church in Boston. The church recently burned down. They are led by an eccentric professor. The students are history grad students.
- Beneath the new church, one of the grad students comes across a previously unknown room. In fact, it's a crypt.
- They enter the room, which is burned and destroyed, and unstable at best. Dirt sifts down from above. Timbers creak. The professor finds an unusual leather pouch of coins buried with one of the corpses. He picks up the bag.
- Immediately the room starts to collapse. The students make it out, but the professor is killed. His hand, the only part of him not buried, is still clutching the bag of coins.
- The six shocked students attend the professor's funeral.
- Days later, the six students gather in tribute to their killed professor. They gather inside his office at the university, drinking, remembering the old man.
- The professor's wife arrives, grieving. She hands them the bag of coins found on the professor's body. Since the coins are part of the excavation, she wants the students to have them to further their research.
- They open the bag and count out thirty silver coins, all ancient.

Could they be *the* thirty coins used to betray Christ? Some of the students scoff at the idea, but others believe it.

• One of the students, Gerald, an intern at the Boston Museum, has had considerable experience in dating artifacts. He tests the coins and concludes that they are over two thousand years old.

• Valery, a student at the Harvard Divinity School, uses history books to place the coins. She's confident that they are from the time of Christ.

• Two of the students, Robert and Piers, go out on the town. Robert immediately gets into a fight at a local club and is stabbed to death.

• The remaining five friends are in shock, horrified. Two deaths in one week. Julie, who's into the arcane and the occult, does some more research. She discovers that the Judas coins are thought to be cursed, and she's beginning to believe it.

• Sheila brings in a numismatist, who states that the coins could potentially be worth millions if sold to the right collector. The coins have only been rumored to exist. They have on their hands a major find.

• The students argue over who should oversee the coins, now that they know the coins are valuable. They quickly begin losing trust in one another. They decide to use the museum's safe.

• Later, Piers and Julie, who are engaged to be married and have known each other since they were kids, suggest that they sell the coins and share the money. But Sheila reminds them that the coins are not theirs to sell. They belong to the parish, and she thinks they should give the coins back.

• That night the others find Sheila dead, fallen from her fifth-floor dorm room. Her death is ruled a suicide by the police.

• The remaining four students secretly wonder if Sheila's death was truly a suicide. None of them have alibis.

• Piers is losing it. He believes the coins are cursed and need to be destroyed. Julie and Gerald go to the museum to find the coins—but the coins are gone.

• They all suspect each other of stealing the coins, which leads to another murder.

• The three remaining students decide to toss the coins into the Atlantic. Just as they are about to do so, Gerald turns a gun on them.

• They fight and Gerald is killed, falling overboard, leaving only Piers and Julie.

• Piers turns around to see his fiancée Julie holding a gun on him.

She wants the coins. He tosses them to her, and she promptly pulls the trigger.

• Alone, with five of her onetime best friends now dead, Julie turns the sailboat back to shore.

• In the distance a storm is coming, and the seas are choppy. Lightning illuminates the entire sky, revealing ominous thunderheads. The little sailboat rises and falls on the massive swells, standing little chance against nature's fury—and the curse of the coins.

THE END

Treatment *v.* Outline

The words *outline* or *reblocking* are used to describe a list of the scenes in a cinematic story, much like the beat sheet. Outlines of this kind are especially useful in the development process because they reveal the flow of the scenes, without elaboration, at a glance. An outline can be thought of as a skeletal treatment. Where a treatment may contain dialogue to dramatize a particular moment, the outline will not. Its purpose is strictly diagnostic, to allow the executive, the director, and the producers to chart the direction of a story and to make course corrections before the writer is fully committed to writing or rewriting.

The following example is a partial outline for our Disney film, *Meg:*

1. Seventy million years ago. T-Rex attacked and destroyed by *Megalodon*.
2. Professor Jonas Baxter finishes lecture on Meg. Terry Tenaka tries to get his attention.
3. Jonas attends media awards party. Learns his wife is cheating on him, walks out. Terry Tenaka is waiting for him.

In the next chapter we will discuss how to write an original treatment for motion pictures, while at the same time examining the basic elements of fiction and drama.

2

The Big Screen:
Original Treatments for Motion Pictures

• • •

Make it new.
—Ezra Pound

Walt Disney Pictures has paid $700,000 against $1.5 million . . . for the first hundred pages and treatment of an unfinished novel.

After heated bidding during the past few days, the publishing house of Bantam-Doubleday-Dell obtained the rights to two novels by a first-time novelist for $2.1 million—one of which is still in treatment form.

Wouldn't you love to read those words about your story? Our client Steve Alten did! His dream of making it as a writer came true when after twenty rejections for representation, his "idea" for a novel titled *White Death* about a prehistoric shark found its way to our office. Steve spent ten years researching the sixty-foot *Megalodon Carcharodon* while working days at a meat processing plant in South Florida. His awesome idea was swimming in the depths of 450 dense pages complete with every known fact about the *Megalodon* and its environment. We clearly saw the potential, but Steve needed to work on a treatment that would assist him in developing his idea into a thrilling commercial plot showcasing provocative characters. It took a dozen drafts over a period of six months, plus the assistance of thewriterslifeline.com's David Angsten and screenwriter Tom Wheeler, to come up with the final 15-page treatment and 100 sample pages of the novel that AEI and Zide Films, with the assistance of Jeff Robinov, then of International Creative Management, sent to Disney Pictures.

Is there a mysterious secret to accomplishing this dream scenario? No. Once you've got the basic talent it's simply a combination of being persistent, having access to Hollywood (via your manager, agent, or producer), knowing the basics of the business and your craft, and then honing your skills and going for it! Kevin Costner, as reported by Peter Keough in the *Chicago Sun-Times*, once drew an analogy between the artist's dedication and people jettisoning all the weight to keep a plane from going down. He said, "I think one of the first things to go as people's lives start to go down is their dreams. Dreams should be the last thing to go—dreams are the things you go down *with*. If you're left clinging to a piece of driftwood in the middle of the ocean, I'd put on it the word *dreams*."

Okay, so let's get started making your dreams come true.

What Makes a Great Treatment?

A treatment can be useful in getting your story straight, getting the details of the screenplay you wish to write clearly spelled out. When you begin creating the details of the script, it's all too easy to lose track of the backbone of the story. But the treatment *focuses* on the story's backbone, allowing it to be seen clearly.

Not only is a treatment good for keeping track of the forest instead of the trees, but also the writer has less invested psychologically in a treatment than he does in a full screenplay. Having to redo a portion of a treatment is far less agonizing than having to rewrite a portion of a script. For the same reason, it's often a better idea to do a short treatment than a longer one.

Using a treatment to develop the story before writing the screenplay, moreover, parallels the actual film development process in which the director, producers, and/or the financing company's executives want to make sure they "buy" the story's overall shape before committing to the time and financial expense required by a script. Experienced screenwriters may go to one story development meeting after another without writing down their ideas until everyone involved has agreed upon the main elements.

A treatment re-creates the story development process in the privacy of your own workshop. Your treatment is your own private story development meeting. With it you can be sure that the four elements of drama—character, action, setting, and point of view—are being mapped out clearly scene by scene, act by act. Having these elements clearly outlined in the treatment allows you to sit down to write the screenplay with the greatest self-confidence possible.

The main structural work involved in the script-writing process will occur during the treatment stage. For the treatment to be effective, all the following elements must be in place:

- an **opening** that hooks the audience;
- a final **climax** that satisfies their sense of storytelling;

and in between:

- a **protagonist** the audience relates to;
- a **central conflict**, around which all the action revolves;
- a **central emotional line** that determines the mood and viewpoint of the film;
- all the necessary **main and supporting characters**;
- the **essential structure and content of every scene** from beginning to end.

A treatment for an original screenplay can be any length, but it can't go wrong at five pages and should rarely be more than twenty. It can't go wrong at five pages because if it catches your reader's attention, he'll ask to see a longer treatment—or he'll start talking to you about a script!

The Writer's Storyboard

Directors often use *storyboarding* to plan a shoot. A storyboard is a series of sketches or diagrams illustrating every basic scene and camera setup, thereby providing a visual account of how the film will look before shooting begins. The writer can also adopt this technique to assist him in seeing his story and how it will lay out on the page. Many writers have found it useful to use three-by-five-inch index cards in the early stages of developing the treatment, each card containing a shorthand description of one scene (the dramatic interaction of the protagonist with one or more of the other characters). Others create a color-coding system that makes it easy to keep track of character interaction by assigning each character a different color card. This also helps to keep the entire story in perspective, since you can see its overall shape and identify its holes at a glance as you lay out your cards on a table or corkboard. Using this system, one scene might consist of a beige and a blue card, each cut in half, because in that scene Alex (beige) interacts with Heidi (blue). In another scene, where Alex and Heidi are joined by Susan (violet), the scene card might be beige, blue, and violet.

Laying the cards out in acts on the corkboard allows you to flesh out the story before committing it to a prose narrative. What's on each card? Whatever's required to remind you of the heart of the proposed scene: "Alex and Heidi confront Mai-Ding about the missing body. Susan bursts into tears, runs out the door." The setting should also be noted, and whether the scene is an interior or an exterior, and if it's day or night. When working with clients on treatment cards, we use a black border around night scenes, and indicate interiors by cutting the left corner of the card:

> *Alex & Heidi confront Mai-Ding*
> *about missing body.*
> *Susan leaves in tears.*

The development of scene cards in a step-by-step order detailing a brief description of every scene from beginning to end involves the expenditure of creative energy, thought, and imagination. The creative process is not logical and need not be done in chronological order. Put cards on the board as they occur to you. When they stop occurring to you, take a break and come back to your work when you have new ideas for scenes. Allowing the creative process to follow its nose in this fashion makes it fun, and generally more effective than sitting in front of the corkboard until you've thought up all the scenes. If you're collaborating with someone else, a typical writing session at this stage might be nothing more than brainstorming together until you start filling your storyboard with scene cards.

Don't be afraid to take cards *off* the board and toss them. Director Paul Mazursky (*Diary of a Mad Housewife, Down and Out in Beverly Hills, Scenes from a Mall*) says, "I've storyboarded every picture. I throw out some of it, but I use a lot of it." That's the advantage of the storyboard. Its flexible structure allows the story to develop without committing it to the linear reality of a computer screen or paper. This storyboarding process is the heart of constructing a film treatment. If you succeed, and your film is made, a director will re-create your storyboard with his own.

Don't be impatient with this process. It may take many sessions. Good stories grow slowly, gestating into their own natural shape until they're ready to be born, or until they click. Taking the time now will allow the actual writing of the treatment, and then of the script, to be almost automatic. You'll just be filling in the blanks that you created in your storyboard sessions. Yes, it's time-consuming, and yes, it's difficult. But that's what makes screenwriting the most challenging of all writing careers. If you're in a hurry, find something easier to write!

When you finally arrive at an order that seems to click, check to see that every scene:

- expresses conflict, and
- moves the plot forward another step.

If it doesn't express conflict, either add conflict or cut the scene. If it doesn't move the story forward, either collapse the scene into one that does, or cut it. Only scenes that move the story forward are allowed. Imagine yourself sitting in the theater, wondering, "What was the purpose of *that* scene?"

Once you've completed your storyboard, and your story is laid out with all its necessary scenes, it's time to write the treatment. Now all you do is turn the sketches written on the cards into clear, simple, vivid, and dramatic prose that allows the reader to *envision* your story. For example:

> Alex and Heidi confront Mai-Ding about the missing body.
> Susan bursts into tears, runs out the door.

becomes:

> Harsh light illuminates the face of Mai-Ding. In the shadows, on either side, Alex and Heidi hold her arms.
> "Where's the body?" Alex demands.
> "We know you moved it," says Heidi.
> "If you don't tell us, we're calling the police."

Let's take a closer look at the qualities that make up a good film and, thus, must be represented in your treatment.

Action or Story

> Ideas have to be wedded to action; if there is no sex, no vitality in them, there is no action. Ideas cannot exist alone in the vacuum of the mind. Ideas are related to living.
>
> —Henry Miller

If the action of your story doesn't reveal itself within the first few paragraphs of your treatment or the first two or three pages of your script, most people in the entertainment industry will stop reading. Agents, producers, directors, and story editors are all looking for the same thing: great storytelling. A great storyteller knows the story must begin immediately, not "at the beginning," but "in the middle of things." Aristotle was the first to point this out, crediting Homer for starting *The Iliad* and *The Odyssey* "in the middle of the action"; more recently, William Goldman advises writers, "Begin as far into the scene as possible, and get out of it as soon as you can." In the first few minutes of the movie *Witness*, after the death of an Amish man, his widow and young son leave on a train journey. In the station in Philadelphia, the little boy witnesses a murder. In the first ten minutes of *Independence Day*, humongous alien ships appear in the sky entirely shadowing the cities below, an immediate threat. As the White House is alerted to the crisis, helicopters are dispatched to make contact—and they are blown to smithereens. Now we know: These aliens ain't friendly!

A good story instantly hooks even the most jaded people in the business. What's your story about? What's its *one-liner*, the tag that might be used to sell the film to prospective buyers?

- *"Die Hard* in a tunnel." *Daylight* with Sylvester Stallone.
- "What happens to a friendship after you sleep with your best friend?" *When Harry Met Sally* with Meg Ryan and Billy Crystal.
- "When two men get into a minor accident on the FDR Drive the ensuing feud escalates into a sinister game of cat and mouse." Ben Affleck and Samuel L. Jackson's dark thriller, *Changing Lanes.*
- "Everyone has their limit. Self-defense isn't murder." In the vein of *Sleeping with the Enemy, Enough* with Jennifer Lopez.
- *"Searching for Bobby Fischer* meets *Dead Poets Society." Finding Forester* with Sean Connery.

Here's a checklist that might help you sharpen your story:

- Does your story make a statement? Does it make your audience think or feel strongly about its subject matter?
- Does it say something important about today's world?
- Is its statement clearly reflected by the protagonist's character?
- Does the protagonist learn a lesson in this story that can be shared by the audience?
- Does your story ask a question important for today's audiences?
- How do you want your audience to feel when they leave the theater?

Not Just Action, Dramatic Action

There are two kinds of action in a treatment:

1. **Something that happens** to a major character to move the story forward.
2. **Dialogue** that moves the story forward.

"A black limo rounds the corner," is *not* action. "A black limo rounds the corner and heads directly for Mary" is. Whether the limo hits her or not, if Mary is one of your major characters, that's action.

When a minor character gets hit by the limo, it's dramatic action only if the collision is a *necessary* part of your story, causing the major character or characters to react. Not everything that happens to a major character is dramatic action. When Mary runs up the steps just before opening the door and being blown away, running up the steps is action only if it has a direct purpose in the story, such as building suspense. If you show her pouring milk into her coffee before she goes off to her final rendezvous, you're probably going to remove that scene along the way. In a perfect film, putting milk in the coffee works only if the milk or the coffee is poisoned. Even the smallest actions must have meaning, or they distract from the forward movement of the story.

In 1928, Walt Disney wrote instructions from New York to Ub Iwerks, his chief animator in Hollywood:

> Listen—please try and make all action definite and pointed and don't be afraid to exaggerate things plenty. It never looks as strong on the screen as it appears on the drawing board. Always work to bring the GAGS out above any other action—this is very important.

Over the years Disney repeated to his animators, *"Make it read!"* meaning, make the action distinct and recognizable. No contradictions, no ambiguities.

Once the character work-up is done, you can turn back to your story's action line. Even though many of your action elements may have occurred to you before this point, you'll now discover that they come into focus because the characters are in focus. The most important thing to recognize about your dramatic action is that it must be *rhythmic*, arranged in a fashion that constantly holds your audience's attention. There are as many ways of creating good dramatic action as there are writers, but in successful film storytelling the *pattern* must be compelling.

The pattern of dramatic action can be determined by giving each scene in your story what we call an *intensity rating*. Rate each scene of your story on a scale of one to ten, one being least dramatic, ten being most. The hard part about writing action is maintaining your perspective to help determine where your script is strong and where it's weak as far as story pattern is concerned. The intensity rating is part of a diagnostic tool we've invented at AEI that helps writers visualize their action line and turn weaknesses into strengths.

Here's how it works:

On a single sheet of paper, as in the accompanying illustration (see p. 33), write "page 1" at the top left-hand corner, and "page 115" at the bottom left-hand corner. Then start filling in the most important scenes of your action line, with only a few key words to describe each—and drawing a dashed line under each scene with the number of hyphens from one to ten that fits the intensity rating. At the end of each hyphenated line, type a right karat (>, usually found at the far right of the bottom row of your keyboard. It's best to write the scenes down from memory, on the principle that if you don't remember them they aren't dramatic enough to include in your overview.

In the sample Intensity Rating illustration, we've written only scenes we've thought of so far, and we've been random and arbitrary about the page numbers—which are simply guesses at the present stage of our thinking about the process. We learn some things, though, just from doing this much:

1. Nothing very intense happens until Jack breaks out of prison.
2. Nothing very intense happens between pages 15 and 30.
3. Susan killing Jack, on page 96, is just as intense as Jack jumping Elmer on page 70. Maybe that should change. (And so on.)

We learn even more about our action line if we turn the page sideways and view the arrows as vectors in a "roller-coaster graph." Now the shape of the action line, as we've established it so far, becomes clear. And it can use improvement. Wouldn't it be better, for example, to begin with a 10 instead of a 1? The idea, after all, is to hook the audience immediately. So Jack's prison break might be a better opening. By the same token, maybe the ending should be rethought immediately. After the killing of Jack and the near-death of Elmer, do we really want our story's action to trickle off into a sunset dinner? One come-down moment might be fine, but three will leave the audience without the intensity we've gone to all the trouble to bring them to.

Nothing beats doing this for yourself. Watch your favorite film on videotape, stopwatch in hand. As story action occurs, stop the tape and note how far into the story this particular scene falls. Create a one-page chart, just as we've described, for *Jaws* or *Jurassic Park* and you'll understand why these films knocked the box office for a loop.

You'll want to make sure that the high and low points reflected in your overview chart correspond with *act breaks*. Obviously you'll close each act, not with a "2" scene, but with a "10" scene. This closing scene is known as a *cliffhanger* from the many films that literally leave the protagonist at the edge of the cliff at a momentous turning point in the action line. We're not going to duck out to the bathroom just as Indiana Jones opens the ancient pyramid to discover it's writhing with snakes. If you can't think of dramatic closes for your acts but are very good at thinking of dramatic beginnings, chances are you have a very small problem. Simply move your act break. If act 3 opens with a 10, but act 2 closes with a 4, cut the 10 scene in half and place the first half at the end of act 2. Presto! you now have a cliffhanger ending for act 2 as well as a dramatic opening scene for act 3. Remember, your goal is to keep your audience on its toes so that they never know when to expect the next shock. In general, the more turns, twists, and cliffhangers in a story, the more involving the story. Of course, none of these action moments mean anything if they're not completely related to the character and don't derive clearly from the character's motivation and his mission.

So see the Intensity Rating illustration on the facing page.

INTENSITY RATING

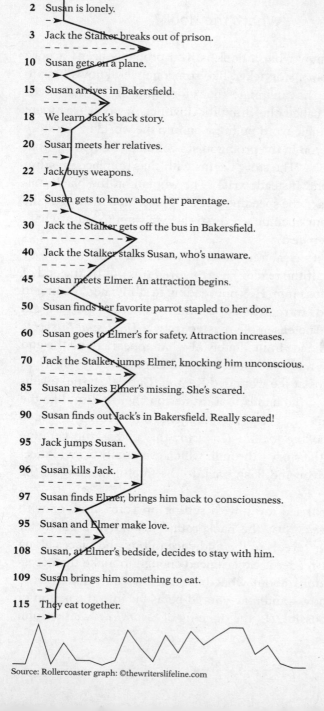

1   Elmer is lonely, in Bakersfield.

2   Susan is lonely.

3   Jack the Stalker breaks out of prison.

10   Susan gets on a plane.

15   Susan arrives in Bakersfield.

18   We learn Jack's back story.

20   Susan meets her relatives.

22   Jack buys weapons.

25   Susan gets to know about her parentage.

30   Jack the Stalker gets off the bus in Bakersfield.

40   Jack the Stalker stalks Susan, who's unaware.

45   Susan meets Elmer. An attraction begins.

50   Susan finds her favorite parrot stapled to her door.

60   Susan goes to Elmer's for safety. Attraction increases.

70   Jack the Stalker jumps Elmer, knocking him unconscious.

85   Susan realizes Elmer's missing. She's scared.

90   Susan finds out Jack's in Bakersfield. Really scared!

95   Jack jumps Susan.

96   Susan kills Jack.

97   Susan finds Elmer, brings him back to consciousness.

95   Susan and Elmer make love.

108   Susan, at Elmer's bedside, decides to stay with him.

109   Susan brings him something to eat.

115   They eat together.

Source: Rollercoaster graph: ©thewriterslifeline.com

What's the Hook?

If you don't know what a hook is, you probably aren't a born storyteller. A born storyteller, like someone who knows how to tell a good joke, has an innate knack for capturing his audience's attention; it's called the dramatic instinct. A good treatment wastes not a single word pulling you into the world of the story and involving you in the protagonist's conflicts. Remember that commentary like "The story begins with" has no place in a dramatic treatment. Instead, write "The woman on the black stallion races toward the speeding train." It's essential to *intrigue* the reader with your opening words so she will want to know what's going to happen next.

Make sure it's clear very early in your treatment what your story is about. If the reader hasn't figured this out by the end of page 1, you'll lose him. He's not reading to study; he's reading to be entertained. Introduce the central conflict as soon as you possibly can. The ensemble mystery movie *The Usual Suspects* hooks the audience immediately at what appears to be the end of a story. The audience views the bodies of several men. Then the movie stops at the wounded Keaton (Gabriel Byrne) awaiting his death at the hands of a mysterious figure. But, like the savage opening murder of the main character played by Diane Keaton in *Looking for Mr. Goodbar*, this end is the genuine beginning of the story—through which eventually we will meet the only survivor and flash back to the fateful meeting of the suspects.

Don't get carried away with setting up your story, or with presenting *back story*, the background history of a character that the writer reveals to the audience in bits and pieces along the way. Your reader is experienced enough to make the necessary assumptions about what has brought your character to where he is now—and *now* should be as far into the action of the story as possible. In the opening of *Swordfish*, we see John

Travolta's character engaged in a highly dramatic bank raid. By the time he makes his escape, we know exactly who he is and what he's all about: an extraordinary, death-defying terrorist, willing to risk his life on an impossible mission.

The Thematic Core of Your Story

Not every story needs to explore a theme, or even convey a message. Many excellent movies, like *Heist* or *Eraser*, are written as pure entertainment and have no intention of showing anything more than what's on the surface. Yet the greatest films, and the ones every agent or manager wants to set up, revolve around a central theme that seems to shape every aspect of the story's characters and action. The urban drama *Set It Off* produced by Dale Pollack (*Blaze*, *Saturday Night Fever*) and Oren Koules depicts the self-destructive heroism that comes from desperation. *The Professional*, on the surface about killing and revenge, also explores love's ability to grow under the most unlikely circumstances. Each scene in the best-told story reflects that story's theme, examining it from yet another dramatic angle. But don't be surprised if the theme of your story isn't clear when you begin the storyboarding we described earlier. It won't be. Let it emerge as the story itself emerges from the depths of your unconscious where myth makes its home.

The theme will emerge only when the characters are clear. Yes, it's a chicken-and-egg situation. You must storyboard the story to know what it's "trying to tell you." Then you must understand the individual characters, their motivations and missions. Only then can you bring the theme, what Lajos Egri called "the premise," into final focus. The children's writer Phyllis Reynolds Naylor advises that if you sometimes confuse plot with theme, you can keep the two elements separate by thinking of *theme* as what the story is about, and *plot* as the situation that brings the theme into focus. You might think of theme as the message of the story, the lesson to be learned, the question that is asked, or what it is the author is trying to tell us about life and the human condition. Plot is the action by which this truth will be demonstrated.

In the 1979 movie *Kramer vs. Kramer*, for example, the thematic core of the story raises the question, Who's the better parent: the transformed, self-involved, ad exec father (Dustin Hoffman)? or the mother (Meryl Streep) who, after leaving behind her child in a quest to reclaim her own identity, returns to fight for custody? In *Seven* (Brad Pitt, Morgan Freeman), a serial killer uses the seven deadly sins to choose his victims. The thematic core suggests that no one alive is immune from the impact of the deadliest sins, and that only someone detached from life can escape their psychological and emotional horror.

THE TREATMENT AS TRAILER

The treatment offers a way to get the story straight quickly and efficiently. Often writers come up with ideas that spark my interest and in order to get the support of my coworkers and help gauge their enthusiasm I'll ask for a brief treatment to pass along. While treatments vary in length, my favorites are ideally around three pages with one act per page. This delineates the concept quickly and hits upon the important beats within each act.

The best advice I've heard came from a colleague who instructed a writer to think of the treatment as a great trailer. Not only should it sell the basic story, characters, tone, and the world, but most important, it should contain unforgettable moments that make you not want to wait a minute longer to see the movie. Like cutting a great trailer, treatment writing has become an art form that requires a delicate balance. One must know how to reveal just enough information to whet the appetite without giving "the powers that be" too many opportunities to say no.

—Terrence Myers, Director of Development,
Laurence Mark Productions

The Centrality of Characters

The personages in a tale shall be alive, except in the case of corpses, and . . . always the reader shall be able to tell the corpses from the other.

—Mark Twain

No matter what kind of movie you're writing a treatment for, your work begins with characters. Characters are the most important element of the story and should generate the action, the setting, and the point of view. Characters are not, after all, human beings; they are created by the dramatist to attract and hold an audience's attention. Your job as a writer is to give us insight into each and every character in your story, no matter how evil or virtuous his actions may be.

Characters are the heart of drama, and a treatment in which the characters aren't clearly drawn and compelling is too dull to read. Today's viewing audience is extremely sophisticated and demands well-constructed characters whose actions reflect their motivational pattern. As the television producer Norton Wright puts it, "Character is revealed by action. Action is motivated by character." Precisely because real-life people behave inconsistently and with motivations only vaguely understood, we demand in our fictional men and women actions that are easily related to recognizable "character patterns." Martin Riggs (Mel Gibson) in *Lethal Weapon* acts the way he does because he's torn between his suicidal tendencies, based on his love for his dead wife, and his instincts as a cop. While it might take years of psychotherapy to fully understand such behavior, the theater audience must get it in the first half hour—or they will feel the character is unclear. And dramatic characterization must be done from the inside out. You can't just tell us your character is angry. You must provide action that shows his anger.

In development meetings the most important first step is to

bring the protagonist (also known as the main character, or hero) into dramatic focus. It's his or her story, which means that every scene in your treatment must relate to his *character arc*, a term used to describe the various "beats" by which a character develops or evolves from the beginning to the end of a story. In well-constructed stories, the major characters change or grow. In poorly constructed stories, the protagonist remains the same at the end as he was at the beginning.

Types of Characters

There are four basic types of dramatic characters. In reverse order of importance, they are:

- function characters
- minor, or *tag*, characters
- supporting characters
- major characters, including the protagonist and the antagonist

Function Characters

A function character is one who performs a single function in the story without being involved in the motivational pattern of the major characters. Linda Emery's mother in *Dragon* (played by Michael Learned) has only one function: to disapprove of her daughter's marriage to Bruce Lee. The elderly next-door neighbor in *Sliver* serves only one purpose: to warn newcomer Carly Norris (Sharon Stone) that the high-rise she's moving into is haunted. The function character has no distinguishing characteristics. Less is better. Too much description is the bane of screenwriters. The minute you give a function character a distinguishing characteristic, you've turned him into a minor character.

Minor, or Tag, Characters

A minor character's *tag* or neurosis is a single defining attribute that distinguishes him and makes him memorable. For Serge (Bronson Pinchot), the gallery receptionist in *Beverly Hills Cop*, it was his heavily accented exchange with Eddie Murphy that had the audience laughing out loud. Where a function character is shaped to be forgettable, a minor character is written to be instantly recognizable. A minor character may have motivation (he's addicted to power), but he doesn't have a mission in life. Dan Aykroyd as the son in *Driving Miss Daisy* gives new meaning to gentility as he strives to keep his mother in check.

As a rule neither function nor minor characters are ever highlighted in the treatment. They need not even be mentioned unless they serve an indispensable function in moving the story forward. If you can tell the story without mentioning function or minor characters, do so. Otherwise, include them only where necessary.

Supporting Characters

Think of the supporting character as a recurring minor character. Like the minor character, he has a tag that identifies him immediately. But, like the major character, the supporting character *evolves*. When the power-hungry character dies in the midst of his quest for power, he's still a minor character. When he's reduced to impotency before he dies, he's become a supporting character. His tag has developed or evolved. The memorable, fast-talking, ever-grinning government witness played by Joe Pesci in *Lethal Weapon 2* serves at first merely as an exasperation for the Mel Gibson and Danny Glover characters, but eventually he becomes their ally.

Major Characters

> I understand one secret: The way you get screenplays on the screen is you write parts actors want to play.
>
> —Larry Ferguson, screenwriter, *The Hunt for Red October*

"If you write a big action piece that showcases a great character for Harrison Ford to play, you stand a better shot of selling it," says former William Morris agent Dave Phillips. The most important major character, of course, is your protagonist. But both hero and villain, protagonist and antagonist, are major characters. The *protagonist*, a term used first by classical Greek tragedians, is the first actor, the one who dominates most of the action. The *antagonist*, who's sometimes but not always a villain, is his opponent, the one who acts against the protagonist. Creon is Antigone's antagonist in Sophocles' *Antigone*, but he is by no means a villain. In Shakespeare's *Richard III* or Jerzy Kosinski's *Cockpit* the protagonist is villainous.

Depending on the complexity of your story, there may be a number of major characters. Once you have your protagonist figured out you'll want to go through the same brainstorming process with your second main character and especially with your antagonist. It's a rule of thumb in the industry that the best stories draw their strength from the antagonist because the audience is excited when a protagonist faces an extraordinary challenge from a fascinating and complex opponent. Audiences love to hate great antagonists:

- Mitch Leary (John Malkovich) in *In the Line of Fire*
- Cruella de Vil (Glenn Close) in *101 Dalmatians*
- Eric Qualen (John Lithgow) in *Cliffhanger*

Keep in mind that your antagonists don't necessarily have to be human. Consider:

- the storm in *The Perfect Storm*
- the creature in *Alien*
- the spiders in *Arachnophobia*
- the fire in *Backdraft*
- the tornado in *Twister*

It's a truism of drama that the stronger the antagonist (whether human or not), the stronger your protagonist will look. Yet although it's sometimes easier to create a believable antagonist than relatable and admirable protagonists, you won't want this strength to become overbalanced in favor of the antagonist.

Who's the Protagonist?

The protagonist or hero of your story is the major character whose motivations and mission shape the action. He or she is the central focus, the actor who is on camera most of the time and through whose eyes the audience learns the story. The protagonist is literally the center of attention, the star: Dave Kovic (Kevin Kline) in *Dave*, Mrs. Doubtfire (Robin Williams) in the film of the same name.

In a story treatment for a mainstream film, the protagonist is

- someone the audience is able to identify with, or relate to, although not necessarily sympathize with;
- someone eminently castable, a part a star would want to play.

Identification with a protagonist means that the audience is able to experience emotion through that character. You create audience identification by making your protagonist someone for whom we feel sympathy, whose flaws and foibles we understand; by making him likable; by giving him internal and external conflicts; and more than anything else, by placing him in jeopardy from the first moment to the last. Introduce your protagonist as soon as possible, preferably in the opening lines of the treatment.

A protagonist is convincing when all of the following four dimensions of his makeup are clearly focused:

1. his **motivation**
2. his **mission** in the story
3. the **obstacles** he faces in pursuing this mission
4. the **change** he undergoes from the beginning of the story to the end

Let's examine these dimensions one at a time.

Motivation

When a real-life person does something strange, you find the behavior believable because you know it has happened. A dramatic character doesn't have the same advantage. The moment he acts out of character, he throws the entire story into jeopardy. The reader, who suspends his disbelief when he begins reading the treatment, immediately recovers it when a character's behavior jars him. That doesn't make sense, he says to himself, and tosses the treatment aside. The spell is broken.

In order to make the major character's development from beginning to end convincing, his motivation must be believable and well defined. Usually motivation is a simple matter, although it's not so simple to create a character as convincingly motivated as the grandfather in *Heidi* or Romeo in *Romeo + Juliet*. After reading your treatment, the buyer should clearly understand the main character or characters and their relation to the dramatic elements of the story.

Motivation is the mechanism that makes your character tick. A minor character can be motivated by love, hate, greed, despair, or anxiety; that is, by any recognizable emotion. To sustain our interest, a major character usually requires a combination of two motivating emotions. Greed and love warring within your protagonist, for example, automatically provides both internal and external tensions that lend themselves to scene-by-scene dramatization.

At the heart of every good story is the question, What would happen if a character like X found himself in a situation like Y?

THE BIG SCREEN / 43

What would happen if an irrepressible and exuberant little girl found herself the ward of a bitter and cynical old man? That question powers *Heidi*. *Moonstruck* asks what would happen if a woman about to be married went to convince her future husband's estranged younger brother to attend the wedding and they were instantly, passionately drawn to each other. Aristotle was the first to point out that the greatness of drama is that it shows us not just what happened, which is history's job, but what *might* happen under certain circumstances. If a noble man, acting in character, is faced with a threat to his nobility, he would die rather than act ignobly. Drama allows us to participate vicariously in fateful actions without being burned by them ourselves. In a sense, your character is *forced* by his motivational mechanism to act the way he does. Examples from recent films include these:

• The powerful motivation for **revenge** works well in films like *The Specialist* (Sylvester Stallone, Sharon Stone) and *Desperado* (Antonio Banderas). In *The Quick and the Dead*, Ellen (Sharon Stone) must survive a quick-draw contest in order to exact revenge against the evil Herod (Gene Hackman) who presides over the town of Redemption.

• **Greed** mixed with a **need for family love** is the driving motivational complex of Tom Cruise's character Charlie in *Rainman*. After he discovers that his deceased father's millions have gone into a trust to support an autistic older brother he never knew he had, Charlie vows to bring his brother back to California as a way to control the inheritance. Along the way, Charlie finds the family love he never experienced growing up.

• **Redemption** motivates Clint Eastwood's character Frank Horrigan in *In the Line of Fire* and Sylvester Stallone's Gabe Walker in *Cliffhanger*. Both films examine what would happen if a man who made a mistake that ruined his entire life got the chance to do it all over again and set things right.

• The strongest motivation is often simply **survival**, the instinct to avoid death, which motivates the protagonists of *The Pelican Brief* (Julia Roberts) and *Seven* (Morgan Freeman).

Mission

Your story goes into high gear when the character is given, or decides to undertake, a mission. Your major character has a mission in life, expressed through and determined by his motivational makeup.

The character's mission in the story is usually related to his mission in life: *A deeply cynical private detective with an inflexible personal code is hired by a woman who does not fully reveal how deep her troubles are. His loyalty is to this woman, but when evidence turns up that seems to incriminate her, his code is put to the test. His mission in life, being true to his code which does not tolerate clients who lie to him, is now in conflict with his mission in the story—to discover where guilt lies. Succeeding in the investigation reconciles this tension by allowing him to justify his trust in the woman.* This is the mission setup for *Chinatown* (Jack Nicholson, Faye Dunaway).

Drama becomes even more dynamic when the primary mission of the story's protagonist directly challenges or interferes with the mission of others—especially that of the antagonist. Robin Hood's mission is diametrically opposed to that of the Sheriff of Nottingham, as is Luke Skywalker's to Darth Vader's in *Star Wars*. The conflict can be resolved, therefore, only when protagonist and antagonist face each other in a duel. The key to creating powerful drama is establishing a clear-cut mission for protagonist and antagonist, and making sure that each of these opposes the other.

Obstacles

The obstacles in the way of fulfilling the protagonist's mission comprise the bulk of your story material—that daunting "middle part" that connects your dramatic opening with your conclusive ending. The protagonist must face serious challenges, hurdles, and dangers in the motivated pursuit of his mission. Barriers of all sorts must stand in the way of his reaching his objective—or your treatment will be judged to have insufficient conflict and complication. Before you begin writing your treatment, you'll want to know that you have enough obstacles to give your protagonist plenty to do and plenty to think about.

The most convincing dramatic obstacles aren't usually "invented." They're *discovered* by brainstorming about the nature of the protagonist's mission. Brainstorming is exactly what happens in a development meeting when you simply throw out ideas, anything that comes to mind, opening the floodgates of imagination and creativity. One idea leads to another, and before you know it your story is unfolding. If your protagonist needs to deliver a prisoner across country, as in *Midnight Run*, what might stand in his way? Jack Walsh (Robert De Niro), a skip tracer, and Jonathan Mardukas (Charles Grodin), an accountant who embezzled millions of dollars from the mob in Vegas and then jumped bail, face all the normal hazards of a cross-country trip:

- The FBI is trying to capture them.
- The Mafia is trying to kill them.
- They hate each other's guts (at first).
- How will they travel (train, car, etc.)?
- What will they eat?
- Where will they sleep?
- How will they avoid the Mafia in order to keep Mardukas alive?
- How will they keep the FBI at bay so that Walsh can deliver his "meal ticket"?

And there is the added twist of Walsh actually beginning to like Mardukas, who never misses an opportunity to explain why Walsh should let him go.

If you don't come up with enough exciting obstacles you'll

find yourself in deep trouble when writing the long middle portion of your treatment, act 2. The best stories use the momentum of escalating obstacles in act 2 to carry the reader toward an exciting climax in act 3. Obstacles are the successful writer's stock in trade and why he gets paid the big bucks. In *Cliffhanger*, Sylvester Stallone's character, Gabe Walker, must overcome his internal obstacle, memories of his failure to save the girlfriend of his former friend and present climbing partner, Hal Tucker (Michael Rooker), from plunging to her death. His external obstacles are the icy cliffs and antagonist Eric Qualen (John Lithgow). Can you imagine *The Wizard of Oz* without the Wicked Witch of the West? *D.O.A.* takes its heightened conflict from the ticking clock. College professor Dexter Cornell (Dennis Quaid) is deliberately poisoned by a radioactive substance, giving him only twenty-four hours to live and to discover the identity of his killer.

Obstacles can be found in the natural environment of the protagonist as he undertakes his mission, whether it's the high-tech voyeur's dream of a modern condominium tower in *Sliver*, the sordid urban underbelly of *Blade Runner*, John Nash's schizoid visions in *A Beautiful Mind*, or the artistic isolation of Australia in *Shine*. Nothing is more helpful than visualizing your story; the visualization process lets you see your protagonist on the battlefield where he will encounter the dragons you've invented to thicken the plot. Once, for example, you've set the *Nautilus* as your stage in *20,000 Leagues under the Sea*, it's just a question of vicariously experiencing what dangers—from loss of air pressure to giant squids—the *Nautilus* will confront in its natural setting.

If you don't know whether your protagonist's battlefield is high or low, curved or flat, seething with tropical heat or frozen with arctic winds, on the moon or under the sea, you're not ready to begin writing your story treatment. Imagine *Lawrence of Arabia* without the desert, *Alien* without outer space, *Monster's Ball* without the southern town, or *The People vs. Larry*

Flynt without Los Angeles. Obstacles are generated as much by the setting as they are by the characters.

Your treatment, having provided the initial framework of your character's motivation and mission, should offer only the most dramatic scenes where your character meets progressively more dangerous obstacles that finally lead him toward a dramatic decision or resolution. Along the way, reveal as many cliffhangers as you can to propel the reader from one act to another and, within the long act 2, from one part to another. Director Merian C. Cooper calls this "the three D's: danger, distance, difficulty. Or better still, difficulty, distance, danger. And if you go through those three D's you get a picture at the end of it." Obstacles!

Your story's action line is divided into acts: first, second, and third—beginning, middle, and end.

- Act 1 is the grabber, introducing the protagonist and his mission or quest.
- Act 2 develops the story, as the protagonist faces one obstacle after another.
- Act 3 shows him succeeding or failing to accomplish his mission.

Whether you're writing a thirty-second commercial or a four-hour miniseries, telling a joke, or inventing an excuse for calling in sick to work, the overall three-act pattern is natural. (As we'll see in the next chapter, television films have seven acts because they divide act 2 into five parts).

Change

The best-crafted major characters change as they move through obstacles to accomplish their missions. Don Quixote becomes more realistic after tilting at so many windmills, replacing his initial idealism with fatalism; Sancho Panza, his sidekick, progresses in the opposite direction, assuming the mantle of crusader at his don's deathbed. Stallone's Gabe Walker (*Cliff-hanger*) evolves from a man who's lost his nerve to one who's regained his courage and self-respect. Falstaff in Shakespeare's *Henry IV* learns that there's an end to frivolity, and that his friend Prince Hal must replace folly with responsibility. Tom Cruise's Charlie (*Rainman*) begins as a self-involved, grasping workaholic. At the end of the story, through his relationship with his autistic brother, he has become more sensitive, learning to listen and care. Amélie's disbelief, in *Amélie*, that anyone could get to know her enough to love her turns to the sweetest love when Nino does.

Characters that don't change, like Batman, or James Bond, or Lara Croft in *Tomb Raider*, or Indiana Jones, are referred to by critics as "cardboard" or "comic book" characters— dramatically effective with audiences only if they're colorful enough, and the star who plays them charismatic enough, to hold our interest, generally in a story filled with numerous and entertaining obstacles.

Your protagonist's change must be in character, caused by the interaction of his mission with his motivational makeup. In the title role in *Dave*, Kevin Kline's good-humored avoidance of life's important issues evolves into a serious realization that his ingenuous perspective can make a difference for all Americans. Dave Kovic's transformation is "in character."

Dramatic change is at its most compelling when the writer places two strong dimensions of the character's motivation at war with each other and allows the stronger force to win. At the moment of victory, the transformation is complete.

In examining what makes a good film, we've looked at story and dramatic action, opening hook, theme, and the essentials of character. Next, your treatment should have a setting that enhances your action line and a point of view from which your story is being told.

Setting

> Nothing can happen nowhere.
> —Elizabeth Bowen

Your treatment will indicate in a few brief strokes the importance of the story's setting to its action line. Imagine *Midnight Cowboy* or *Taxi Driver* set in a city other than New York. The setting in the best conceived stories is virtually another major character. *Under Siege, Die Hard, Executive Decision, The Guns of Navarone, The Shipping News, The River Wild, Blade Runner*—all these films would be entirely different if you changed the setting.

Your setting doesn't have to be elaborate. Consider *Working Girl* and *9 to 5*, where the setting is an ordinary workplace. In *Eat Drink Man Woman* the setting is a Sunday dinner table in Hong Kong at which every major turning point in the movie is revealed. The setting is suggested in the titles of such films as *The Panic in Needle Park* (Al Pacino), *Boyz N the Hood* (Laurence Fishburne), *The Abyss* (Ed Harris), and *Bad Day at Black Rock* (Spencer Tracy). In each of these films, the setting provides obstacles that keep the protagonist busy throughout the story. When you're "discovering" the obstacles to your protagonist's mission, and running low on ideas, it often helps to consider switching the setting. Look for one inherently more dramatic than the setting you've been having trouble with. An emergency room is more dramatic than a convalescent ward; a criminal court more dramatic than a civil court. Outstanding theatrical motion pictures such as *Witness* or *Babe* present not just a story, but a whole new world.

Point of View

As you begin to write, ask yourself, Whose story is this? Hitchcock was a master at letting the audience know who was telling the story. His haunting classic *Rebecca* unfolds through the point of view of the second Mrs. De Winter (Joan Fontaine). In *Rear Window*, the story is told from the POV of James Stewart's character, the news photographer confined to his room by a broken leg. *Shadow of a Doubt*'s viewpoint is that of the young niece who slowly realizes her suspicions that her uncle is a mass murderer.

The point of view in a dramatic treatment must be unified and, ultimately, identifiable. This is the hero's story, told from his point of view; or it's the hero's story, told from someone else's point of view—that of a friend, a cop, a lover, a survivor. *The Secret Garden* tells its story from a child's point of view in an adult world. *Babe* offers a delightful look at barnyard life (a metaphor for the big bad world) through the point of view of a piglet.

Point of view can be tricky to deal with or even to understand at first, but it basically dictates that no scene you write can exist without relating, directly or indirectly, to the viewpoint you've chosen. Either the viewpoint character—the one from whose perspective the story is being told—is involved in the scene and therefore has firsthand knowledge of what happens within it, or he could have found out about the events of the scene and therefore has a rationale for including it as he narrates the story. Scenes of which the viewpoint character or characters could have had no knowledge destroy the unity of point of view. In *Witness*, scenes in the Amish country *without* John Book (played by Harrison Ford) are allowable even though he is the viewpoint character because, before the end of the story, he could have been told about all the events by Rachel (Kelly McGillis).

Experiments with point of view abound in the art of film, and the more you think about this dimension of drama the more complex it becomes. Movies need not limit themselves to a single perspective. A good example of multiple point of view is *Courage under Fire*. When Denzel Washington's character opens an investigation into the death of an officer (Meg Ryan) to see if she was in fact courageous under fire and deserving of a medal of honor, the audience is offered several characters' points of view of the events relating to her death. The classic example of multiple viewpoint is the Japanese film *Rashomon*, which shows the same sequence of events from four points of view in succession. Suffice it to say here that you should ask yourself as you revise your treatment: (1) Is it clear from whose viewpoint the story is being told? and (2) Does this point of view distract from, or enhance, the story?

Let's review the basics again. Your treatment needs to reflect all the important dramatic elements you intend to develop fully in your completed screenplay. The buyer should be able to recognize:

- the general rhythmic shape of your story's action line
- its act breaks
- the "arc" of the main characters, as they change from beginning to end
- the dramatic impact of its setting
- its point of view

With all this in mind, the following basic structure recommended by most screenwriting authorities should also shape your treatment. This outline is based on a 115-page script and a 15-page treatment.

Outline

Act 1
Who's the Protagonist? What's His Problem?
How Does It Become His Mission in the Story?
Treatment Pages 1–2

In the first two pages of your treatment:

- introduce the protagonist in a way that makes him immediately relatable to the audience, someone we care about and for whom we want to root;
- announce the protagonist's mission in the story in the form of an inciting incident or problem he must solve;
- set up the mood, the movie's tone, its setting, and its stakes;
- suggest why this story is important to all of us—the central question, theme, metaphor, or conflict that will be explored throughout the movie;
- introduce the subplot, or *secondary action line*, that complements or conflicts with the protagonist's main action line;
- introduce the antagonist, the protagonist's chief obstacle;
- introduce a major event that turns the protagonist around completely (what he wants in life is challenged, and now he must react) and launches him or her into act 2.

Act 2
The Protagonist Encounters
Obstacles to His Mission
Treatment Pages 3–10

The bulk of your treatment, from pages 3 to 10, narrates the protagonist's encounters with the obstacles that stand in the way of accomplishing his mission. These obstacles are made dramatic by the rhythmic way you've arranged them, so as to take the audience on a roller-coaster ride of highs and lows, expectations and surprises, escalating complications and increasingly serious and costly confrontations in which, along the way, the stakes grow progressively higher and higher.

Since act 2 does comprise the bulk of your treatment, it's helpful to break it up into three parts, each of which should end with a major cliffhanger or twist.

Act 2, Scene 1
Treatment Pages 3–6

In pages 3 through 6 (roughly):
- As your protagonist reacts to the challenge he encountered on page 2, his major decision leads him into action.
- As he faces the first challenges, we witness his initial development.
- Something happens that also impedes the subplot.
- We're given an inkling of what's to come.

Act 2, Scene 2
Treatment Pages 7–8

The protagonist's reversals continue, until he begins to make headway. Then around page 8, new information, or the triumph over a major obstacle, turns everything 180 degrees to force the protagonist to face an even greater obstacle than he or we had previously imagined. Now your protagonist should be in big trouble, forcing him to reflect and make an even deeper commitment to his mission.

Act 2, Scene 3:
Build to Climax
Treatment Pages 9–10

Now the characters converge. The heart of the movie happens, that quiet romantic or philosophical moment that ups the ante and makes us root for the protagonist's mission even more than before. This is where to hint at the moral of the story. It may be the place where all seems lost. The protagonist may look like he's about to give up.

As the protagonist faces the biggest hurdle of all, both the main action line and the subplot seem to be falling apart. It's the protagonist's darkest hour, his final breaking point, the moment when he realizes all may be lost, and he knows he must deal with that.

Suddenly something happens that changes everything. The universe offers him a break. He seizes the moment and goes for it. Now he has an even bigger picture of what it would mean to accomplish his mission: not just satisfying his quest in the story, but fulfilling his quest in life as well. By page 10, he's standing at this crossroads of action. His next move will be definitive. He faces the climactic turning point. Will he win or lose?

Act 3
The Protagonist Achieves His Mission
Treatment Pages 11–15

The final pages of your treatment contain the crisis, the climax, and the story's resolution.

• The **crisis** is the scene or sequence of scenes in which the final outcome of the story is determined by the protagonist's actions. When you get to this point, write it as though it were a separate story, giving it its own beginning, developed middle, and end. "Milk it for all its worth," the producers tell the director. The milking begins with your treatment of a complicated crisis, filled with its own twists and turns.

• The **climax** occurs at the end of the crisis, its final moments: the Terminator in *Terminator 2: Judgment Day* finally destroys the bad guys. Now, all that's left is—

• The **resolution**, when, to save the human race, the Terminator destroys himself in the fiery cauldron.

When it's over, let it be over fast. Don't hang around with lots of words that only take away the dramatic punch of a strong and satisfying resolution.

In chapter 3, we take a look at the treatment for television films.

3

Breaking into Television:
Treatments for Television Movies

. . .

Imagination is thinking of something that hasn't been on
television.

—someone in Hollywood

There was a time when writing for television actually held a
stigma. Not so today. All the big filmmakers have their
fingers in the lucrative TV pie. Barry Levinson's *Homicide*,
Steven Spielberg's *High Incident*, and Michael Crichton's *ER*
have garnered critical acclaim. According to the Writers Guild
of America (WGA), the vast majority of its members work in
television. Television writers enjoy a type of recognition not
easily bestowed on film writers. TV offers much more immediate gratification; whereas a large percentage of film screenplays
never get made, you can see your work produced and aired on
television six weeks from the time you turn in your completed
screenplay.

There's more opportunity than ever for newcomers. In addition to substantial monetary rewards, TV provides excellent
discipline for a new writer—the competing demands of art
and commerce create an environment that makes it one of the
best possible training grounds. But you must take it seriously,
providing what Warren Littlefield, former president of NBC

Entertainment, identifies as the two most important factors in program acquisition: relatability and point of view, a subject matter that appeals to the network's audience presented with a viewpoint they haven't seen already, or at least lately.

Writing for TV v. Writing for Feature Film

Someone once said there are only two kinds of films, good ones and bad ones. Aesthetics aside, television films are distinct from motion picture feature films in some notable ways:

• Feature films are generally stories that need to be told on a larger canvas, requiring larger production budgets than television films (whose budgets range from $500,000 to $5,000,000);

• Feature films are generally able to be more graphic with regard to sex and violence;

• Feature films have different target audiences, depending on the film. Television's target audience depends on the channel and time of day;

• In general, feature films tend to be less formulaic than television films, which often follow patterns that have proven to attract high ratings;

• Feature films have a different dramatic structure: three acts as opposed to the seven acts in network television films;

• Feature films can be experimental; films for television rarely are;

• Television films in general have a narrower focus;

• Whereas television films are often topical and tied to a "pre-sold" event or character, motion picture features (because of their much longer development period) are more rarely topical;

• Motion picture features vary in length from 75 minutes to 180 minutes or longer; because of programming slots and commercials, TV films are generally standardized to 96 minutes;

• Television films tend to employ popular, familiar television casts. Motion picture features in general rarely use television casts, though it's true that many TV stars have successfully crossed over: film star Tom Hanks once starred in a hit situation comedy, *Bosom Buddies*; Marisa Tomei was a regular on the soap *As the World Turns*; Will Smith came out of NBC's *The Fresh Prince of Bel Air*; George Clooney came from *ER*; Denzel Washington walked the halls of St. Eligius Hospital on *St. Elsewhere* from 1982 to 1988; Brad Pitt had a recurring role as Randy on *Dallas*, and Halle Berry played Debbie Porter on its popular spin-off *Knots Landing* from 1991 to 1992; Ben Stiller hosted a weekly behind-the-scenes look at the world of TV comedy, which aired on MTV in 1990.

• On the other side of the coin, some TV programmers seek to employ big box-office stars. HBO, for example, prefers feature casts to TV casts: Emma Thompson in *Wit*; Halle Berry in *Introducing Dorothy Dandridge*; Dennis Quaid and Andie MacDowell in *Dinner with Friends*; Judi Dench and Olympia Dukakis in *The Last of the Blonde Bombshells*. But HBO doesn't limit itself to actors; it has scored feature talent in other arenas, such as screenwriter Alan Ball, creator of *Six Feet Under*, and the Tom Hanks–Steven Spielberg producing team for *Band of Brothers*. Showtime, A&E, CBS, and ABC are keeping up with the Joneses: Angela Bassett starred in *Ruby's Bucket of Blood* for Showtime and *The Rosa Parks Story* for CBS; Judy Davis portrayed Judy Garland in *Life with Judy Garland: Me and My Shadow*; and Sissy Spacek played Zelda Fitzgerald in Showtime's *Last Call*; not to mention Academy Award–winner Marcia Gay Harden and Richard Dreyfus on CBS's popular series *The Education of Max Bickford*.

Though these distinctions are generally useful, don't forget that entertainment is by nature an industry of exceptions. A film whose subject matter would be suitable for TV is sometimes produced and released as a feature simply because a big star has agreed to do it. *Malice*, a film about an insurance scam between a patient and her surgeon lover whom she sues for malpractice, was made as a feature because Alec Baldwin and Nicole Kidman agreed to do it; *Dangerous Minds,* about a female ex-marine who becomes an English teacher in the inner city, became a theatrical motion picture because of Michelle Pfeiffer; and Julia Roberts's interest pulled *Erin Brockovich* into theaters and Oscar competition. A film can be produced for television but then elevated to feature status by the quality of its execution. *The Last Seduction,* an HBO original starring Linda Fiorentino, as a woman who double-crosses her doctor/husband after he sells drugs illegally to pay off a shylock, was released theatrically because of its unusual concept and taut execution.

Many stories straddle the line between material for television and the big screen. The true story of Pamela Smart, the high school teacher who had an affair with her student and then talked him into killing her husband, did become a movie for television called *Murder in New Hampshire: The Pamela Smart Story,* but it was also the inspiration for the fictional black comedy released as the feature film *To Die For,* with Nicole Kidman, based on Joyce Maynard's novel. The television movie *Bodily Harm* with Joe Penny and Lisa Hartman followed the exact same plot as the feature film *Malice.*

If a treatment is submitted to a television movie production company or broadcaster, it will be considered only for television. But an agent, manager, or independent producer who reads your treatment will always have an eye first toward making it work as a feature; only if that's not a productive route will the story be considered for domestic television (keeping in mind its potential for foreign motion picture release).

When AEI takes a television film project out to sell, we create a treatment ranging from one or two to twelve or more pages. Nearly everything we've said in chapter 2 about preparing a dramatic treatment for a motion picture film can be applied to the television film treatment, but there are some important differences.

THE TREATMENT AS A
"LEAVE-BEHIND" FOR THE PITCH

In the working world of television the treatment is usually the second item that tells the buyer what the project is—the "pitch" being the first. It's the treatment that allows the buyer the opportunity to replay what was pitched in the words of the writer or producer who gave the pitch. When the pitch meeting is over and the writer or producer is wondering whether the buyer "got it," the hope is that the treatment, which is usually left behind after the pitch is made, is able to support and possibly even further elucidate the essence of the pitch.

The treatment should be the tool that gives the buyer not only the fundamentals of the pitch but the further textures and colorizations of story and character. There is no real form to follow. A treatment can be as long or as short as the writer thinks it takes to get the necessary points across. Every writer, like every pitch, is different. So, what might be the right approach for one treatment might differ in another treatment by virtue of what it is that the writers want communicated. There's a cliché that "ideas are a dime a dozen." That may be, but it's the treatment that takes the idea and lends it the layers of content that may very well bring the added value to put it over the top with the buyer.

—Steve Weiss, William Morris Agency

The Seven-Act Structure

The ancient Greek dramatists wrote plays in one continuous act with choral interludes; the Romans moved toward crafting their plays in three acts; and Shakespeare and his contemporaries in five. Shakespeare and his fellow Elizabethan dramatists improved the dramatic impact of their plays by dividing act 2 into three separate acts, each with its own beginning, middle, and end. Network television movies outdo Shakespeare in this one particular: they're written in seven acts. Although movies for pay-cable broadcasters like HBO, Turner, USA, and Showtime are structured in three acts like feature films, free TV has replaced the traditional three-act structure with a seven-act form to coincide with its commercial station breaks; the goal is to end each act with a cliffhanger to make sure the audience returns after the station break. (Fox movies have eight acts, to allow for an additional commercial break.) The psychology of the audience demands constant involvement, emotional connection, and stimulation. In our world of remote control, even the slightest deprivation thereof forces an immediate flip to another channel. The seven-act structure, with its first six acts ending in cliff-hangers, compels the viewer to stay tuned during commercial breaks, and it has the welcome side effect for the writer of making that endless middle of the story easier to deal with.

The first act in any form of drama is the hook that involves the audience with the protagonist and his story. The final act brings the story to a satisfying climax and resolution. Beginnings and endings are easy for experienced storytellers. The challenge is always that middle. How do I keep the audience stimulated without risking being too shrill for too long, or being repetitive? The TV film answer is to divide the middle of the story into five acts, each of which must have its own compelling beginning, well-developed middle, and provocative ending to hold the audience through the act break. Whether writing treatments for pay cable or free TV, a screenwriter can only improve his craft by learning the rationale behind the seven-act structure. Even though your reader may never know that your three-act treatment was actually written with seven acts in mind, he will be impressed that your second act has so many dramatic twists and turns to keep him glued to the page (because you secretly broke act 2 into five parts).

The Inciting Incident

Let's look at the TV treatment more closely. A story for a two-hour television film begins in the same way as a story for a theatrical motion picture: with an unforgettable character, a situation fraught with drama, and a premise that bears dramatic exploration. As you develop your treatment beyond its immediately involving beginning, you expand the setup into five well-developed and rhythmically orchestrated middle acts, and a conclusive and satisfying ending in act 7.

The First Hour
Act 1 is different from the other six acts of a television film in the following ways:

- It's approximately twenty minutes in air time. The other six acts are approximately twelve minutes each.
- It consists of twelve (instead of six) scenes, the twelfth being the cliffhanger.
- It sets up as quickly as possible all the dramatic elements of the story: character, setting, and what's at stake in the drama.
- It presents, no later than scene 2, the inciting incident that cranks the plot into action.
- The story's progressive complications begin in scene 3.

In acts 2 and 3, the shape of the action line emerges through progressive, escalating complications punctuated by twists and the act-end cliffhangers.

The Hour Break
These cliffhangers get progressively more exciting with each act, with the most thrilling climax appearing at the end of the third act. The end of act 3 is also called the *hour break*. The act 3 cliffhanger needs to be strongest because program changes on competing channels occur on the hour, as in, "Honey, can we please switch to NBC at eight?"

The Second Hour
In the second hour, which opens with act 4, protagonist and antagonist face each other with maximum intensity and build to the crisis that occupies act 6. Between scenes 41 and 42

the crisis reaches its turning point, where the protagonist must make the dramatic decision that will lead to the climax of the story. The climax occupies act 7, and the story's resolution occurs in the final scenes, 47 and 48. Knowing the story-scene numbers will help you flesh out the outline for your treatment, but you don't need to write the numbers into the treatment itself; marking the act breaks is enough.

In developing TV treatments, producers use a worksheet like the one illustrated on pages 67–69 of this chapter to chart clearly and easily the dramatic elements of a story. The worksheet (which we ourselves learned about from TV producer Norton Wright) may be useful in helping you track the escalating progression of obstacles you'll want to set up in your treatment. It is especially effective when adapting a book or true life story, which nearly always needs to be rearranged into an effective dramatic structure. At the Writers' Lifeline, Inc., we also use the worksheet as a diagnostic tool; it quickly helps us determine whether a story we're coaching through rewrite has enough "story material" to create a film.

When using the worksheet, fill in the scene blanks with one or two lines describing the characters, the layout, and the flow of action. Once you've filled out your worksheet, you'll be ready to begin writing the treatment itself.

What a Treatment Looks Like

While far less critical than the characters and story line, the physical format of your treatment can enhance its salability. The treatment should be reader-friendly—typed single-spaced in short dramatic paragraphs that hold the reader's attention. Paragraphs should not be indented but separated from one another with a double space. And, by the way, stop thinking about your treatment (or script) in terms of paragraphs. The unit of drama is the *scene*, not the paragraph.

At least in the first stages of selling your treatment, use the seven-act structure explicitly. At the end of act 1, leave a space and then add a centered heading:

Act 2

before going on to the opening scene of act 2. Even if your agent, manager, or independent producer decides the best market for your story is cable, which has "concealed" act breaks (because there are no commercial breaks), your seven-act format will help show clearly that your story has a strong framework—and sufficient dramatic ingredients and twists. You may be asked to remove the act break indicators later, but we recommend you use them on the first approach. Now let's look at the specifics of the physical format.

Title
The best TV film titles are abrupt and a little provocative, and manage, in the broadest sense, to summarize the story and/or its importance. When NBC tested the title of AEI's movie based on K. K. Beck's novel *Unwanted Attentions*, they found that the test audience responded better to the title *Shadow of Obsession*. NBC retained the title of our *Amityville: The Evil Escapes*, from the novel by John Jones, because "Amityville" is a pre-sold concept. Titles of movies for television generally parallel their log lines (see page 65): *Woman with a Past*, *A Mother's Justice*, *Fear Stalk*, *She Said No*, *Shadow of a Doubt*, *In Broad Daylight*, and *Without Her Consent*.

Your Name and Story Type
Following the title on page 1 of your treatment, type your name:

Amityville: The Evil Escapes
Treatment for a movie for television
by Jonathan Biloxi

On the next line, note what *type* of television story this is. Possibilities include:

Based on the novel by John Jones
if it attempts to follow the novel faithfully;
Adapted from the novel by . . .
if it takes great liberties with the novel's characters and/or story line;
An original story
if you made it up;
Based on a true story
if it's based closely on actual events;
Inspired by . . .
if it's based loosely on actual events.

This information orients the buyer to read your treatment with an eye toward judging its market value.

Your Story's Log Line

A *log line* is a one-line description of a story aimed at making someone want to watch it. After the title and your name, include a log line that tells the reader, in *TV Guide* language, what this movie is about. Think of the log line as an advertising hook, as in these top-rated movies for television:

• *Deadly Care.* A critical-care nurse addicted to drugs endangers her patients' lives.

• *Deadly Intentions.* A young wife discovers her husband's intention to murder her.

• *The Fear Inside.* A woman must overcome her agoraphobia in order to escape a killer stalking her in her own home.

• *She Fought Alone.* After a date rape by the high school quarterback a teenage girl fights for her reputation.

• *Shadow of Obsession.* Stalked by an obsessed admirer for fifteen years, a beautiful college professor becomes the prime suspect in his murder.

Your log line needn't mention character names. A strong character trait will do—with a dramatic teaser about the story:

> A woman running from love finds herself . . .
> A man trying to forget his past is forced to face it when . . .

Television loves specific catchwords that quickly tell the reader what the story is about. Is it about love, greed, obsession, murder, family turmoil? A woman or family in jeopardy? An ordinary woman in extraordinary circumstances? A woman against nature or the system? A woman on a mission? Escaping from something or someone she loves? Once you've settled on one or two words you can push out from there and add a few more economical adjectives and verbs to make up your log line.

The Body of Your Treatment

Next follows the body of the treatment, beginning in the middle of an exciting opening scene; progressing through accelerating complications and obstacles; and ending with a satisfying crisis, climax, and resolution. As in a motion picture film treatment, the television movie treatment summarizes the main characters' conflicts and personal development and lays out the primary flow of the drama in brief but very dramatic paragraphs. In addition, the TV treatment makes the film's act breaks clear, ending each act with a cliffhanger.

All you need now is a good story, and you're ready to get started.

MOVIE FOR NETWORK TELEVISION
7-Act Format Worksheet

ACT I	
1	
2	
3	
4	
5	
6	
7	
8	
9	
10	
11	
12	(cliffhanger)

ACT II	
13	
14	
15	
16	
17	
18	(cliffhanger)

ACT III	
19	
20	
21	
22	
23	
24	(biggest cliffhanger!)

Act I approximately 20 minutes long with 12 scenes to cliffhanger.
Scene 1, get to know or become interested in the protagonist.
Scene 2, inciting incident that cranks plot into action.
Scene 3, progressive complications start here.
Acts II and III each approximately 12 minutes long with 6 scenes, ending with a cliffhanger; Act III ends with the biggest cliffhanger.

HOUR STATION BREAK

ACT IV	
25	
26	
27	
28	
29	
30	(cliffhanger)

ACT V	
31	
32	
33	
34	
35	
36	(cliffhanger)

ACT VI	
37	
38	
39	
40	
41	
42	(crisis cliffhanger)

ACT VII	
43	
44	
45	
46	
47	
48	

Each act about 12 minutes long with progressive, escalating complications and crises, ending in a cliffhanger.
Act VI: scenes 41 and 42, crisis and a decision.
Act VII, story reaches climax.
Scene 48, resolution.

7-Act Format Worksheet
UNWANTED ATTENTIONS

[aired as *Shadow of Obsession*]

Act I
Scene

1. Benjamin becomes mesmerized with Rebecca at library.

2. Benjamin follows Rebecca to her dorm.

3. Benjamin befriends Wendy from Rebecca's dorm, to be close to her.

4. Benjamin hears about campus party, harshly breaks off relationship with Wendy.

5. At party Benjamin arranges to give Rebecca a ride home.

6. Benjamin passes the turn for the campus. Rebecca begins to panic.

7. They struggle, he strikes her, threatens her with a knife ordering her to partially disrobe. He forces her to say she loves him, then returns a shaken Rebecca to dorm.

8. Rebecca files charges, appears in court. Charges are dismissed as she is humiliated by judge.

9. Benjamin follows Rebecca in his car, watches her through her window. Scratches heart on her car.

10. Rebecca reads and destroys letters from Benjamin.

11. Rebecca keeps moving. He finds her each time, calling her. Rebecca is frantic with fear.

12. Suddenly Benjamin stops calling. Is he gone?

Act II

13. Rebecca is now in love with Philip. He tells her about threatening telegram. It's from Benjamin.

14. She tells Philip about Benjamin. He's shocked.

15. Rebecca shows Philip articles about women who were stalked. They're all dead.

16. Rebecca seeks help from her attorney friend Angela. She suggests a PI, Michael Caruso.

17. Michael is immediately attracted to Rebecca. She confesses she wishes Benjamin dead.

18. Michael finds Benjamin's apartment. Michael discovers room dripping in blood.

Act III

19. Michael calls police. They go to see Rebecca. She's openly relieved that Benjamin is dead.

20. Police search her apartment and car. They find blood in the trunk.

21. DA begins investigation.

22. Evidence against Rebecca mounts.

23. She hires criminal lawyer Trevor Keegan. He questions her innocence.

24. Blood in car matches Benjamin's. Rebecca is indicted for murder.

HOUR STATION BREAK

Act IV	
Act IV	38. Rebecca makes breakfast. Attacks Benjamin with frying pan, then injects him with syringe.
25. Benjamin's mother takes the stand and accuses Rebecca of being obsessed with her son.	
26. Keegan refuses to cross-examine. Rebecca is angry.	39. Rebecca frantically searches for keys to van. Can't find them. Rebecca escapes on foot through woods.
27. A guilty Caruso attends trial.	
28. Angela takes stand. Testimony backfires, seems to offer motive.	40. Rebecca makes it to roadside hotel, calls Keegan. Call overheard by Caruso. He shows up at hotel.
29. New DNA evidence is introduced by DA. Philip becomes convinced of Rebecca's guilt.	41. Caruso reveals how Benjamin faked his own murder and that Keegan is going to set her up.
30. Philip refuses to testify and breaks engagement. Rebecca collapses.	42. Caruso insists they return to cabin. When they get there, Benjamin is gone.

Act V	Act VII
31. Keegan serves Philip with a subpoena. Keegan is ruthless when Philip takes stand.	43. Rebecca begs to leave. Caruso notices Benjamin hiding, mentions hotel.
32. Caruso continues to investigate on his own.	44. Rebecca gives in to Caruso's persuasion. Sheriff's dept. calls. Caruso leaves to meet the sheriff.
33. Trial ends. Jury retires. Rebecca returns home to wait for verdict.	
34. Rebecca is attacked in her bathroom, drugged and kidnapped.	45. Caruso realizes mistake. As he returns to hotel room, he's knocked out.
35. Rebecca awakens in van. Benjamin is driving.	
36. Benjamin allows Rebecca to go to a ladies' room. She discovers in old paper she's been convicted of murder.	46. Benjamin lets himself into room, then takes Rebecca to cliffs to throw both of them over.
Act VI	47. Before Benjamin can go over edge, Caruso shoots him. Benjamin falls off cliff.
37. Benjamin imprisons Rebecca in cabin in the woods. Rebecca thinks about a way to escape. Benjamin barricades her in her room.	48. Rebecca stands before judge while he vacates judgment, dismisses case. Caruso waits for Rebecca outside the courthouse.

The treatment based on this outline appears on pp. 82–87.

WHAT MAKES A TREATMENT WORK
FOR TELEVISION?

A damn good story. A damn good story one of the networks happens to want.

Used to be the only buyers were ABC, CBS, and NBC. All three made approximately the same kind and number of movies—22 to 45 a year—so producers still had two places to shop if one passed. Today, though, ABC and NBC make only 4 to 6 films yearly, while CBS makes about 20 yearly.

Fortunately, the cable networks now exist, making the chances of a sale slightly higher. They're strictly "niche" buyers, though. Lifetime Television, for example, makes movies only for women.

Treatments that work best for television:

- Fill a niche. A behind-the-scenes story about the music industry might appeal to VH1 but not Disney.
- Generate publicity. Controversy, especially based on true stories, can be a slam-dunk.
- Are easily promotable in a short snappy sentence, with a clearly defined concept.

The networks also prefer:

- Primarily American characters
- Relatable protagonists
- Emotional themes

One last piece of advice:

- Write for a smaller scope, a smaller world, and fewer characters.

Now forget I said that, because I'm first a fan of good literature. Don't sacrifice colorful, endearing characters just to make a television sale. Write what you need to say. What we need to hear. The rest will work itself out. . . .

—Judy Cairo, President, Cairo/Simpson Entertainment

Where to Find Story Ideas

Talent borrows. Genius steals.
—T. S. Eliot

If your career goal is not only to find ideas but also to sell them, you must begin to see everything through a storyteller's lens. Begin to perceive life's ups and downs from a dramatic point of view. Everywhere and anywhere, in the media and in your daily existence, always ask the question, Could this be a movie?

Stories are found in all corners of the globe, and in nearly every corner of human experience. Rarely, however, do they come entirely from your own imagination—even when you think they do. Something, sometime, planted that idea in the back of your mind, although you may have entirely forgotten how or where. The imagination works best when stimulated by an outside feeling, event, or challenge. A stray thought, based on something you've glimpsed during rush hour, leads you to wonder, "What would happen if . . ."—the primary formula that underlies nearly every good story. Something that made you chuckle, something that made your skin crawl or set your teeth on edge, a look on a stranger's face that made you wonder what lies behind it—any one of these can start the dreamworks inside your head turning to search for a story that fits it.

Open yourself to incoming stimuli, then allow the brainstorming to begin. Work in the garden, go for a drive, wash all the dishes, paint the house, or take a walk. Read the papers. Listen to the news. If you aren't able to leave the house, use your remote control to surf the TV channels, or surf the Internet from your computer keyboard, always in search of something that will provoke your creativity and give birth to a story idea. Extracting a singular idea from a long novel without adhering too closely to the full story is another productive technique for coming up with and focusing on your own ideas.

The best stories aren't invented. They're discovered, then retold from the storyteller's unique viewpoint. What makes the story yours, what makes it original, is not the idea behind it but your "angle," the way in which you *treat* the idea: your treatment.

Your Own Backyard

Your family and friends, coworkers, or neighborhood characters are often wonderful story sources as well. Keep an eye out for eccentric characters in your own family or among your friends' families, whose hard-luck or triumphant stories of their relationships, their jobs, their migrations, their criminal activities, their civic and personal accomplishments and defeats might be the basis for a film treatment. Darren Star's *Melrose Place* was inspired by the Los Angeles apartment complex where he lived while a struggling writer in Hollywood and the assortment of aspiring actors, actresses, writers, and others, who were his neighbors. Fran Drescher's hilarious mother in *The Nanny* is an accurate characterization of her own mother, big hair and all. While this part of the process is mostly inspiration, it's the impetus for the perspiration to come.

Published Books, Stories, and Articles

Books and articles provide reliable story sources. You can mine them for a well-wrought plot and change the characters and detailed action line to suit yourself. Professional writers have long understood that there are a limited number of possible plots in effective storytelling. William and June Noble's *Steal This Plot: A Writer's Guide to Story Structure and Plagiarism* is an excellent introduction to the way in which writers borrow a successful plot to flesh out their "original" takes on a story, and how this borrowing differs from plagiarism.

You can also try to acquire the dramatic rights to a story, so that you can actually adapt the book, short story, or article for a screen treatment (we discuss adaptation in greater detail in chapter 6). Suffice it to say here that if you want to adapt your favorite novel, you must try to option it or find another way of getting the novelist's permission to create a screen treatment from which you, as well as the novelist, can profit. Usually in order to option a book you must contact the agent who handles what are called the *dramatic rights* (the rights to turn the book into a film or a stage play), and find out how much money he and the author require in order to give you the right to adapt the author's book and sell your treatment or screenplay. We receive screenplays based on novels all the time, only to discover that the screenwriters have wasted their time writing them without inquiring about, much less securing, the right to adapt.

The cost of an option depends on the popularity of the book and who else wants it. Most options last for twelve to eighteen months with renewal clauses for additional time at higher or lower option payments. How do you find out who the agent is for a particular book? Just call its publisher and ask for the subsidiary rights department. They can tell you who handles the book's dramatic rights. The networks have ongoing contracts with bestselling authors like Judith Krantz, Jackie Collins, and Sidney Sheldon so that they have the first shot at adapting novels by these authors as movies or miniseries. But any novel, nonfiction book, short story, or article that has a "self-promoting" or "pre-sold" subject or title that will appeal to television audiences and sponsors—one they will recognize without the need for a large promotion campaign on the part of the broadcaster—is a desirable story source. Joe McGinniss's bestselling and controversial book *Fatal Vision*, about the murder trial of Dr. Jeffrey MacDonald, the Marine Corps physician convicted of murdering his whole family, easily became a television movie; the Nancy Kerrigan story, the Menendez brothers, AEI-client Jesse Ventura's election, and the Simpson-Goldman murders were automatic "instant movies."

Local Heroes

Most beginning writers can't afford to buy the rights to blockbuster books. The enterprising writer keeps his eyes open to local possibilities—a new play in a neighborhood theater, an old out-of-print paperback novel you run across at a used bookstore, an offbeat story in a literary magazine. *Shattered Innocence* was a fictionalized movie for network television based on a PBS documentary about the life and death of a young porno star. *First Steps* was a movie for television inspired by the *60 Minutes* profile of Dr. Jerrold Petrofsky, who experimented with computerized muscle "brain." Paul Auster's feature *Smoke* was based on a *New York Times* op-ed piece. First-time producer Stuart Regan found the out-of-print novel *Leaving Las Vegas*, by John O'Brien, in a secondhand bookstore. Regan optioned the book for $2,000 and, in 1995, brought this bittersweet autobiographical story to the big screen starring Nicolas Cage and Elisabeth Shue—garnering both actors an Academy Award nomination, and the Oscar for Cage.

Public Domain

Public domain is a copyright term for a work that is not, or is no longer, protected by copyright. Any book published before 1911, for example, is in the public domain. When you browse the secondhand bookstore or the library, you can discover little-known novels, out-of-print novels, or forgotten classics that are in the public domain. If you're not sure about their copyright status, call or write the Library of Congress Copyright Office in Washington, D.C. (www.copyright.gov); for a nominal sum, they will perform a copyright search that will corroborate the public domain status of the book in question. Despite the Bono Law (see chapter 8), many great works come into public domain each year.

Off the Beaten Path

University presses and small, offbeat publishing houses often publish novels and biographies that are out of the mainstream and therefore may have been overlooked by big production companies and story scouts. If you find one of them, a unique and affordable project could be yours to develop. The beautiful television film *My Antonia*, based on the novel by Willa Cather, was optioned from the University of Nebraska Press, which had republished and copyrighted it.

Failed Features
Television likes "almost feature films" as well—books that originally had film potential, but for one reason or another didn't fly in the world of theatrical motion pictures, as happened with *Scarlett*. Though highly publicized, this sequel novel to Margaret Mitchell's *Gone with the Wind* didn't stir up much excitement in the feature film industry. But television snapped it up, seeing the potential for pulling in its predominantly female readers as viewers. *Shadow of Obsession*, one of AEI's movies for television that aired on NBC, was based on the novel *Unwanted Attentions* by K. K. Beck, which had been in development as a theatrical motion picture at Warner Brothers for years. A feature script had been written but for some reason never got made. When the studio's option lapsed, we picked it up.

The Printed Word
Reference books such as encyclopedias, biographical directories, old catalogs, even phone books contain provocative facts that can inspire an idea for an interesting story. Reference books that relate to television, film, and radio past and present are another promising source. Newspapers, news wire services, and magazines are another obvious and endless treasury of topical material. True-life adventures interest television programmers because they are based on reality, which, for reasons unknown, interests the general TV movie audience more than invention does. Network executives are especially excited when the event or adventure behind the story has been highly publicized, providing an opportunity for network news follow-up interviews of the real-life people behind the story you've just watched.

Become Your Own Tracker

The minute a story hits the front page of the *New York Times*, the *Los Angeles Times*, the *Chicago Tribune*, or the *Washington Post*, it's usually way too late for you to try to secure its television rights. All the production companies, broadcasters, and independent producers have *trackers*, individuals whose job it is to track down stories as they are happening. These trackers, in turn, rely on scouts and spies at the major newspapers and TV news bureaus. The critical time to get the scoop on a TV story is within the first twenty-four hours of its occurrence. You're at an advantage if you live in a smaller city or town.

Develop your own tracker system by getting to know law enforcement officials, attorneys, and newspaper people. Tell them you're a TV writer and want to know the moment something that has potential story value occurs. Immediately after they call you with a lead, get in touch with an independent producer, agent, management or production company and tell them you've got access to a story that might interest them. *The Hollywood Creative Directory*, the *Studio Directory*, and *The Hollywood Agents and Managers Directory*, all listed in the recommended reading section at the end of this book and on www.aeionline.com\resources, are useful sources of names and numbers. Make sure you do indeed have the access, and that you've "covered yourself" with the source *by tying up the rights* so that someone else doesn't go around you on the basis of your tip-off.

Nailing the Rights

In the case of a crime, TV producers pursue what's known as a *hierarchy of rights*. Rights sought, more or less in order of importance, include:

- the victim's rights
- the perpetrator's rights

- the investigator's rights, the rights of the families of both the victim and the perpetrator
- friends' and neighbors' rights, etc.

Ultimate security, of course, lies in controlling all these rights, so that no other company can base a film on the same material without coming to you. For example, we marketed a true-life treatment by AEI's client Charles Brown, called *Murder by the Book*. The story relates a Motown executive's hiring of a hit man to kill his child and wife. The hit man buys a handbook about being a hit man and proceeds to commit the crime. His lapses from the handbook's detailed instructions lead to his capture. As we began to shop the treatment, a competing agent secured the rights to the hit man's handbook and began shopping them simultaneously! We should have optioned the handbook ourselves, simply as security.

When a crime is highly publicized, securing even one of these rights may provide sufficient basis for a TV film. So heated was the scramble for story rights to the Amy Fisher case (the Long Island teenager who attempted to murder her lover's wife) that three different versions based on three different rights—the perpetrator's, the victim's, and the journalist's— became television movies. What made this particular crime of passion so special? We think the scramble was caused by the newspaper headline writer who came up with the tag *Long Island Lolita*. The designation became a household phrase throughout the United States. This phenomenon translates to a "pre-sold" concept, which made network executives salivate for a share of the audience.

Life Rights

Another kind of true-life story worth pursuing for television is that of the local hero, a man or woman the viewer can relate to, who triumphs over great odds. The rights involved in this kind of story are called *life rights*, allowing the writer or producer the right to make a film from the hero's life story. You need to secure an option on the life rights against a *purchase price* that will be paid when a broadcaster actually puts the story into production. Although the sky is the limit on the value of such a story, which depends entirely on demand in the marketplace, most life-rights stories sold to television earn between $15,000 and $50,000 per hour of programming ($30,000 to $100,000 for a two-hour movie). Options can run from zero to $10,000 or more for six months, with two twelve- or eighteen-month renewals built into the option agreement.

Fictionalizing True Stories

If you aren't able to secure the rights to a story that excites you with its TV potential, consider fictionalizing it. Many TV movies are "look-alikes" based on treatments of true stories whose rights situation is too complicated or too expensive to deal with. In the fictionalizing process, you simply use the true events as your plot pattern, but invent your own characters, settings, and variations in the action.

Industry Sources

If you're serious about writing for television or film you should start reading the trade publications, especially *The Hollywood Reporter* and *Daily Variety*; or subscribe to www.filmstew.com. Notice what's being bought, optioned, developed, and shot. Read the film and television reviews. Reading these announcements will save you the time and frustration of submitting an idea that's already well covered in upcoming films. Often an idea that seems new and current to an outsider is, in fact, already well along the way toward production.

Don't Forget to Watch TV!

We're always amazed at how many would-be TV writers readily admit they "don't watch TV." No wonder they're getting nowhere in the business. One of our favorite sources for television film ideas is the educational and arts cable channels. Once we watched a documentary on Arts & Entertainment on the life of undercover agents. After they successfully completed an assignment and testified against the criminal, they suddenly found that they were marked men or women. They had to enter the Federal Witness Protection Program, where they could not speak to or contact anyone from their past. We thought, What if something very personal and dramatic required one of these people to return to his previous life despite the dangers? This idea led to an AEI treatment called *The Danger Zone*, which eventually led to an outstanding novel by AEI bestselling client Shirley Palmer.

Getting to a Deal

As we've mentioned, it's difficult for inexperienced writers and producers to make a deal directly with the networks or cable companies. You'll succeed most quickly by allying yourself with an insider: agent, manager, attorney, or credited independent production company (all of them listed along with their credentials in the various quarterly publications of *The Hollywood Creative Directory*; the *Studio Directory* also lists industry insiders). The insider will then pitch your story treatment to the buyers. As a recognized supplier, your insider contact makes the conservative broadcaster-buyer feel comfortable with:

• his or her ability to *deficit finance*, which means ensuring the difference between the film's entire budget and the amount of money paid to the producers by one particular buyer;
• his ability to add creative elements (called *attachments*), such as stars and a well-known director;
• his ability to supervise you in the process of turning your treatment into a script, and in the process of rewriting the script as it nears production.

Once the excitement of the "buy" dies down and the realities of development and production set in, no one's particularly enthused about dealing with the naive first-timer, unless he's allied with an experienced pro. Even if you somehow manage to get the attention of a network executive—by sitting next to her on the plane, for example, or meeting her at a party—she'd almost surely ask you to join up with an experienced insider, to whom she might refer you if the story idea has potential.

Though the observations we've made in this chapter are not hard-and-fast rules, the following checklist may help you decide whether your treatment is strong enough to sell:

• **Do you have a strong protagonist?** Your story should be focused on one castable main character who is on-screen nearly all the time, and whose conflicts and motivation drive the action from first to last.
• **Is your protagonist identifiable?** The television audience must be able to relate to the heroine; that is, the viewer must be able to put herself into the heroine's shoes so that she can experience the heroine's emotions vicariously. She loves to watch stories of ordinary women in extraordinary circumstances.
• **Is your protagonist's motivation clear and compelling?** The protagonist's pattern of behavior, which we call her motivation, must be clearly apparent at the outset of the story: What happens if a woman like *this* faces a problem like *that*? Perhaps her insecurity drives her to forgive men too easily, or her love for her mother drives her to turn a blind eye to reality.
• **Does your protagonist have a clear-cut and dramatic mission?** The effective heroine has a heroic purpose in the story, which throws light on her goals in life. This is what we've earlier described as her mission, determined by her motivation.

• **Are the obstacles to your protagonist's mission progressively more dramatic?** In the well-made story, the protagonist must face serious challenges, hurdles, and obstacles in pursuing her goal. Something has to stand in her way. And don't forget that the stronger the antagonist, the stronger your heroine will appear.

• **Does she exhibit courage?** In facing these challenges, hurdles, and obstacles in pursuit of her goal, the protagonist must demonstrate her courage, either physical or emotional—preferably both. Here's where drama is different from reality. It's not a good story just because something traumatic occurs to someone relatable; it can be a good story only if your relatable protagonist deals, in the end, *courageously* with what happens to her.

Now that we've talked about treatments for television movies, the next chapter shows you how to construct a treatment for an episodic series. The following pages show the treatment for the NBC film *Shadow of Obsession*.

TREATMENT FOR A MOVIE FOR TELEVISION

UNWANTED ATTENTIONS
[aired on NBC as *Shadow of Obsession*]
Treatment by Chi-Li Wong
Based on the Novel by K. K. Beck

Log Line: Stalked by an obsessed admirer for fifteen years, a beautiful college professor becomes the prime suspect in his "murder."

Act I

It is 1973 and **BENJAMIN KNAPP** feels the onslaught of another headache. He goes to the library and tries to concentrate on a history assignment. When he first sees her, he knows: there will never be another.

Benjamin follows her to her dorm and learns her name, **REBECCA KENDALL**. He pretends to befriend Wendy, also from the same dorm, and uses her to get closer to Rebecca. When he learns Rebecca will be attending an upcoming off-campus party, he harshly breaks off with Wendy, telling the stunned freshman that he is engaged to someone else. Through careful manipulations at the party, he arranges to give Rebecca a ride home.

Benjamin is driving. Rebecca notices that he has passed the turn for the campus. When she inquires, Benjamin refuses to take her home. There's a struggle, he strikes her, and with a knife hovering inches from her throat, orders her to partially disrobe—and forces her to tell him she loves him. Satisfied, Benjamin returns a shaken Rebecca to her dorm.

Rebecca brings Benjamin to trial on assault charges. Lacking evidence, the charges are dismissed, but not before the judge humiliates Rebecca, blaming her for Benjamin's advances.

Over the next fifteen years Benjamin remains in Rebecca's life. He follows her in his car on dark lonely roads. He watches her from her fire escape. Rebecca finds a heart scratched onto her car door on Valentine's Day. A series of letters, each one harsher than the previous, arrives in her mail, admonishing her for not responding and, finally, threatening her. Rebecca has the post office return them unopened. He starts calling her. Even though she has a series of unlisted numbers, Benjamin always manages to find her. She keeps moving. Suddenly Benjamin stops writing and calling. Is he gone?

CUT TO:

Act II

Rebecca, now a college professor, reveals to her fiancé, stockbroker **PHILIP PATTERSON**, the details of her haunted past. At the mention of Benjamin's name, Philip reacts suddenly and reveals a telegram he received, warning him not to marry her. Rebecca is stunned; she hasn't heard from Benjamin in two years.

Philip presses for an explanation from Rebecca. Her obvious discomfort in discussing the incident that forever changed her life only makes Philip press harder. Nervously, Rebecca recounts the ride home with Benjamin Knapp, fifteen years ago.

Philip is shocked by the story. However, when Rebecca shows him articles she has collected over the years of women who were stalked by obsessive men, he is horrified. "Rebecca, all these women are dead."

Fearing for her life, Rebecca enlists the help of her attorney, **ANGELA CASARETTI**, who was a prelaw student during Benjamin's assault trial. She is unable to get a restraining order on Benjamin because they can't locate him. She suggests Rebecca hire a private detective and recommends her friend **MICHAEL CARUSO**.

Caruso, who is immediately attracted to Rebecca's beauty and sophistication, successfully tracks down Benjamin's address and brings the news to an anxious Rebecca. Curious, he baits her with his comment, "I hope you'll go easy on the guy," and is met with an icy reply from Rebecca: "I wish I could kill him."

Spurred by his curiosity and rapidly growing interest in Rebecca, Caruso pulls Benjamin's address from his pocket. When he arrives at the apartment, he finds the door ajar. Much to his horror, the walls, floors, and bed are dripping with blood.

Act III

Caruso immediately contacts the police and informs them that he believes Benjamin Knapp has been murdered. Caruso accompanies the police to Rebecca's, having informed them of her chilling comment that she wanted Benjamin dead.

Not surprisingly, Rebecca is openly relieved when she hears the news that Benjamin is dead. Feeling free and easy for the first time in fifteen years, Rebecca allows the police to search both her apartment and car. Her relief quickly turns to shock as they discover the car trunk is soaked with blood.

D.A. **CARL APPLEGATE** begins the investigation. Comments from Benjamin's mother indicate Rebecca was obsessed with her son for years. Although there is still no body, the evidence against Rebecca is so strong Angela suggests that Rebecca hire the sensational criminal lawyer **TREVOR KEEGAN**.

At a tense first meeting, Keegan confronts Rebecca with the cold truth: Given the evidence, it will be easier for him to defend her if she agrees to plead guilty than if he tries to convince a jury of her innocence. Angrily, Rebecca proclaims her innocence. D.A. Carl Applegate indicts her for murder. Even in death Benjamin Knapp still has a hold on her.

Act IV

At the trial, Benjamin's mother takes the stand, recalling the assault trial and the fact that the charges against her son were dropped. Rebecca cringes as she remembers all of the notes she received from Mrs. Knapp, urging Rebecca and Benjamin to "patch things up." Rebecca thinks that Mrs. Knapp is truly insane for believing she and Benjamin ever had a relationship.

Much to Rebecca's dismay, her attorney chooses not to cross-examine Mrs. Knapp. Later he reveals to Rebecca that doing so would have made him appear callous.

Ever present at the trial, Caruso is taking more than simply a professional interest in Rebecca; he feels responsible for her being brought up on charges, but most of all his gut tells him something is wrong.

Keegan calls Angela Casaretti to the stand. She is the attorney who has been working with Rebecca for the past fifteen years trying to stop Benjamin's constant harassment. Angela's testimony recalls the terror that Benjamin brought to Rebecca. As the evidence showing an obvious motive builds up against her, Rebecca wonders if this whole trial, the murder, and her arrest are not another form of Benjamin's harassment.

Just before Philip is to testify, D.A. Applegate asks that the court allow the introduction of new evidence. An expert testifies that Benjamin Knapp had his blood DNA-typed in order to prove his innocence in a paternity suit. His DNA type matches the blood found in both Benjamin's apartment and in Rebecca's car.

This information convinces Philip that Rebecca is guilty. He breaks off their engagement and refuses to testify. Rebecca collapses in Keegan's arms.

Act V

Keegan, well aware that Philip's reaction was inevitable, serves him with a subpoena that he filed at the start of the trial. Rebecca is crushed. She realizes that her relationship with Philip was a mistake fueled by Benjamin's harassments. Knowing this will only make Rebecca appear guilty, Keegan again insists that she change her plea to guilty. She refuses.

Keegan is ruthless when Philip takes the stand. Philip had access to both Rebecca's car and her apartment. Given the threat to his impending marriage that Benjamin provided in the telegram, he had every reason to want Benjamin dead. Now that Philip is in jeopardy, it is all too easy for him to accuse Rebecca.

After closing arguments in which Keegan hopes the jury will think that Philip may have been the murderer, Rebecca waits alone at home. Unable to rest, she prepares a hot bath to ease the tension. Standing before her mirrored closet doors in her slip, she is suddenly knocked to the ground by a man's arm. As she struggles, she feels the prick of a needle sliding into her flesh. She falls into a pit of blackness.

Rebecca awakens to the uneven rhythm of a moving vehicle. Bound and gagged, she can make out the driver, now hidden beneath a sandy beard and mustache; it is Benjamin! The vehicle stops. She feigns unconsciousness as the van door squeaks open. Another needle slips into her arm.

Something is bothering Caruso. Even though he heard Rebecca say she wanted Benjamin dead, the case is too neat. His years of experience tell him that murder cases are never this black and white. He starts to go over the case.

Benjamin allows Rebecca the use of a bathroom at a roadside stop. He gives her ten minutes. Desperately, Rebecca tries to find something to leave a note on. Her frantic search uncovers the morning paper. As she reads the headlines, she learns the horrible truth: the jury has convicted her of murder.

Act VI

Benjamin keeps Rebecca isolated in a windowless cabin deep within the woods, wondering what will happen next. Hoping to catch him off guard, she agrees to listen to music with him while he reveals how he had planned his own death in order to blame her. Rebecca scans the room for a weapon while Benjamin talks. A poker in the fireplace. But can she do it? Can she get close enough? She bends to kiss him on the cheek. Instead of kissing her in return, he slaps her across the face, accuses her of being a slut, and barricades her in her room.

The following morning, he greets her as if nothing happened. She seizes the opportunity and offers to cook him breakfast. As she displays the bacon and eggs before him, she splashes his face with scalding grease. He screams in pain as she smashes him over the head with the skillet. He falls to the floor, unconscious.

Frantically, she searches the house for the keys to the van. Her heart pounding, she finds the syringe. Fearing he could awaken at any moment, she injects him. Still unable to locate the car keys, she runs away from the cabin until she comes to a road. In the distance, she sees a column of smoke. With new hope, she runs toward it and comes across a small lake resort.

Caruso is waiting for Keegan when he hears the phone ring. He overhears Keegan telling Rebecca to stay calm and to talk to no one and wait for his arrival. As he arranges a float plane to take him to the resort, he has his secretary alert the press. This is going to be a big boost in Keegan's career. However, Caruso has a different plan. He disables Keegan's car and posing as the attorney's assistant boards the plane himself.

Rebecca is startled by Caruso's arrival. He warns that Keegan believes she is guilty and is planning to bring in a psychiatrist to declare that she's insane.

As she leads Caruso back toward the cabin, he explains how Benjamin could have used blood doping—a technique of storing one's own blood—to fake his own death. The only problem is that they need Benjamin to prove it.

Rebecca is terrified to enter the cabin, fearful that Benjamin is waiting for them. However, as they enter the kitchen, there is only the splattered breakfast, the skillet, and the syringe—Benjamin is gone.

Act VII

Rebecca begs Caruso to take her away. As they leave, Caruso notices Benjamin's feet sticking out from under the shed. He baits him, proclaiming that Rebecca is his prisoner and that he's taking her back to the inn.

When they return to the inn, Rebecca gives in to Caruso's charm and care. He admits that his investigation continued because he had fallen in love with her. Their first kiss is interrupted by a phone call. It's the sheriff's department. They want to speak to Caruso in the lobby.

As Caruso heads toward the lobby, he realizes he made a costly mistake. He's never heard Benjamin's voice. He races back toward the room, but as he turns a corner, a figure steps from the shadows and smashes him on the head. The keys to the room fall to the floor.

Rebecca rushes to the door when she hears the keys in the lock. She turns, thinking it's Caruso: standing before her is Benjamin. He drags her from the room.

Her horror intensifies as he brings her to the edge of a cliff, saying that the only way to be united forever is for them to fall together. With waves crashing below them, Rebecca pleads with him.

Suddenly, Caruso appears, holding a gun. Benjamin, with a sparkle in his eyes, tries to force Rebecca over the edge, but she manages to free herself as Caruso fires. Benjamin tumbles backward off the cliff. . . .

CUT TO:

Rebecca stands before the judge, who readily vacates judgment and dismisses the murder case against her. She bursts through the wall of reporters and into the arms of Michael Caruso, at long last ready to let someone love her.

4

The Bible:
Treatments for
Television Series

. . .

CLIENT: Remember when you told me to be careful what
   you wish for, and I wished to be a staff writer on a successful series?
AEI: We remember. So?
CLIENT: I forgot to wish to be a staff writer on a successful
   intelligent series.

If writing movies for television is the brass ring, the gold ring is
creating and writing series television. Whether family drama,
police or detective series, medical series, legal series, westerns,
adventure, science fiction, or situation comedies, the series—
since the infancy of television—has been the backbone of programming.

Series writing (also referred to as "episodic television") is the
arena of television most difficult to break in to. Although we
don't mean to be discouraging, trying to enter the world of television writing by creating a new series is like planning to break
the bank in Las Vegas with one slot-machine nickel. The reward
is so enormous that the odds are stacked against the outsider.

But, after all, what do you stand to lose? Some of your
time?—which, worst case, has still been well spent on a learning experience.

As a new writer with an eye toward that gold ring, you must arm yourself with all you can learn about the skills and techniques of TV writing—with as much as you can learn about programming. It's not a bad idea to construct a program chart like the type network execs have on their office walls, showing the broadcasters' lineup of shows for the entire week, to familiarize yourself with what kinds of series are airing on each network. Producers are constantly searching for a new, "original" series hit.

So you want to try to pitch a series idea. What do you do? How do you put it together? The most important thing we want to communicate to you, the writer, in terms of how you think about your idea for a television series is that the most critical element is the *characters*. The pilot story is the least important, because if you have a remarkable and outstanding mix of characters who have interesting relationships with one another, yet the pilot story doesn't excite buyers, then it's easy enough to change the story.

HBO's Russell Schwartz gave this example. A writer pitched a series idea to HBO with a five-page treatment for the pilot. The characters he wanted to create were intriguing and the universe he created for them was imaginative and exciting, but the story he fashioned for the pilot wasn't very strong. Clearly the selling point of his pitch was the characters; the pilot could be redeveloped.

Who the characters are and what the relationships between or among them are is the hook that captures an audience—and therefore is the most essential element for you to think about. Character is what distinguishes television series from television movies, where plot is equally as important as character. It's even truer in comedy than in drama. Comedy series tend to be much simpler in plot line than drama series, and what carries the comedy is the characters' relationships, with the dialogue and jokes that spin out of them. *Seinfeld* was the ultimate example.

When Schwartz listens to pitches for series, he says,

I'm thinking about what I'm going to do ten episodes, thirty episodes, fifty episodes down the road. Is there something interesting here that will sustain a series? If all they've done is pitch an interesting pilot, but the writer doesn't know where to go with it, then that's not something I'm going to think I can use. The biggest piece of advice I'd give to someone writing a treatment for a series is to focus on the characters.

If you're dreaming of a staff position, write a spec script of a different successful series, not the one you want to write for. *Frasier* producers will not read a *Frasier* spec script. The only way they'll read one is if it's from an agent they know—though generally they don't even like to do that. Even with a release from you, they're opening themselves up to a submission claim. If you want to write for *Frasier*, write your spec script for a series that you think has a similar sensibility.

When I'm reading an *Everybody Loves Raymond* spec script the only thing I need to discern is, whether the writer can capture the voices of the characters. It certainly doesn't help me to know if he's got a reputation for being a good writer, because he hasn't created anything original for me other than a basic story.

—Russell Schwartz, vice president, HBO Pictures

If you're trying to break in you can cover all bases by (a) doing a spec script from one or two shows similar in sensibility to the one you're applying for; and (b) writing a spec for an original show even if you don't plan to pitch it immediately. Then your submission includes not only a spec script that showcases your originality and creativity, but the writing samples that demonstrate you can also capture a voice.

Realistically, it's unlikely you're going to get a staff job starting from scratch without ever having sold an episodic script, unless you're coming in through a studio program or special personal relationship with the producers. For most outsiders hoping to break in, the best you can hope for is a spec assignment, which in itself is a huge breakthrough, because so few of these are given out—a show hires you to write a script, with the understanding that if they really like it, and your planets are all aligned, then you might have a chance of winding up as a staff writer and proving yourself.

Unfortunately, as we suggested earlier, series producers will not accept unsolicited material (meaning scripts not represented by an agent, manager, or lawyer they know) because the chances of finding something original and interesting are far outweighed by the likelihood of getting sued by someone whose script turns out to be similar to a project which may already have been in development. Your goal in writing your spec scripts is to get someone to read your material and then want to represent you.

What to Write About

For a new writer, it's probably best to base a series on something you know intimately, rather than on what you guess TV might want. When it comes to all the accepted and established subjects, you're up against the pros who've been creating series for years. What they *haven't* been doing is writing about the subject matter that *you* have a special relationship to: you may know and love the tuna fishing business, or come from a family of twelve kids; maybe your spouse tames wild animals, or your grandparents ran an old-fashioned small farm against all odds, or your uncle is a moonshiner. Your passion and knowledge of details, coupled with the originality of your subject matter, give you an edge that might just lead to a sale.

Studying the network lineup also will help you learn about the production companies and producers of each series, so you understand the markets and players. Don't get caught up yet in trying to copy a successful show, or in writing for a particular market—because first and foremost you want to be original—but it can only help to be aware of present and changing trends. Think of something new or something old with a twist. Your goal is to write an original treatment containing imaginative, identifiable characters that audiences will invite into their living rooms week after week, and a compelling story that reflects your talent and creativity.

Is There a Selling Season?

Episodic television is seasonal: in May, June, and July new series are ordered; those shows premier either in the fall (September or October) or at midseason (between January and March). Occasionally you'll see midseason pilots being done in July or August, but, historically, that's been rare. By and large there's been one pilot season, which begins in September. Programmers pick their fall shows, along with a bunch of others for which they say, "We're not passing on these yet—we're going to order some of them to pilot for midseason, and we're going to hang on to some first-round pilots and decide if we want them for midseason."

It's certainly true that networks are premiering more shows midseason than they ever did before. With six networks' worth of new shows being premiered at the same time, the networks have found that they can open them midseason with less clutter. The marketplace for new series reflects the shifting programming priorities of the networks, cable companies, and stations. Those needs change from network to network, from season to season, and from executive to executive.

How a Bible Is Sold

The selling process begins when a *seller*—an independent producer, agent, or manager—finds a bible to get excited about. The seller either (1) options the bible, the industry term for the treatment of a proposed series, by making a deal with the writer that establishes the seller's right to develop the series in exchange for an option payment and promised purchase price; or (2) if he's an agent or manager, makes a representation agreement with the writer. The seller then works with the writer to improve the treatment based on the seller's experience with both dramatic principles and the current marketplace.

Once development is completed to the seller's satisfaction, the seller takes the treatment to a *buyer*—a cable or network programmer. If the buyer shares the enthusiasm, a deal is made to produce a *pilot*. This means that the buyer guarantees the seller a license fee payable upon delivery of the show, allowing the seller to proceed with the production knowing that the bulk of his costs will be covered.

Achieving a series deal with a major broadcaster is almost always dependent on attaching an experienced, successful series writer to the new project as a form of insurance that the project will have the best possible shot at capturing an audience. This pro is known as a *show runner* because successful writers become executive producers and run the show. A new writer has virtually no chance of receiving sole credit for a pilot script, and very little chance of even being involved in writing it. Writing your own first series may not even be desirable financially because, when you think about it, your series has a better chance all around if it's in the hands of a popular show runner. You will, in the end, make more money because he's attached than if you had been the sole writer.

So don't despair. The network-approved show runners who are hired to write or cowrite pilots are the most successful in the industry, and your being associated with them can truly launch your career. When you get to be a show runner yourself, you'll understand. With the enormously successful dramatic series *The Practice, Boston Public,* and comedy series *Ally McBeal* under his belt, David E. Kelley doesn't need to "cowrite" anything. If he agrees to write and produce your series, are you really going to be unhappy?

A former Boston lawyer, Kelley switched careers to become a television producer whose shows are recognized for their quality as well as receiving top ratings. In 1983 he wrote a film script based on some of his legal experiences. *From the Hip* was optioned and he acquired an agent in 1986. It was produced in 1987 starring Judd Nelson, Elizabeth Perkins, and John Hurt. At the time, producers Steven Bochco and Terry Louise Fisher (creators of the successful police drama *Hill Street Blues*) were planning a new series set in a law firm, and looking for writers with legal backgrounds. After seeing David E. Kelley's script they invited him to Los Angeles to discuss writing a single script for *L.A. Law*.

Kelley joined the show's staff as a story editor. The next year he became executive story editor, and after Terry Fisher left the show became the supervising producer. Steven Bochco left *L.A. Law* after the third season, and David E. Kelley took over as executive producer, while continuing to write many of the scripts himself.

He then served as creative consultant on *Doogie Howser, M.D.,* which was produced by Steven Bochco, and as executive producer and writer for *Picket Fences*. He was the executive producer of *Chicago Hope*.

As we go to press he's in preproduction with yet another new series, *Girls Club*, a one-hour drama about three young female attorneys based in San Francisco who are determined to make their mark on the justice system.

What about Credit?

Although your life will certainly change if you get "created by" or "co-created by" credit on a series that gets on the air, those luminous credits are governed by the Writers Guild of America and you can't negotiate for them.

When the pilot is completed and the series ordered, the studio will submit the pilot script to the WGA using a WGA form especially for this purpose. The studio does this for every episode written in a series. The studio will indicate on the form who should get the writing credit on the pilot and who should get the "created by" credit on the series.

Generally, the person who writes the pilot is the person who is going to get the "created by" credit. It's rare when that doesn't happen. If there's underlying material from which the project issued then it may happen that the "created by" credit is shared with the source of the story, or that either the writer of the pilot or the source gets some form of "developed by" credit.

A more common dilemma (though it also doesn't happen too often) is when your pilot script is rewritten by another writer hired by the studio. In that case, the studio must make a tentative decision regarding whether you and the second writer should share the writing credit or whether only one of you should receive it. This is complicated by having to determine two credits: the pilot and the series. It's possible—albeit rare—for the second writer to contribute enough to share writing credit on the pilot but not the series—say, if the second writer doesn't change the characters or settings at all and simply rewrites dialogue. In that case, the final credit might be: "Story by First Writer," "Teleplay by First Writer and Second Writer," "Series Created by First Writer."

All the affected writers are given a copy of the submitted WGA form. At that point the writers have the ability to request an arbitration if they disagree with the studio's proposed determination.

One of the banes of our existence is writers demanding contractual "created by" credit. Under no circumstances, according to the Writers Guild, can you contractually secure a "created by" credit. The studio and the Guild are going to want to see what the final product is before credits can be determined. If the pilot is heavily rewritten by someone else you may not be entitled to receive a "created by" or even a shared "created by" credit.

If your pilot turns out well and captures the enthusiasm of the programmer's executives, an initial order for thirteen episodes will be issued. Then, if the show does well in the ratings, the studio will issue a "back order," bringing the number of episodes to 22. Dramas rarely go beyond 22 episodes a year. Comedies, if they're successful, will go to 24, 25, and occasionally 26 episodes.

What's in the Bible?

Although you would not necessarily include a bible in pitching a television series to a buyer, you definitely would have one to convince an agent or manager to take you on, and you'd definitely have one to pitch a miniseries.

Ideally, for a television series you would write:

- an overview of the series
- character descriptions: Who are these people? What makes them interesting? How are they going to relate to each other? What is it about their relationships with one another that we're going to find comedic or dramatic?
- a brief overview of the pilot in four to five pages

Anything longer than five pages would allow you to wander down way too many side streets—and that's not what's going to sell a TV series. It's really all about the premise and characters.

An agent, manager, or independent producer may want a much more detailed view of your series idea, in which case you would include:

- a one-page overview of your series
- a one-page description of all the major characters
- a four- to five-page overview of the pilot
- extended descriptions of each character
- a one-page description of the "franchise," or setting
- "background" on the series concept, where appropriate
- the pilot treatment
- brief descriptions of four to twelve future episodes

On the next page is, courtesy of HBO, Harry Stein's bible for *Playing Doctor*.

PLAYING DOCTOR
by
Harry Stein

The basic concept is a medical school version of *The Paper Chase*—the interplay among smart, ambitious, fiercely competitive young people and the medical professionals (equally competitive and complex) charged with turning them into doctors. Because much of the action is set in the adjacent hospital where the students undergo hands-on training, the show will also feature the life-and-death, breakneck excitement of an *ER*. The opportunities afforded by such a venue—dramatic, romantic, and comedic—are limitless.

The show will focus largely on two students, David Van Deusen and Craig Frank, uneasy friends, rivals, and occasional outright antagonists, as well as on their and others' relationship with a brilliant professor, Peter Meyerowitz, equal parts mentor and tormentor.

Through these med students we will, in a larger sense, explore a quandary which is more compelling in the hard-driving, unreflective, morally ambiguous present than ever before: the clash between ambition and idealism. How do you hang on to your humanity when leaving it behind can often seem essential to forging ahead? In a brutally competitive field, how can qualities like generosity, kindness, self-sacrifice NOT be liabilities?

The irony here is that medicine calls itself (and in crucial respects is) the most humane of professions. Yet the training for it—acquiring the authority/ability to ultimately make life-and-death decisions—can be brutal and brutalizing. The medical establishment itself recognizes the contradiction and is working to change; and this, too, we will deal with. Still, the bottom-line reality remains: dedicated and idealistic as you are, if you're not tough, you're in trouble. You may survive, but you sure as hell won't stand out. Then again, if you're hard-driving enough to truly excel, what are you left with? Forget about what kind of doctor you'll be: What kind of *human being* will you be?

Week to week we will see this process working on people, changing them—and not always for the better.

SETTING: JOHNS HOPKINS MED SCHOOL

Among the most prestigious such institutions in the country, Hopkins also offers Baltimore's widely diverse array of locales; and, as an innovative and far-seeing school emphasizing early exposure to patients and ethical questions, it is an ideal place to showcase the range of pressures and challenges of the modern med student's life.

CHARACTERS

The Principals:
DAVID VAN DEUSEN: One of our two main guys. On first glance, a charmer—quick, funny, likable. But we soon pick up that the glibness masks real complexity and self-doubt. It turns out he's in med school not out of burning passion but because, as the son of two doctors, he's *supposed* to be; and, hardly the most reflective of people, he is only now beginning to question any of it.

In fact, what we have is a kid (22 years old, but truly on his own for the first time) struggling to belatedly grow up and figure out who he is; yet doing so in a pressure-filled hothouse environment in which many with whom he deals, patients and civilians alike, treat him like an all-knowing god.

A bit of background: David's father—not Jewish, always working, somewhat remote—is a respected general surgeon. His intensely driven mother is a cardiologist. But the family's real engine is his mother's mother, a celebrated, much-beloved German-Jewish Holocaust survivor/writer, who in private is iron-willed and arbitrary, about as far from the reflective, saintlike figure she plays in public as you can get. The family has already been cruelly disappointed once, by David's older brother, Nate, who opted out of the family business in the most in-your-face way: he does massage therapy ("back rubs," in his grandmother's contemptuous view), dividing his time between New York's Alphabet City and rural Jamaica.

The Nate experience has put even more pressure on David. As an undergraduate he attended Columbia, so the family could keep him on a short leash; and he has a pretty good idea he was accepted at Johns Hopkins only through their pull. Indeed, for all his native ability (he's also a good athlete and a good jazz clarinetist), he's long been a grade-A bullshitter, able to hold forth on everything from poetry to American history, and up till now he's really never had to completely earn anything.

Basically, we're talking an unexamined life. But that's about to change: though his family can do a lot of things, they can't do a thing for him when there's a life on the line.

CRAIG FRANK: Our (unlikely) other student principal. At first, there appears little likable, let alone admirable, about Craig. At 27, several years older than most of his peers, married, with a four-year-old daughter, he is as calculating as anyone at the school—an unsubtle self-promoter; *the* ultimate kiss-up—with the uncanny ability to alter his personality to please whomever he's trying to impress. Indeed, he initially befriends David because (unbeknownst to David) he's found out who his grandmother is. Before med school he worked as a journalist for his father-in-law, the manager of a public television station (a do-gooding experience he describes with good-natured scorn), and we soon learn he secretly has a contract for a book recording his med school experiences. But easy as it is to write Craig off as a total asshole, it's not quite so simple. First among his quasi-saving graces: at least he's up front about it—amusingly so—which gives him honesty and self-knowledge points. More to the point, more and more we see that he is a tormented soul. Neurotic and self-hating, Craig truly does know the difference between right and wrong, thinks about it far more than most—indeed, as much as anything it is his desperation for respect that has drawn him to medicine. Still, somehow, when his self-interest is involved, he will invariably end up making whatever choice serves *him* best.

We also come to see where it all came from. His parents were divorced early and, needy from the start, he never remotely got the attention he craved. He continues to revere his extremely liberal, youth-obsessed mother, a successful book editor, but can never quite please her: a WASP wannabe, even she's put off by his relentless climbing, making no secret of her preference for his well-married writer sister.

Of course, he's in therapy; and though he keeps it under wraps, he's vulnerable to every wacky, New Age nostrum that comes down the pike.

In brief, you can't help liking the guy despite yourself. And when he fools you by coming through in the pinch, as he very occasionally does (e.g., I envision a future plot where a wealthy young stockbroker, someone Craig went to college with, belittles Craig, whom he's never liked—then has a heart attack and falls into his clutches), it comes as a genuine revelation.

PETER MEYEROWITZ: The school's superstar, 42, a nationally recognized internist and legendary diagnostician. But among students who crave his approval, this hugely complex figure is equally famous for his erratic personality. Highly principled and capable of enormous charm, a truly great teacher, the Queens-born Meyerowitz can turn on a dime into a caustic, egotistical bully. In his private life, Meyerowitz is childless and working on his third marriage.

As we come to know him better, we will learn that his intensity and fierce dedication to medicine are the result of a near-fatal case of Hodgkin's disease as an undergraduate. He never talks about the cancer—or that the resulting chemo left him sterile—but it was the pivotal emotional event in his life.

Meyerowitz will be as compelling to viewers (and as important in the lives of his students, especially David and Craig) as John Houseman in *The Paper Chase*.

Other Main Faculty:
DICK FISHER: Clinician and teacher. A gifted cardiologist, at 53 he's in the midst of a divorce and a consuming midlife crisis. He masks his deep insecurity with an air of enormous self-importance. Sporting shades and driving a fire engine–red Miata, flirting awkwardly with some of the more attractive students (he eventually has an affair with one), he's an easy target for students and colleagues alike. But, like most others here, there's more to him than it seems—and, in the crunch, he's also extraordinarily good at what he does.

SUSAN HAWKING: English, 45, general surgeon and the dean of students. (Always being asked if she's related to Stephen, which she's not.) Highly dedicated but somewhat brittle, she's a particular mentor to women, a result of her own often difficult student days. For all her professional standing, she must also deal with a complicated home life, and here she's much less in control. Her celebrated sociology prof husband (who fancies himself fully liberated) privately relies on her for his every need, physical and emotional; she's at odds with their sullen, uncommunicative teenage son, who's struggling in school and up to God-knows-what; on top of which, she suspects their cleaning woman's robbing them blind.

Other Main Students:
NICOLE RICHARDSON: From rural Oklahoma, a graduate of SMU, Nicole is salty-tongued, no-bullshit, and smart as a whip. One of David and Craig's gross anatomy lab partners, Nicole is soon caught in the cross fire of their on-again, off-again friendship.

The daughter of a high school coach and an accomplished jock (a seriously competitive softball player), Nicole plans to enter the overwhelmingly male realm of orthopedic surgery—the medical version of carpentry, involving strength and stamina and, drawing as it does an inordinate number of beer-guzzling, nurse-chasing types, a high tolerance for assholes. For their part, the would-be studs, whom she gets a charge out of out-machoing, don't know quite what to make of her; since (like David and Craig) they're at once drawn to her and not entirely sure of her sexuality, increasingly a source of confusion even to her.

Ambitious and hard-charging, as the series begins she's already been at school several months, having arrived in early summer to get a head start. And she's already involved in an unequal relationship with Matt Schulman, a talented but extremely self-absorbed intern.

TIMOTHY SCHNIBBE: David's med school housemate, Tim is the ultimate grind—self-serious and driven. An upper-middle-class African-American, he even listens to bland semi-classical music (which he doesn't much like), since a science project he did back in high school proved it was the ideal backdrop for studying. He loves science fiction, is terrified of dogs, and begins every third sentence with a condescending "Basically . . ."—a verbal tic that drives David crazy.

Though he is generally low key (and not overtly political), in the face of even the mildest of perceived slights, a huge chip emerges on Tim's shoulder. For he is one of those people, gifted yet fragile, who's ever aware of others' assumption that he's gotten where he is through favoritism. The irony is that he himself makes some of the same negative assumptions about other blacks (which gives him plenty of room to grow).

RACHEL QUINDLAN: A Harvard grad and daughter of an academic feminist lawyer (no brothers, father's a new-mannish wimp), she's in open rebellion against what she sees as her mother's archaic views on gender. (The fact is, it's NOT hard being a woman in med school anymore; the place is NOT set up for the benefit of sexist jerks, and even the most normally condescending male faculty usually take care not to step over the line.) Still, as these things go, her mother's influence has had its effect. Though she loves and would be terrific at pediatrics, Rachel feels she should aim instead for the high-powered and far more prestigious field of cardiology (which, in an additional irony, regularly throws her into the orbit of the screwed-up and creepily lascivious Fisher—the one guy who actually does fit the old Neanderthal stereotype).

Her sister, a college junior at nearby George Washington University in Washington, is in even greater rebellion—when she shows up, she turns out (to the guys' delight) to be incredibly sexy in an old-fashioned, kittenish way—and an unbelievable embarrassment to Rachel.

RAJIV PATEL: Tim's friend and fellow grind. Younger than most (he skipped a couple of grades), he's great with minutiae and can memorize anything—which makes him a classic know-it-all. Curtly dismissive of those he considers his intellectual inferiors, uninterested in anyone else's views, his awful people skills mean he has trouble effectively applying any of what he knows to real life.

Like others in his socially inept circle, Rajiv is also subject to bouts of unbeliev-able immaturity—especially in the gross anatomy lab. Still, in his usual driven way, he's *working* at being a regular guy—conscientiously drinking a 4-ounce can of beer every day.

CARLOS EPSTEIN-BROWN: Argentinean, went to Yale as an undergradu-ate. His family (British/Jewish descent) made big bucks as industrialists. Aristocratic in presentation, fair-minded, and straightforward, he's one of David's gross anatomy partners and becomes a friend. This stuff comes easy to him—he rarely attends lectures and is unconcerned with class ranking. Yet he does well anyway because he's endlessly curious and genuinely loves science. He brings the same excitement to a range of passions, from old movies to horse racing. He's gay, but not politically so; tends to have rough-tradish liaisons with young working-class men.

MATT SCHULMAN: Nicole's intern boyfriend. The son of a general surgeon who's aiming even higher, Matt demands total commitment from Nicole—but expects her to understand he can give little back in return. Though fond of her, he flirts compulsively with every attractive woman around (the nurses have his number). For all his emotional immaturity, a gifted young doctor.

Of course, you can make your bible complete by writing the pilot script yourself. But if you do this, make sure you let the seller (agent, manager, producer, or attorney) you work with know that you're willing to step back if a sale proves easier with everyone pretending that your pilot doesn't exist. The upside is that you'll write such a great pilot everyone will immediately identify you as the next David E. Kelley. The downside is that if your pilot is set aside, your ego will have to deal with it—buttressed, you hope, by a satisfactory breakthrough payment.

One-Page Overview
On the next page is the one-page overview of *Port of Call*, an original dramatic series that AEI, represented by the William Morris Agency, first sold to Viacom for development based on a brief initial pitch—simply, "We're working on a new series about the New Orleans Harbor Police, who patrol 13,000 miles of waterways in the largest harbor operation in the world."

ONE-PAGE OVERVIEW

PORT OF CALL: HOT PEPPER
created by
Kenneth Aguillard Atchity

A third-generation New Orleans detective tracking his partner's murderer is paired up with an expatriate French detective.

Disobeying orders that he remain "on leave" until the heat cools down from his last escapade, Harbor Police Detective **ARCHIE CAMERY, III**, makes it to the Harmony Street Wharf just in time to witness his partner Buddy's body parachuting into the Mississippi.

Hard-nosed, by-the-book Captain of Detectives **JIMMY-BIRD JOHNSON** knows just where to find his loose-cannon detective: The Endless Train, a shotgun-style bar frequented by local law enforcement. Jimmy-Bird tries to persuade Archie to stay out of the way of the investigation, despite the lead Archie's already onto from **MELANIE CHATELAINE**, the gorgeous octoroon private detective who was Buddy's lover. Jimmy-Bird is babysitting **LOUIS LARRE**, a Frenchman assigned to New Orleans by Interpol. Larre is on the trail of international smuggler **ENRIQUE BARRACAS**. The Captain teams up the unlikely pair. Louis's high-tech savvy and suave bravado complement Archie's local knowledge and natural wariness.

Checking over Buddy's autopsy report, Archie notices that the red substance found caked beneath Buddy's fingernails is—cayenne pepper! Computer checks with U.S. Customs lead him to a Louisiana "Collectibles & Edibles" merchant on Bourbon Street, who imports the substance from French Guyana for his "Cajun spices." Meanwhile, Louis, now undercover as an importer/exporter, makes a dangerous contact—Barracas's sexy sister, **TALIA**, who has contraband artifacts to sell. As the investigation proceeds, Archie and Louis find their separate searches converging: the cayenne pepper disguises not only cocaine (the find that killed Buddy) but also Barracas's merchandise—a magnificent gold Inca burial mask. As the final twist, Archie discovers that Louis's pursuit of Barracas is based on a personal vendetta—Barracas killed Louis's sister, and nothing can stop Louis from bringing him to justice.

The one-page overview of your pilot story should also make clear:

• who the main characters are (Detective Archie Camery of the New Orleans Harbor Police and Louis Larre of the French office of Interpol);

• what the story is about ("After losing his partner, a New Orleans Harbor Police detective finds he can still cut the mustard");

• what the main motivational conflicts of the character(s) are (Archie's motivation is to find his partner's killer; Louis Larre's is his relentless pursuit of an international smuggler somehow linked to the partner's murder);

• the dramatic potential of the series, based on a totally involving opening and closing scene that provides a glimpse of the series's ongoing potential.

Leading Characters

Next, to allow us to see your dramatis personae at a glance, give us the leading characters in a single page. Each one should be described in a few lines, emphasizing the character's identifying attributes, motivation, and directions for growth.

THE CONTINUING CHARACTERS

PORT OF CALL

Leads:
DETECTIVE LIEUTENANT ARCHIE CAMERY, III, 35–40, of the Harbor Police Department of the Board of Commerce of the Port of New Orleans.

LOUIS LARRE, mid-40s, red hair, blue-gray eyes, half French-Canadian, half French. Louis was trained by the French *Douanes*—now working for Interpol, and assigned to New Orleans by request of the French consulate to serve as liaison "in the Americas" for international smuggling.

Supports:
JACQUELINE AGUILLARD CAMERY, Archie's wife, a dark-haired, flashing-eyed Cajun.

JIMMY-BIRD JOHNSON, Captain of Detectives and Chief of the Harbor Police, a happy, portly, African-American (late 40s to early 50s).

MELANIE CHATELAINE, an extremely attractive octoroon private investigator. Her ties with the African-American, Cuban, and Creole (and, yes, voodoo!) communities make her an invaluable resource for the Harbor Police, as well as for the New Orleans Police Department.

Extended Character Description (also known as *character workup*)

The next section of your bible should devote an entire page each to an extended description of your series's *major characters*; a half page each to its *continuing characters* who play supporting roles; and about a quarter of a page for *minor continuing characters*. For many executives in the series television industry, as in feature films, action line has become secondary to character development. Audiences tune in not for the benefit of stories but to watch characters they like. *Murder, She Wrote* survived year after year because of Angela Lansbury's character; *Seinfeld* lives on because of Jerry.

Once your bible makes it into the broadcaster's development process, the characters will become even more the focus than you've already made them. What motivates them, their missions in life, their feelings toward others and toward life itself—these are central issues. The more you can do in your extended descriptions to indicate directions for character development, the more excited a prospective buyer will be. Obviously, the ideal is to have a compelling action line each week, combined with totally involving characters.

The next page has the extended description of each character for *Port of Call*.

Extended Description of Each Character

PORT OF CALL

Leads:
DETECTIVE LIEUTENANT ARCHIE CAMERY, III, 35–40, of the Harbor Police Department of the Board of Commerce of the Port of New Orleans. Archie is convinced he's seen it all—and what he hasn't seen, he's heard about. His weariness and conviction stretch back two generations before him. His father and his father before him were both detectives.

Archie's wife is a dark-haired, flashing-eyed Cajun, **JACQUIE AGUILLARD CAMERY**, who has decided she won't speak to him until he quits the force—and can't keep herself from telling him so at every opportunity. The truth is, he himself wants to retire; he has his eye on a ramshackle cabin on Grand Isle (on the Gulf), where he'd like to raise their twins, fishing and leading a saner, safer life. He's always about to go fishing—when something else comes up. He's moody, sometimes quixotic—has trouble with anger. Even anger makes him angry, and he's been known to burst into violent behavior. But a woman's anger totally baffles him—he responds by going away.

He has trouble with any kind of machine, inheriting his distrust from his grandfathers. Archie went to Loyola, the Jesuit high school, and, encouraged by Jesuit discipline, started out to study classics at Tulane—when environment triumphed over education and he switched to the family's tradition of criminology.

Between his wife's Cajun proverbs, the Camery family's New Orleans wisdom, and his background in the classics, Archie has a saying for everything, from the sublime to the ridiculous (sample: "White hair is beautiful, but not in my soup.")

Jacquie married Archie because she recognized his "Cajun qualities"—he does everything the hard way.

LOUIS LARRE, mid-40s, red hair, blue-gray eyes, half French-Canadian, half French (his mother a famous singer from Montreal, his father a French industrialist and vintner). He is as relentless and methodical as he is self-confident and charismatic.

Women fall in love with Louis before he can even wink at them—his looks, charm, and style. But Louis, most of the time, is not interested. A secret known only to himself holds him back from them, makes him unable to commit.

Louis, trained by the French *Douanes*, is now working for Interpol and has been assigned to New Orleans by request of the French consulate to serve as liaison "in the Americas" for international smuggling. We find out that he in fact requested his assignment and is not yet ready to tell Archie why he wanted to leave France and has no desire to visit Montreal (he will do both, later in the series).

Unlike Archie, Louis is high-tech—wired into every database, fitted with the latest devices of communication and surveillance. Whatever hurt him long ago has led him to replace hunches with gimmickry—another distancing mechanism. As his relationship with Archie progresses, Louis will learn to trust his instincts again.

When Louis chooses a place to live, it'll probably be in a converted streetcar near the old streetcar yards—because it's the kind of place American "investigator types" are supposed to live in. Plus, it gives him a perfect perspective for surveillance.

Louis can't swim. Archie calls him "Tropics."

Supporting:
JACQUELINE AGUILLARD CAMERY, Archie's Cajun wife, says they've been "married so long we on our second bottle of Tabasco!" She loves him passionately and presides vociferously over the sprawling, exotically landscaped "river cottage" on once genteel, now shabbily elegant Dryades Street that has belonged to Archie's family for nearly 100 years. She and Archie now rent out the two upper stories to the Giammos, a large Italian family to whom she is second mother.

Jacquie is *not* interested in being a widow, does not consider Archie's liaisons on the dance floor with any woman but her "in the line of duty," and is not shy about adding her two cents to his investigations. Plus, she has a secret weapon: the "bayou telegraph," linking her Cajun relatives from swampland to farmland throughout South Louisiana.

JIMMY-BIRD JOHNSON, Captain of Detectives and Chief of the Harbor Police, a happy, portly, African-American man in his late 40s or early 50s, an insatiable romantic with a passion for sweets—who considers himself to be one of the best bakers in the Crescent City. Born in Charleston, South Carolina, Jimmy-Bird went to Tulane Law School and decided to stay because, compared to New Orleans, he found Charleston "too damned civilized." He's always bringing homemade beignets and pies in to H.P. headquarters to "keep up morale" (most of it stays in his office). He laughs so hard he gets leg cramps.

MELANIE CHATELAINE, an extremely attractive octoroon (probably with Latin blood) private investigator who lives above T-Neg's Restaurant and has to sneak in and out at the risk of being forced by its proprietor (Pero Noiret) to eat. Her ties with the African-American, Cuban, and Creole (and, yes, voodoo!) communities make her an invaluable resource for the Harbor Police, as well as for the New Orleans Police Department. Most people who don't know her assume she's a high-priced call girl, and Melanie isn't worried about dispelling their views. Her aim is simple: she's waiting for the "big one," so that she can retire to an island where no one knows what the word *race* means.

Minor:
DETECTIVE MARIA ROSA FONG, half-Latina, half-Chinese, born in Harlem, proud of being the first woman to make detective for the Harbor Police— but paying for it on a daily basis, both from her fellow cops and from her Latin friends. Maria Rosa is vivacious and constantly being propositioned by the lowlife hauled in to the H.P.'s net. Maria Rosa is always trying to stop smoking—she's failed a "million" times, but is always onto something new.

DETECTIVE CHARLIE FEIBLEMAN, gaunt as a scarecrow with a personality to match, is a blue-blood aristocrat of old New Orleans shipping and cotton-trading money who's abandoned his heritage and playboy past to do something to "keep him off the streets." Charlie's unflappable.

E. J. CADY, Captain of the New Orleans Police Department, often working in tandem with the Harbor Police, is a dark-haired ex-football player who takes us in and out of the world of New Orleans sports—football, basketball, races. Cady is often seen in the company of high-rollers, and we suspect he himself may be a gambler.

ASHBEL LONG, District Attorney of the City of New Orleans, colorful, straight out of an old Orson Welles film, but *not* related to the "King Fish" family of governors and senators. He is a cutthroat prosecutor, with a heart of gold he does his best to hide.

"SHERM" (short for "Sherman") LINCOLN, African-American officer of the Harbor Police, in charge of the boats. Sherm is superstitious, especially about music—and plays ragtime piano on Pirates Alley behind the cathedral in the Vieux Carré on his nights off.

BOSTON, the retired Louisiana state policeman who runs The Endless Train, the "cop bar" on Girod Street in the Warehouse District. Even Boston doesn't know why he's called Boston.

"SIGMUND" REES, the East Indian pathologist who got his nickname from giving psychological background on the organs he autopsies.

PERO NOIRET, wiry Cajun proprietor of T-Neg's, Buddy's and Archie's favorite restaurant (Melanie lives upstairs), the "information center" of the old part of the city. Pero is convinced that there's no ailment that can't be cured with the exact right food and drink, the living opposite of "New Age herbal-holistic astrojumbalaya," as he calls it.

CONRAD, the impoverished but dignified (he refuses to take welfare) old, African-American streetcar conductor who becomes Archie's pal after the chase in "Hot Pepper"—and provides a perfect location for clandestine meetings as well as a constant flow of information. Archie has to find creative ways to compensate Conrad, and has Jacquie look after him.

BERNIE ADASHEK, Chief Inspector, U.S. Customs, Port of New Orleans. His Polish-Jewish family settled in New Orleans to control the textile trade. He wasn't interested in continuing the merchant tradition and now monitors it instead.

What Makes a Good Series Character?

All your talent and skills are needed to create characters who are easily identifiable yet have sufficient depth to allow each episode to deal with new situations that will hold an audience's interest. We can't say enough about the construction of a good character. Let's look again at the four dimensions that build a good character, this time focusing on series examples:

1. Motivation. A major character is usually motivated in two conflicting directions that compel the audience's involvement and sympathy. Archie Bunker in *All in the Family* was torn between his extraordinary bigotry and the kind heart he tried to hide beneath it. Superman is torn between his sense of duty to Metropolis and his need to reveal himself to Lois to gain her love.

A supporting character usually has a single motivational tag that makes the character seem real to the audience when, in fact, the very opposite is true. Real people are too complex to be good fictional characters, as the recent *Kissinger and Nixon* and Oliver Stone's *Nixon* demonstrate. Phoebe in *Friends* is the airhead flower child; Cliff Claven in *Cheers*, a bumbling trivia nut; Mrs. Kravetz in *Bewitched*, a busybody.

2. Mission. Each episode of a series is set up so the major character is involved in a mission, usually his own, sometimes that of another character. In one episode of *Seinfeld*, Elaine's mission was to get a new poster signed by the "third tenor." In the comedy *Cybill*, Cybill's best friend Maryann's ongoing mission in life is discovering new ways to stalk her ex-husband, Dr. Dick.

3. Obstacles. In each episode of a series, character development unfolds through a sequence of obstacles the protagonist must deal with in his effort to achieve his mission. The way in which the character deals with an episode's obstacles is what makes the audience feel that something has been learned, some progress has been made, something important or comical has been conveyed. In *Ellen*, Ellen Degeneres's character is suspicious of her mother's video date and wants to take a look at the tape, but the dating service will not allow viewing by nonmembers. Ellen tries to outwit the agency's receptionist, the first of several obstacles she faces to accomplish her mission.

4. Change. Although series characters don't change to the same extent as movie characters must, they're best when they've been created with room to grow and stretch. As the series *Friends* developed, Jennifer Aniston's character Rachel changes from not recognizing the aimless pining of Ross (David Schwimmer) to suddenly realizing after he leaves for a trip to China that she's attracted to him—only to find it's too late when he returns with a Chinese girlfriend. Now Rachel's the one pining. The growth and change of the series characters compels audience involvement. People tune in again each week to see what progress the cast of *ER* is making in their attempts to deal with the stress of the emergency room on their psyches and daily lives; the audience is hooked. The extended presentation of your characters in the bible should reflect possible growth in each character, but not extended to such a detailed road map of the future that the person you're pitching to feels he has to either accept that road map or not do the project.

Instead, you want to give a strong sense of who these people are—their conflicts, their relationships and how they may be explored, their baggage and how they deal with it—but not get into anything too specific, unless in response to being asked to do so.

Even your short description of characters on the one-page overview discussed earlier should indicate the primary motivation that drives their actions through the story. If your series has more than one leading character (and there probably shouldn't be more than two or three; if there are, the series then becomes an ensemble piece like *Friends*), give an example of how the focal point can shift from week to week. This will also underline your show's variety and versatility. Expand on your characters' identifying attributes, using anecdotes to dramatize them. Character is revealed in action, not description. Include a line or two in your extended description to indicate potential ongoing interactions or conflicts between your major and supporting characters.

5. Conflict. This is the key to both characterization and action, as well as the core around which scenes, the units of drama, are constructed. Your character involves the audience's sympathies when he or she faces conflict (provided by major and minor obstacles). We want to see how, on *Frasier*, Frasier will deal with Lilith's re-entry into his life, or what Ross of *Friends* does when he learns his ex-wife is having his baby with her lesbian lover. When you clearly know what would happen if a character like Sydney Briston of *Alias* finds that her mother, whom she thought was dead, is very much alive—and a double agent—you're on your way to capturing an audience. Success in this regard explains why ardent series fans are constantly sending in ideas to the producers. They know the characters so well they can accurately imagine what they'd do in stressful situations.

Along the way, don't forget that the first impression your character makes on your bible's reader is the most important. Once you've done your draft, use all you know about good drama to go back and sharpen:

- each character's introduction
- each act's opening scene
- each act-end

Trying to accomplish all this in bible form takes hard work and skill. But the key is to know your characters so fully that in one or two sentences you are able to give a credible and complete character study with just enough flexibility to show that this character is going to be real and interesting whatever the plotline or story. Having a particular film or TV star in mind can assist in selling the character to a network exec, or production company exec, but nothing beats originality.

Next you want to create the world, the setting, in which these characters move, almost as if it were another character itself.

Setting
Here's the place in your series bible to make us understand how exciting the setting you've chosen, known in episodic television as the *franchise*, is for dramatic exploitation—how much potential it has for repeat episodes, as in:

- the emergency room of *ER*
- the contrasting streets of New York in *NYPD Blue* and *Sex and the City*
- the forensic lab in *CSI*
- the Victorian family home in *Charmed*
- the offices of *The Drew Carey Show*
- the courtroom of *Judging Amy*
- the funeral home of *Six Feet Under*

What is the environment in which your characters will operate most of the time? What will be the main set? Study the importance of setting in the hospital in *Scrubs*, the radio station in *Frasier*, *Boston Public's* school setting, and the coffeehouse in *Friends*. Be logical as well as creative, keeping production costs in mind. Location shooting, where filming takes place outside a studio soundstage, although it enhances what's known as *production quality*, is also difficult and expensive. Creating a show that can be filmed in the controlled environment of a studio immediately gives you a leg up when it comes to selling your series bible.

Of course if you're creating a series that strongly relies on the vitality and drama of locations in a big-city setting, then make it clear that many scenes can be shot with economy in mind. *Baywatch*, in its earliest days, was shot on a relatively shoestring budget, using the Southern California beach as the single franchise where all the characters come together. That's not to say that these characters can never be seen outside of this *primary environment*, but a precise and distinctive setting can support and add to the overall flavor of the series concept. Other examples include the settings for *The King of Queens*, *The Gilmore Girls*, *Sex and the City*, *Law and Order*, *Malcolm in the Middle*, *Six Feet Under*, *The Sopranos*, and *Providence*.

SETTING BACKGROUND

PORT OF CALL

It's important to realize that, despite the depiction in movies like *The Big Easy*, *Shy People*, or *Southern Comfort*, there are *three* distinct Louisianas:

NEW ORLEANS "The City That Care Forgot" (because of its determination not only to live life but to celebrate it), or "the Crescent City" (because it's shaped that way, by the serpentine curve of the Mississippi River, 2,300 feet wide at Canal Street): cosmopolitan, international, delta city (like Alexandria, Egypt). New Orleans is the largest port in the United States (based on annual tonnage). Its diverse architecture reflects its Spanish, West Indian, French, and American Greek Revival roots. The city is 110 miles upriver from the Gulf of Mexico. The sun rises in New Orleans over the West Bank district—and the West Bank is south of downtown.

FRENCH or SOUTH LOUISIANA (now also referred to as ACADIANA) Outside New Orleans, where the Cajuns live, are the swamps and waterways and farmlands and towns we'll visit as the series continues: Carencro ("buzzard"), Marengouin ("mosquito"), Carville (the leper colony), Napoleonville, Thibodaux, and Breaux Bridge.

NORTH LOUISIANA North of Alexandria, places like Shreveport, and Pineville (the state insane asylum), the "piney forests"—still a Southern place, but one where *bayous* become *creeks* and Catholics, Baptists (and worse!). It's where the English-speaking people were forced when the French-speaking refugees from Europe and Canada settled in South Louisiana.

Not a lot of love is lost between North and South Louisiana, though New Orleans, a narcissistic, voluptuous, magnetic, promiscuous city unto herself, could basically care less.

The Creoles are, generally speaking, white descendants of the French and/or Spanish colonists, French-speaking city dwellers, sophisticated and educated ("Creoles of color" include African blood—from the West Indies—in their mixed ancestry).

The Cajuns (also known as Acadians) are French-speaking country people, mostly farmers or fishermen, originally driven by the British in 1755 from the province of Acadia in Canada. Longfellow's *Evangeline* is a romantic poem about one of the emigrés—Evangeline Parish and Evangeline Maid Bread (the latter the bleached-white-bread equivalent of Holsum or Tastee) are two reminders of her in everyday Louisiana life.

The PORT of the City of New Orleans   Probably the second busiest in the world, it consists of 13 miles of wharves sprawled along 44 miles of water-ways (the Mississippi itself, the Industrial Canal, and Mississippi River/Gulf Outlet). It is *not* a compact area that can be easily secured or patrolled.

Superintendent Joseph Cannatella of the Harbor Police Department calls it "an open port," precisely because it is impossible to limit access to scores of wharf entrances.

There are 2,000 annual ship arrivals and 100,000 barges passing in and out of the port—carrying $8 billion worth of cargo.

Traffic in the lower Mississippi area is so heavy that upriver pilots refer to the area between Baton Rouge and the Gulf of Mexico as "The War Zone."

The Pilot Treatment

Following your description of the setting comes the *pilot treatment*. This concise and dramatic treatment should give the reader a glimpse into what he might expect to see fully drawn out in the pilot script.

The *pilot* is a sample episode of your proposed series, introducing your leading and continuing characters in the kinds of situations in which they will typically be involved. The pilot also announces your series's general style. The full pilot treatment shows us the dramatic through line of the pilot episode.

Use brief paragraphs, and emphasize the primary characters as well as the excitement of the action. Don't forget the cliffhangers, which should stand out dramatically and propel the reader from one act to the next.

The seven acts of a dramatic pilot movie should be easy to identify. Even if the pilot is made as a one-hour, having six strong cliffhangers as *act-ends* will only help sell the story. Too much action and too many twists are rarely a problem.

A comedy pilot would have seven acts in a half hour. In the initial stages of a comedy pitch the acts are usually not described as such; you pitch the premise, relationships, and basic pilot story. Only when a studio wants to do the pilot and they bring you in to pitch it to a network will a network request an outline or a beat sheet (although not all networks do this). At that point they'll give you notes for the "approved pilot outline" and you'll proceed to script.

Keep in mind that your pilot treatment, like all treatments, should be written in the present tense and, though condensed, should still pay attention to the basic act structure starting with the hook, or teaser, proceeding through a scene-by-scene presentation of the entire action line, and ending with a climax that leaves the audience dying to see more of these characters in this fascinating setting.

Your pilot treatment should run between four and eight pages.

It should be the best writing you're capable of, and should include samples of dialogue at key points in the story.

<u>OPENING CUTS</u>

PORT OF CALL

-**MARDI GRAS**—the Vieux Carré—SEXY women—all races—exotic, erotic, revealing costumes!

-**Aerial shot:** The Crescent City (New Orleans), the NATCHEZ (an old-time stern-wheel riverboat) makes its stately way on the serpentine Mississippi gleaming in the high-noon sun.

-A **COTTON-LADEN BARGE** moving upriver, a classic columned plantation home in the background.

-**Aerial:** The bridge across **LAKE PONTCHARTRAIN**.

-An **AFRICAN-AMERICAN FUNERAL PROCESSION**, led by a jazz band.

-**Aerial:** A Saints' game in progress in the Superdome.

-A **CAJUN PIROGUE**, its owner running his crawfish nets along a backwater while an oceangoing supertanker looms by in the background downriver.

-**Aerial:** Ship after ship, loading and unloading, lined up at wharves on both sides of the river.

-A **FLIGHT OF WHITE EGRETS** takes to the air.

-**Aerial:** The cypress swamps.

-**BOURBON STREET**—a **BLUES TROMBONE** played by an old African-American man.

-**Aerial: OIL RIG** off the coast, swaying under hurricane gales.

-**CAJUN DANCING** at a neon nightspot.

-**Aerial:** Jets in and out of the international airport at Kenner.

-**THE FREE FERRY,** docking in Algiers (across from N.O.).

-**Aerial:** An ancient **STREETCAR** wends its way through the Garden District.

PORT OF CALL
Created by
Kenneth Aguillard Atchity

A third-generation New Orleans detective tracking his partner's murderer is paired with an expatriate French inspector when the suspect is a diabolically vicious international smuggler.

DETECTIVE LIEUTENANT ARCHIE CAMERY, III, of the Harbor Police Department of the Board of Commerce of the Port of New Orleans inherits a weariness and tenacity from two generations before him, encapsulated in his love for Cajun proverbs. His father, and *his* father, were both detectives. Archie's wife is a dark-haired, flashing-eyed Cajun, **JACQUIE AGUILLARD CAMERY**, who's pushing him to take early retirement but can't help assisting through her access to the "bayou telegraph."

Disobeying orders that he remain on leave until the heat cools down from his last escapade, Archie hangs around the Harmony Street Wharf waiting to meet up with his partner, **BUDDY**, who's on a hot lead. Suddenly the hum of a light plane catches Archie's attention. He starts to look away when a brightly colored parachute appears from the clouds. As the parachute turns in the evening breeze, the words *Cuba Libre* can be made out before the parachutist hits the dark river. Minutes later Archie watches the U.S. Coast Guard go to the rescue. The Coast Guard radios Archie on the patrol boat—they want him to go aboard the cutter. The dead man is Buddy.

Archie's first stop is to see **MELANIE CHATELAINE**, an extremely attractive octoroon private investigator whose ties with the African-American, Cuban, and Creole communities make her an invaluable resource for the Harbor Police—as well as for the New Orleans Police Department. She's also Buddy's lover. Melanie isn't surprised to see Archie. She'd been waiting for this day. His look says it all. Melanie's stoic reaction doesn't disguise how much she loved Buddy. She sends Archie away.

Hard-nosed, by-the-book Captain of Detectives **JIMMY-BIRD JOHNSON** knows just where to find his loose-cannon detective drowning his sorrows—at The Endless Train, the shotgun-style bar frequented by local law enforcement. Jimmy-Bird sympathizes with Archie's painful loss of his friend and partner, but he's up to his ass in alligators because of it, and he wants Archie to stay out of the investigation. Archie wants to know who's gonna handle it.

Jimmy-Bird is babysitting a French member of Interpol. He half-jokingly, as he leaves, suggests the Frenchman.

LOUIS LARRE is half French-Canadian, half French. He's as relentless and methodical as he is self-confident and charismatic. Louis was trained by the French *Douanes*, is now working for Interpol, and has been assigned to New Orleans by his own request. Louis is on the trail of international smuggler **ENRIQUE BARRACAS**. Archie and Buddy were already alerted that a man named Barracas was operating in New Orleans. Though they pursued him in the line of duty, Louis is after Barracas with a vengeance because he murdered a Cuban diplomat and Louis's French girlfriend at a casino in Monte Carlo.

The captain teams up the unlikely pair. Despite the initial friction between the two new partners, Louis's high-tech savvy and bravado complement Archie's local knowledge and natural wariness.

The inscription on the parachute leads Archie to the Cuba Libre bar in the Vieux Carré—it is a combination of Havana nightclub and New Orleans showgirl bar. Despite his conviction that the connection is "too obvious," Archie grills the Cuba Libre's owner, **RODERIGO**. In the middle of their confrontation, Louis saunters in, following a skirt. Unrecognized by the locals, and infuriating Archie, Louis proceeds to hit on the skirt—a sexy Latina named **TALIA**. Archie looks on in disbelief without blowing Louis's cover. Unlike Captain Johnson, who's corralled every Cuban in town, Archie knows the Cubans are not responsible for Buddy's death, but he demands Roderigo's help in finding the plane. Roderigo's community liked Buddy. He'll help. Meanwhile Louis and Talia have disappeared.

After a night of passion Talia and Louis make a perilous liaison. Louis introduces himself as an importer-exporter of anything expensive and dangerous. Talia sees opportunity.

Archie delves into the stacks of files and history-littered drawers of Buddy's desk looking for a clue. He studies a dog-eared dime-store ledger and finds a $500 notation to "Downer." A payoff for what kind of a tip?

In one of the thousand bayou-formed lakes downriver, African-American **"DOWNER" WHITNEY** is camouflaging the blue-and-white seaplane. Archie and Louis, positioned behind a giant cypress stump, watch until Downer leaves. Later onboard the plane Louis does a quick inspection, finding a drawer filled with glossies of exotic figurines and statuettes—Incan, Aztec?

Archie pores over the medical examiner's report on Buddy. The red substance found caked beneath his fingernails was—cayenne pepper! He enlists Louis's help to break into CRESCENT—the U.S. Customs computer program for cross-listing and preclearing cargo shipments into the Port of New Orleans from "reliable" carriers. CRESCENT tells them that the cayenne came in six days ago on the *Epice du Mer* from French Guyana. Its bill of lading reads: Louisiana Collectibles & Edibles.

It's dark by the time Archie and Louis pay a visit to Collectibles & Edibles. They wait for the African-American clerk to finish dealing with his last customer. The clerk is Downer. Confronted and intimidated by Archie and Louis, he sends them to the warehouse of the owner, **MR. GROVER MARCHAND**. Sneaking out the back door, Downer is met by one of Barracas's henchmen. He gives Downer a serious warning to be delivered to Marchand. Mr. Barracas does not appreciate waiting when his goods have already arrived. Archie and Louis head for the warehouse. Back at headquarters Jimmy-Bird puts a stop on the departure of the *Epice du Mer*.

Archie contacts Melanie. She has a lead. The plane is listed as being owned by **TITUS CASSIUS WASHINGTON**. He's bad, he's powerful, he's crazy. Titus dominates the African-American sex-and-drugs scene. Titus and Downer are connected. Hours later when Jimmy-Bird goes to Downer's house to question him he finds Downer dead.

Back at the warehouse in the woods Archie sees Marchand, apparently alone, mixing his potpourri of spices. Archie quietly walks in, nearly scaring Marchand out of his skin. "What else you got in that crate?" he asks. "Hot pepper, is all," Marchand explains. "It's the basis of my Cajun potpourri." "What else?" "What you mean?" "No one gets killed over hot pepper."

Archie pushes Marchand out of the way, ties him up, and checks the crate—pokes into it, trying to keep the pepper from his eyes. He spots Marchand watching the clock. "Expecting someone?" Archie has now poked around enough to realize there's a box within the pepper box. Marchand confesses he was smuggling in a "little nose candy" for a party friend. The friend is on his way right now. "His name Titus by any chance?" Archie asks. Marchand realizes he's in for it. Marchand pleads for his life. Archie has an idea. "I'll tell you exactly what we're going to do," Archie says.

Titus—a tall, thin African-American, dapper and dangerous—arrives in a white Jaguar limo. He comes in alone for his stuff. Marchand is nervous. Outside his men load the crate. Titus notices how nervous Marchand is.

Marchand tries to signal him: "Police." Titus reaches for his gun. Marchand falls to the ground, a bullet square through his forehead. Titus thinks he's surrounded. Turns and fires into the woods. Archie comes to the door. Titus's security guys fire at him with sawed-off shotguns. Archie fires back. Titus makes a run for it and gets away. Archie runs back into the shed. Marchand is dead. Archie and Louis look at each other. The bullet that killed this man did not come from one of Titus's guns. It came from the woods.

A manhunt is going on, through the woods, with dogs. Archie watches the crate of coke being loaded into a Harbor Police van. Louis approaches the crate. Puts on a glove, dips into it, and takes a sample of the cayenne— putting it in a plastic evidence bag, back into his pocket. "You never know," he says to Archie. But Archie isn't listening. He is pensive. "We in the right location, but in the wrong place," he finally says. "What do you mean?" Louis asks. "That plane is less than a mile from here."

Archie and Louis in an airboat speed across the water under the full moon. They get there in time to see Titus boarding his plane. Chasing the seaplane with Titus onboard they manage to shoot the pilot. The plane lurches to one side, sheering off the right wing. Titus takes the controls, as the plane starts spinning crazily from the unbalance. Aims the plane toward another tree— sheers off the left wing. The plane outspeeds the airboat but crashes anyway, bursting into flames. Titus is charred. Buddy's killer is dead!

At headquarters, Chief Johnson congratulates Archie and Louis for getting Titus at no cost to the taxpayer. Archie is glum. They got Buddy's killer, but haven't solved whatever Buddy was working on. On his way home he gets a call from one of the detectives telling him that Louis's sexy contact is Talia Barracas! Enrique's sister!

Archie races over to the Cuba Libre. In the middle of the dance floor, entangled in an erotic tango, are Louis and Talia. Talia sees Archie out of the corner of her eye and discreetly excuses herself to go to the powder room. Louis looks up to see Archie at his table. "Do you have any idea who your girlfriend is?" "She's Barracas's sister." Archie is astounded. "You knew?"

Meanwhile—
Talia is escaping out the back door. Back inside, Cuban thugs have stationed themselves at every door. Archie turns over the table, Louis falls to the floor, and they try to shoot their way out. They're totally outnumbered. It's looking grim—until what appears to be the entire New Orleans police force bursts in to the rescue.

Louis explains to Archie that he was using Talia to get to Barracas. Archie: "She's using you to find out how much we know about her brother's operations." Louis: "There's no operation without me." Louis's beeper goes off. Archie reaches for the radio. "Omigod," he says.

They arrive back at the Tchoupitolas and 3rd Street headquarters to find the place surrounded by fire trucks and emergency vehicles of every description. Inside is devastation: "Four dead officers, three others wounded." In the evidence room a guard lies dead on the floor. The place is undisturbed—except for the cayenne crate containing the cocaine. It's split open, the white powder spread in all directions in footprints leading away from the scene. What were they after if it wasn't the coke?

Louis realizes the setup by Talia. With nearly all the force coming to their rescue at the Cuba Libre, headquarters was left vulnerable. Looks like Marchand was smuggling coke for Titus, artifacts for Barracas. Downer was selling information to everyone concerned—including Buddy. Which explains the Incan photographs found on Titus's plane—Downer was lining up prospective customers, no doubt on commission.

At his hotel Louis finds Talia is waiting for him. He's not surprised. He greets her as though nothing has happened. "I was worried about you. What did the cop want?" she asks. "He wanted to strut for Roderigo, see if they came up with anything that could help his case." Talia accepts this. She has something for him. She asks for the rest of the money. Louis asks to see her package. Talia opens the package and reveals a magnificent Incan burial mask. "Give me the money. I have to go." "There's no hurry," he says. Louis empties his pockets, including the bag of cayenne, places all on his night table, kicks off his shoes. Moves to the portable bar, opens it.

Louis and Talia are making love, the gold mask now lying on the night table. The door to the suite is shot open—with a silenced bullet. Louis reaches for his gun—but Barracas has him covered. Talia is terrified of her brother. Enrique turns to her. "You were supposed to come right back with the money." "I was coming right back," she says. "And the money?" Talia looks at Louis. "There is no money," Louis says. Enrique looks at his sister. "I didn't think so." And shoots her in the forehead, silently, emotionlessly.

Enrique commands Louis to hand him the gold mask. Unseen, Louis's finger touches one of the function buttons on his pocket computer as he hands over the artifact. "You are a very stupid man," Barracas says, "to get so close to me and then to tangle with my stupid sister."

"You killed Françoise."

"The diplomat's girlfriend? I see. My sister for your sister? Except, amigo, you forget that I have many more sisters, more dependable sisters."

Louis: "You killed your sister for a piece of gold." Enrique's eyes suddenly blaze. "Gold—you call this gold? This is the death mask of an Incan emperor, the face of a god, shaped a thousand years ago and captured by my ancestors from the Indians who worshiped the man who wore it to his grave." Louis: "You're a grave robber." Enrique: "A million dollars here in democratic America for a king's buried dignity." Enrique laughs. "Talia stupidly thought you were paying her that much for it." Louis: "You knew better?" "Of course," Enrique responds. "The mask is priceless. I would never sell it for a million dollars. I knew who you were the first time you came into the Cuba Libre. I knew the fastest way to catch you with your pants down was to let her lead me to you."

Louis's signal has alerted Archie. He's on the radio as he races to the hotel. Barracas's guards watch as Archie and a patrol car arrive, then speak into a tiny radio.

"You smuggled the artifacts from Peru by way of Venezuela—inside cocaine?" Louis asks Enrique, stalling for time. Barracas spits. "Cocaine. When I deal with drugs I deal with tons at a time—hundreds and thousands of kilos. Anyway, as you know, I prefer to deal in heroin. And I do not trust anyone who's not my family to do my work for me. The masks were to be covered with the cayenne from Guyana. But Marchand was a greedy petit bourgeois. Scamming me on the side. Doubling up the powder with my gold. That boy was selling information, coke, and gold in all directions." Barracas laughs. "Like a spinning top, out of control. That had to be stopped!"

Archie is rushing up the stairs, taking them two at a time. Archie bursts through the door as Louis blinds Barracas with a handful of cayenne. Barracas shoots wildly as Louis rolls off the bed—and the lights in the entire hotel go out. Archie tries to make out the shadows and shapes, crying out for Louis. In the hallway the exit door opens. A shape disappears down the staircase—followed by another—as the lights go back on.

Inside Louis's room, Archie sees Talia's body. Louis and Barracas are gone, the door to the hall open. He checks the body for signs of life, finds none, then runs into the hall.

Louis runs down the stairs after Barracas. Barracas turns and fires—causing Louis to duck, hold back. Barracas fires until the gun is empty. Louis then pursues again. Gets to the ground level and out the door—in time to see the black limo taking off down the alley with two men in it. Louis stands and aims carefully. Shoots the driver in the back of the head. The limo crashes into a wall, flips over it and into the air, hurtling on its side—and blowing up. Louis rushes toward the car to check for Barracas.

He hears, beyond, the sound of running feet. Catches a glimpse of his quarry. Runs after him.

Archie comes out the hotel side door, sees the burning car, orders one of the cops following him to deal with it, and then runs after Louis and Barracas with the other cop.

On a very long wharf, a life-and-death foot race is in progress. Louis stops to shoot his last bullet as Enrique reaches the end of the wharf. Barracas jumps into the dark Mississippi. Louis rushes to the side of the wharf, stares help-lessly into the night.

Archie and the cop catch up a few minutes later. Louis stares into the water . . . but the muddy Mississippi has no trail to offer, no clues. Out of breath, Archie reaches Louis and asks, "What happened?" Louis: "He jumped." Archie: "You were standing here watching him jump, or what?" Louis looks at his new partner. "I can't swim," he says.

Jacquie is teaching Louis how to dance to Cajun music while Melanie and Archie help themselves to a huge platter of oysters and a heaping bowl of dirty rice. Louis sits down, exhausted, but happy, with Jacquie. "What have you decided?" Archie asks. "I have decided to look for a cool place to live. This is the place I've chosen. I will continue my hunt from here. Barracas will be back." Archie answers with a smile, "Hunting together is smarter than hunting alone."

Brief Description of Four to Twelve Future Episodes

In a well-written bible, future episodes will suggest themselves automatically to the buyer who's reading your series proposal for the first time. In the pitch stage you won't need this, but should you get to the point where your pilot has been bought you might be requested to provide brief descriptions of additional episodes. Then it's your job to make your series's *legs* (industry term for "continuing potential") crystal clear by offering glimpses of future stories beyond the pilot. These glimpses can range in length from one-liners to a paragraph each and are meant to tantalize your reader.

The Bible as the First and Last Word

Every television project is born of a good script. A good pilot treatment, like a good teleplay, not only tells the first story in the series, but also evokes the ongoing style of the shows, introduces the important characters and their motivations, and in general sets the tone and mood. As part of the bible, the pilot treatment is referred to constantly by staff writers on the series whose goal is to recapture its energy and freshness for their weekly episodes. *If the script is the series's birth, the pilot treatment is the seed that leads to that birth.*

FUTURE EPISODES

PORT OF CALL

When **MELANIE CHATELAINE** ends up in Charity Hospital in a coma because of what looks to be a suicide attempt, **ARCHIE**, at her intensive care bedside, tells **LOUIS** he doesn't believe Melanie wants to do herself in. She cherishes life too much. Revisiting the Cuba Libre, Louis stumbles onto a lead that proves Melanie was the victim of a homicide attempt. As she comes out of her coma, Louis finds himself falling in love with her.

ARCHIE and **LOUIS** are called on to consult with local police in the tiny Cajun town of Marengouin, where a railroad tie has been split open and found to contain cotton soaked with heroin. They scour cargo declarations until they find the needle in a haystack—the one ship out of 3,000 that is shipping railroad ties. But it's already left the port and is steaming downriver, about to escape into the Gulf. They enlist the help of the DEA with its naval helicopter, but are attacked midair by antiaircraft fire from the smugglers.

The jealousy of the New Orleans Police Department for the Harbor Police explodes into action when **JIMMY-BIRD JOHNSON** discovers from an informer on another case that NOPD has been withholding information from him. He sends his new recruit **MARIA ROSA FONG** undercover to infiltrate NOPD training school with **LOUIS** and **ARCHIE** as her anchors. When she discovers graft and corruption among the highest officers of NOPD, the Harbor Police are faced with the most dangerous challenge in their history.

In the middle of the night, while **ARCHIE** and **LOUIS** are staking out a Korean ship suspected of exporting contraband, shooters break into Archie's home and wound his wife, **JACQUIE**, leaving her for dead. She manages to crawl to a phone, thanking God that the children were with her grandparents in Eunice. Archie and Louis arrive as she is being loaded into an ambulance; her quick reactions saved her. As they follow the ambulance to the hospital, they learn that the Korean ship is leaving port. Louis is convinced that the attack on Jacquie was simply a ruse to get them to drop the stakeout. He heads back to the water, convincing **JIMMY-BIRD** to pursue the ship with the H.P. cutter. When they announce to the ship that they're going to board it, the ship attempts to ram them.

Never forget that the most important object of the bible is to sell your series concept. A successful concept usually presents an extraordinarily interesting locale, occupation, or situation, and characters who will clash in some inherently funny or dramatic way. Producers talk through their concepts at breakfast or lunch with financiers or network executives to secure their interest. The best concepts are forceful, unique, and memorable. If the concept elicits initial interest, the conversation immediately turns to potential casting of the lead characters, length and scope of the pilot story, and the potential for interesting a network in the series—along with an analysis of possible respectable time slots on the network's schedule. Armed with the information he gleans from this conversation, the producer can further develop and refine characters, settings, and situations.

In the next chapter we examine the treatment for a true story.

5

Stranger than Fiction:
Treatments Based on True Stories

. . .

'Tis strange—but true; for truth is always strange;
Stranger than fiction.
—Lord Byron, *Don Juan*

True stories drive the networks' and cable broadcasters' schedules and capture the imagination of motion picture filmmakers. The ongoing appeal of reality-based drama, coupled with a continual need for product, makes this an ideal area for the unproduced writer to break into. Being able to say that your treatment is *"a true story," "based on a true story,"* or *"inspired by a true story,"* gives your story immediate marketing strength.

Yet in order to sell it, even the true story must have all the story elements outlined in previous chapters:

- a protagonist we can root for
- clear-cut act breaks with sufficiently dramatic twists, turns, and cliffhangers
- a satisfying, "up" ending

Every week we are pitched projects that may be in actuality "true stories," but are not truly stories in dramatic terms (as audiences define a story), with a *compelling beginning*, *dramatically orchestrated middle*, and *conclusive end*. Sometimes we can doctor them up enough to make a sale, but more often than not they're hopeless: "I was attacked physically in court by another woman"; "My husband tried to kill me"; "I was standing in the bank when the robbery went down"—so what? These all describe a distinct piece of action, isolated and momentary. An incident, however painful, does not a story make.

Real life seldom conforms to the neat, single-thrust impact of a well-made movie, with the appropriate positive or uplifting outcome. Real-life events and situations generally just go on and on, evolving or dissolving rather than resolving. A true story may be more effective as a documentary or a news item than as a ninety-six-minute TV movie or two-hour motion picture. Often a true story achieves its most dramatic and effective telling in a segment of *20/20* or *60 Minutes*, or an article in *Playboy*, and trying to adapt it to the movie format will stretch it too thin.

Keeping these cautionary words in mind, true stories can be a strong source of potential film material, even for a beginning writer. In television, many of the most effective true stories depicted are not about legendary or well-known figures, but rather about everyday individuals caught up in situations that bring out their courage and humanity, or their villainy (like *Small Sacrifices*, about an Oregon woman who may have murdered her three children in 1983, or movies about serial killer Ted Bundy, or about Rasputin, the mad monk who dominated the royal family before the Russian Revolution). The possible sources for real-life story material are indeed myriad.

How to Get the Rights to a True Story

In many cases, you can submit a treatment for a true story that is drawn entirely from the public domain (the legal term, as we mentioned earlier, that describes intellectual property that is not protected under copyright, trademark, or other private claims and is therefore available to the public). All court proceedings, by nature part of the commonwealth of the state or federal government, are in public domain. Nearly everything involving celebrities falls within the public domain, with the exception of materials that may be libelous; one of the perils of fame in this country is the sacrifice of your right to privacy. If the characters you're interested in writing about are dead, there's no need to obtain rights to their stories—unless you're using written material that the public has no access to, such as diaries or letters that belong to the deceased's family.

But unless an incident involving a noncelebrity has become part of the court process it is considered to be in the private domain, and rights should be secured before you can deal with it in a television or motion picture treatment. With or without the help of an attorney, you may have to track down the people involved, get to know them, and obtain the rights to their story, either by optioning those rights, or by exchanging them for promised compensation that will be paid by the ultimate buyer of the story. If the incident you're researching is a true crime, for example, desirable rights, as described in chapter 3, include the victim's rights, the perpetrator's rights, the victim's family's rights, the leading law enforcer's rights (district attorney, police detective, sheriff, etc.), and the rights of anyone else involved who could possibly assign rights to someone other than you and your eventual network buyer.

But just how do you go about tracking down these story rights? The investigative instinct is nothing more than applied common sense. Coupling common sense with determination and focus, you can uncover the information you need. Start by calling the journalist who wrote the article that tipped you off in the first place. Let the writer know how his or her article affected you. The writer may be willing to give you all the information you need to write a treatment, or you may need to get him on your team as a cowriter. Talk to the police. Check court records. Use the library reference desk for leads on how to track a source. When you get a phone number, call and tell them exactly why you're interested. You'd like to write a TV treatment of the story, and you want to know if they'd be interested in cooperating. If they agree to meet with you, your next mission is to get them comfortable enough with you to give you the rights to use their information in the treatment.

If they won't cooperate, you're not defeated yet. You can still write a treatment that is "based on a true story," changing the names, the locale, and some of the events to "protect the innocent." The degree to which you fictionalize the facts is what determines whether a story is "based on a true story" or "inspired by a true story." If your research has yielded enough information, you may even prefer writing a "based on" story to the strictly "true" story; not only will you avoid the rights hassle, but you may also free yourself to create a stronger story, still true to the dramatic essence your instincts recognized when you began this project.

How True Is a True Story?

No FCC rule governs the definition of a television movie advertised as a true story. Each network has its own definition. It's a case of different words for a basic concept, generally an issue for the network's standards and practices department and what they feel comfortable with in regard to their network. The definition only becomes a legal issue if a true story contains fictionalized segments that may be considered by the subject or family of the subject to be defamation of character.

There are no clear-cut lines when a true story is adapted for a movie. Broadly explained, the categories are:

• the favored **"based on a true story,"** which means there is no fictionalization or a very insignificant amount of fictionalization;

• **"inspired by a true story,"** which means there is a significant amount of fictionalization;

- the weakest **"suggested by a true story,"** which is predominately fiction.

Look for stories with enough flesh on their bones to make a full-length movie, but take the development executive's critical approach and search for the seven acts immediately—or invent them. You may find the track of a story in a magazine or newspaper article, a radio or TV documentary or news show, a police blotter, a case file, or something you overheard on the train you took into work this morning.

If the seven acts aren't immediately obvious to you, it's time to begin the process of research. Find out as much about the event or situation as you can, enough to convince you that there is a full story with protagonist, antagonist, and dramatic and interesting complications.

Elements of Drama for the True Story

Fiction, as we know, isn't the same as reality. Instead, dramatic fiction, by suspending our disbelief, gives the *impression* of reality—what Aristotle in his *Poetics* described as an "imitation" of action that may not be "strictly true" but is "more philosophical than history" because it is true in a poetic, or universal, sense. In many ways, as audiences, we prefer the poetic imitation to the reality. Well-wrought poetry and fiction have definable shape and satisfying closure. When you read a good book or see a good play or film, you walk away with a feeling of having experienced something definite, something conclusive. Unfortunately, life itself doesn't often provide such a well-rounded feeling.

Truth *can be* stranger than fiction, but fiction is not strange—it's recognizably dramatic and makes sense to the audience. In developing a true story, more often than not the writer needs to take dramatic license and reshape events and characters, adding plot to the events that already exist in fact. As we've discussed in detail in chapter 2, dramatic fiction is a mechanism, something created; consequently it has mechanical parts. New writers often overcomplicate writing fiction by trying to put in too many ingredients (for example, including every relative just because they existed, whether or not their involvement in the story is dramatically necessary). Often, with a true story, the challenge is removing all those details so a clear story line emerges. "Less is better," as Robert Frost said.

Once you have your true story you're ready to adapt it for the specific needs of television. We receive many stories with only a good opening and/or close—but no twists, turns, and cliff-hangers in between. "Tell the truth," says director Milos Forman (*The People vs. Larry Flynt*), "without being boring." We also get interesting stories that are well developed but have no likable characters in them. Because a true story isn't necessarily good drama all on its own, maintain your focus on being "truer" to your treatment (by concentrating on the dramatic elements of storytelling) than you are to your original source. You have much less leeway to do this with a true story than you do with fictional material. Even to maintain that your treatment is "based on a true story" requires considerable allegiance to the actual events. But generally you will want to consolidate or amplify certain characters and situations to increase the emotional impact of the story without sacrificing the overall authenticity and spirit of the event that inspired you. Let's look at the elements of fiction and drama outlined in chapter 2 from that most difficult—and most challenging—perspective.

Character

The main character must be developed in such a way that the audience can relate to her and her problems ("That could happen to me or to my child!"). A character is constructed from only a few elements. But what do you do if you're writing about a real-life person? Your nonfiction subject must be transformed into a believable fictional character. Recognizing the difference between art and reality, you'll have to simplify the real character until his motivation becomes dramatically clear and compelling. Fictional characters are simpler and less complicated than real people, which is why we love stories so much. The protagonist's motivation must be clear in the treatment, since it is the engine that drives your screenplay and energizes its every aspect.

Dramatic Action

Dramatic action isn't just plot. Creating powerful dramatic action comes from recognizing and embracing your story's natural pattern or shape, and allowing a compelling rhythm to emerge. Because of TV's seven acts, it will be necessary to restructure the chronology of events so that the most exciting ones will serve the need for an involving beginning, a climactic ending, and, of course, the cliffhanger pacing required by station breaks. Each scene must dramatize your protagonist's motivation and must show conflict. If a scene shows no conflict that moves the story forward, cut the scene, or *conflict* it up!

Setting/Background

Just as audience identification with the protagonist of your story is essential, commercial impact is served when the audience can identify with the story's setting—its time and place. Contemporary stories that take place in urban or suburban America are prevalent on television because they are relatable to the largest audiences. Limiting your setting is also beneficial because it puts more pressure on the dramatic situation (Aristotle's followers called this "the unity of place"), not to mention the budgetary benefits of concentrating the drama in one location or at least in one city.

Point of View

The three Amy Fisher television films provide a perfect example of how the same story can find a different point of view in which to retell itself:

1. *The Amy Fisher Story.* This account took an objective viewpoint drawn from a variety of sources to dramatize the relationship between Amy and her married lover and her subsequent attack on his wife.

2. *Casualties of Love.* The "Long Island Lolita" story told from the Buttafuocos' point of view portrays Amy Fisher as a fatally attracted teenager who nearly destroyed a happy family.

3. *Lethal Lolita—Amy Fisher: My Story.* This account is Amy's story, portraying her as an incest victim who gets involved with an opportunist who drags her into an illicit affair and prostitution, until she is driven so insane that she attacks his wife.

The Hook

What is it about your story that will lure the buyer and ultimately the viewer? Good story ideas can be stated in a single sentence (usually the one that ends up in *TV Guide*), known as the story's *premise*, *hook*, or *concept*. The hook most often follows the formula we've discussed: What happens when a woman like this meets a situation like that? The hooks in the following television movies are apparent:

• *Billionaire Boys Club.* Based on the true story of a group of rich preppie friends who commit murder.

• *The Burning Bed.* The true story of an abused wife who murders her husband.

• *The Positively True Adventures of the Alleged Texas Cheerleader–Murdering Mom.* True story about a Dallas housewife who hires a professional hit man to dispose of the mother of her daughter's chief cheerleading rival.

• *Infidelity: A Love Story.* The striking account of the effects of men's affairs on their wives and daughters, based on one woman's true family story of three generations of infidelity.

• *Sex, Lies and Obsession.* The true story of a married man's chronic problem with sex addiction and how it affects his family.

• *Conspiracy.* The true story of the 1942 Wannsee Conference, in which Nazi and SS leaders gathered in a Berlin suburb to discuss the "Final Solution to the Jewish Question," resulting in what would become known as the Holocaust.

Checklist for Undertaking a True Story

When choosing a true story to write and sell, consider the following:

• **Can it be done for network television?** If a true story has elements that are *very* sexual or *very* violent networks will pass. They rarely buy unhappy endings, or stories in which all the characters are distasteful. Networks generally also pass on stories on purely minority subjects requiring primary minority casting; that is simply not their audience. Try the cable broadcasters instead.

• **Casting.** Will a TV movie's subject attract a feature star or popular, well-liked mainstream TV star? Are the two main characters parts that would excite or challenge an actress or actor?

• **Has it been done before?** If you're selling a true story that's been done before, you have to sell what's different about this particular murder story, kidnapping story, or stalking story. This is called a "new take" or "new angle" on the story.

• **Is this story high-profile?** Any item with national news exposure that captures the public imagination is a potential movie-for-television sale.

• **Is this an internal or an external story?** Buyers, like audiences, want dramatic action, not just "internal" stories dealing with a heroine's state of mind.

• **What is the scope of the story?** Factual stories that involve a cast of thousands are difficult to follow in a two-hour format—not to mention being impractical from a budgetary standpoint.

We've focused this chapter on television because the great majority of true stories made into films are made into television films. Turning a true story into a feature film—*Nixon, Lorenzo's Oil, Missing, Erin Brockovich*, etc.—means shifting the structural elements of your treatment to fit the feature film principles outlined in chapter 2. Now let's take a look at how to go about writing a treatment based on a novel or other existing material, a technique known in the industry as *adaptation*.

6

From Book to Film:
The Adaptation Treatment

. . .

When the film adaptation of Hemingway's *For Whom the Bell Tolls* was ready for release, the producers sent a telegram to the author, who was on Bimini:

> "FILM IS FINISHED. YOU WILL LOVE IT.
> ALL WE NEED IS A SHORT, SNAPPY, SEXY TITLE."

Hemingway wired back:

> "HOW ABOUT FUCK?"

Transforming a novel, short story, stage play, or existing screenplay into a new film is called *adaptation*—a practice of flattery by imitation that's been thriving since the Roman playwrights Terence and Plautus freely adapted the Greek comedies of Menander and Aristophanes; and since Shakespeare adapted *Julius Caesar* and *Antony and Cleopatra* from Sir Thomas North's exuberant translations of Plutarch's *Lives of the Noble Greeks and Romans*. Eugene O'Neill's masterpiece *Mourning Becomes Electra* is a retelling of Aeschylus's trilogy *The Oresteia*, the scene shifted from post–Trojan War Mycenae to the United States during the Civil War.

From Cecil B. DeMille's *The Ten Commandments* to *To Kill a Mockingbird*, based on the novel by Harper Lee, adaptation has been a mainstay of the movies. Some of the most brilliant films in history, such as *The Godfather* and *Doctor Zhivago*, are adaptations. The success of such recent films as Ang Lee's *Sense and Sensibility*, Oliver Parker's *The Importance of Being Ernest* (with Reese Witherspoon), and Wes Craven's *Doctor Jekyll and Mr. Hyde* indicates that the adaptation of classics is alive and well, and will continue to be a source of film material for as long as writers can find stories to adapt.

Moreover, the person writing an adaptation has the added advantage of inheriting an already developed plot instead of having to put one together from scratch. For a new writer who's strong in dialogue and character development and weak in structuring action line, adaptation is an excellent training ground.

While novels and short stories are obvious materials to adapt, note the following additional sources for popular movies:

- *Spider-man*, *X-Men*, and *Scooby-Doo* are just three of many examples of adaptations from comic books and a cartoon.
- *Peter Pan* and *The Red Shoes* (Hans Christian Andersen's story about a young ballerina torn between love and success) are adaptations of fairy tales.
- *Lara Croft: Tomb Raider* is based on the popular video game series, *Tomb Raider*, which features the adventures of a female Indiana Jones, an antiquities hunter-for-hire whose expeditions are always chock-full of action, danger, and intrigue.
- *Tron Killer App*, a sequel to the computer game classic and one of the first computer-generated movies, is about a hacker who transports himself into cyberspace to pull off the ultimate hack.
- *The Pirates of the Caribbean* and *Haunted Mansion* are derived from the Disneyland Park theme rides.
- *Clue* and *Super Mario Bros.* were adapted from games— one a board game in which the players must unravel a murder mystery, and the other the Nintendo video game featuring two Italian plumber brothers.
- *The Fast and the Furious*, a fierce and frenzied look at rival

Los Angeles street teams who use street racing, as a means of establishing power, was adapted from a magazine article by Ken Li.

• *The Billionaire Fugitive*, the true story of Robert Durst, accused of several murders including the one of his ex-wife, was adapted from a *Vanity Fair* article for Bruce Willis and Arnold Rifkin's Cheyenne Enterprises.

• *Christiane F.*, the gripping story of a bored German girl's decline into drug use and prostitution, was adapted from a West German magazine article.

• *The Last American Hero* was based on articles by Tom Wolfe about a former moonshine runner, Junior Johnson, who became one of the fastest race car drivers in the history of the sport.

• *Henry and June* was adapted from the diaries of writer Anaïs Nin, and *I Remember Mama* was based on Kathryn Forbes's memoirs, *Mama's Bank Account*.

• *My Friend Irma* was based on the radio adventures of a not-too-bright blonde and her sensible pal; the 1953 film *The War of the Worlds*, and its Paramount–Cruise/Wagner remake, about the invasion of Earth by Martians, was based on Orson Welles's radio broadcast; which was in turn based on H. G. Wells's classic novel.

So you see there is no limit to what you can adapt into a film. All you need is imagination and ingenuity.

Adaptation and Storytelling

The same story can be told in more than one way because the words and structure used in storytelling are, in a sense, arbitrary and dependent upon the storyteller. Witness the transformation of a good joke as it passes from one teller to the next, each elaborating on it in his own unique style. It's no surprise then that a primary vein for the storyteller's mining of material consists of previously told stories. Many films, for both features and television, are retellings of already published or produced stories. Producers scour *Publishers Weekly*, the trade magazine of the publishing industry that announces forthcoming books and trends, and *Kirkus Reviews*, which gives brief reviews of forthcoming books, and cultivate relationships with New York agents and publishers, hoping to be first in line to acquire a promising new novel or true crime story. AEI's NBC films *Amityville: The Evil Escapes* and *Shadow of Obsession* were based on novels, the first by John Jones, the second by K. K. Beck. AEI's 1996 deals with New Line, Propaganda Films, and Walt Disney Pictures were based on novels that had not yet even been sold to publishers. If you've written a novel that could make a good film, whether it's published or not, write a five-page treatment of it and send it to a film or television producer whose listing indicates they are open to developing novels for film.

If the story you want to adapt is in the public domain, either by a failure to register copyright or because it was published before 1911, you're free to adapt it without securing rights. As a member of the public, you have the right already. Just use common sense. Adapting *The Scarlet Letter* again after the 1995 adaptation's failure at the box office, though legally you're free to do it, is probably not a good use of your time.

If the story was published after 1911, the year that modern copyright laws went into effect through the Geneva Convention, someone most likely owns the copyright, and the author or his estate's permission must be obtained before you attempt to sell your adaptation treatment. We're approached regularly by writers who've spent considerable time adapting a work without securing its rights and who are then bitterly disappointed to learn the original story is protected by the very law that serves them as well. But obtaining the rights to an obscure novel you found in a secondhand bookstore or library may not be so difficult. We suggest you do so in one of two ways.

First, check the publisher's imprint, located on the copyright page at the opening of the book, and call or write the publisher's subsidiary rights department to ask who controls the dramatic rights to this novel. If the publisher controls them, tell the rights manager you're interested in optioning the novel to write a treatment of it. If the publisher no longer exists, you need to find out who took over its rights. The *Literary Market Place*, the all-inclusive "yellow pages" of the publishing industry, available at the reference desk of your local public library, may be helpful. If you can't find out any other way, do a search at the Library of Congress's Copyright Office. The Copyright Office will either direct you to the current rights holder, or will tell you that the rights are now in the public domain.

Another avenue is to call an independent producer such as AEI and tell us what you've found and what you want to do. We'll ask you to write a brief treatment, register it, and send it to us. If we're intrigued by the story, we'll handle the optioning of the rights for you after making a deal to clarify and protect your role in the project.

Adaptation, with all its obvious advantages, can sometimes be even more difficult than creating an original story. Your challenge is not only to create a drama that's compelling but also to remain true to the original. A well-done adaptation, like those of Pat Conroy's *The Prince of Tides*, Jane Austen's *Sense and Sensibility*, or Edith Wharton's *The Age of Innocence*, must please the novel's original audience while at the same time capturing film audiences who may never have read, or even heard of, the book. *The Prince of Tides* succeeds in successfully reducing Pat Conroy's sprawling saga to film size by focusing on the psychiatrist's viewpoint, and by eliminating a number of the characters and subplots. Yet it provides the same emotional impact as did the novel. We suggest that when you're faced with a decision, you choose what's good for the drama over what's required to remain strictly faithful to the original. Even William Faulkner, adapting his own novel *The Sound and the Fury* for film, had to make radical changes in his approach to telling the story of the Compson family. Instead of the multiple viewpoints of the novel, he focused his treatment on the point of view of one character, Jason. Yet the film transports us powerfully to the world of Yoknapatawpha County. In other cases, such as William Wharton's novel *Birdy*, the screenwriter was able to follow the novel's structure in crafting an artistically successful film. *The Bridges of Madison County* actually seems a better story in its film version than it was in the original novel.

Guidelines for Adaptation Treatments

Here are some guidelines to remember when undertaking an adaptation treatment:

- Reread the original, looking for scenes instead of chapters.
- Remember that books are literary, films are visual. What you're looking for is visuality, the elements of a book that paint a picture of the characters, the setting, the action.
- Mark the *obligatory scenes* in the story.
- Avoid interior narrative, choosing action over thought; and don't resort to *voice-over* unless you can think of no other way of externalizing and dramatizing a scene.
- Minimize description, even if the source is rich with it.
- Find a way to streamline the plot, reducing the action line to the protagonist's viewpoint with one or two subordinate action lines to complicate the story.
- When in doubt, eliminate an element. Imagine trying to include everything from *War and Peace*.
- Eliminate transitional scenes, and don't worry about making jumps as long as the situation in the new scene is clearly marked.
- Leave metaphor and symbolism, as much as possible, to the director.
- Keep your audience in mind throughout, making sure you

tell a story that can be enjoyed by anyone whether they've read the book or not.

• Apply the principles we've outlined here to the development of your major and supporting characters, action line, viewpoint, and setting. Be as ruthless as necessary to make your drama work, following the imaginatively expansive examples of *A Twist of Fate* (based on *Silas Marner*), *Robin Hood*, or *The Three Musketeers*.

TREATMENTS *v.* TERM PAPER OUTLINES

Don't think of treatments the way you used to think of your term paper outlines: all misery and no reward. Instead, think of them as road maps, but better—not only do they tell you how to get where you want to go, they help you figure out where you're going in the first place.

Some people object that treatments stifle creativity, that part of the process is the gradual unfolding of the author's vision. This may be somewhat true of novels, but not for screenplays. Scripts are a refined form of cabinetry, in which it's crucial to be able to discern the structure before carving the trim.

Treatments also help you to answer the age-old question any writer must ask when beginning a project: Do I want to spend time with these characters? Because if you don't, how do you expect an audience to spend ten bucks and two hours?

    —Michael Walsh, cowriter of *Cadet Kelly*, the Disney Channel's highest-rated movie ever; author of *As Time Goes By* and *And All the Saints* (Warner Books)

Though plays can be as good a source for adaptations as novels, they present a special challenge—that of overcoming the relatively claustrophobic nature of the stage in serving the openness of the film. A film relies on visuals, not on dialogue, and long monologues, generally speaking, must go—we hold our breath to watch Mel Gibson make it through "To be or not to be." Successful movie adaptations of plays include *West Side Story*, adapted from the Broadway musical, itself based on Shakespeare's *Romeo and Juliet*; Franco Zeffirelli's *Romeo and Juliet*; Baz Luhrmann's *Romeo + Juliet*; and *Steel Magnolias*, which managed to "open up" the play by involving not just the beauty parlor but the entire small town.

The following adaptation is one we wrote for network television based on Emily Brontë's *Jane Eyre*. We chose this example because it easily shows you that you can be inventive in adapting a well-known classic novel into something contemporary while still maintaining the original essence of the story.

Adaptation Treatment

SHADOW OF THE CYPRESS
Based on the Novel *Jane Eyre* by Emily Brontë
Story by Kenneth Atchity & Chi-Li Wong

WGAw Registered #561286

Act 1
Kansas City, Missouri

Ten-year-old **JANE GOODMAN**, kept indoors on a snowy November day, feels painfully rejected by her **AUNT SARAH REED**, who clusters her own three children about her. Jane withdraws to the window seat with her sketchbook and pencils. Fourteen-year-old **JOHN** and **ELIZA REED** locate her peaceful nook and proceed to taunt her about being a poor, "illegitimate" relative. They get into a fight. Jane is punished by being locked in her room. **GEORGE REED** nods to his overbearing wife, but gives Jane a sympathetic look. Sarah catches it—and raises hell with him.

CUT TO:

Jane is being interviewed by a social worker for placement in a Catholic foster home. She's turned over to the care of strangers, the **CALEGARIS**. Her aunt leaves her behind without a second look. Jane walks over to a corner and begins to sketch.

CUT TO:

Ten Years Later: Jane, now an attractive and determined young woman, prepares to leave her foster home. Packing clothes and gathering up her large art portfolio, it's obvious she has no plans to return. On the table lies an acceptance letter to the New Orleans Art Institute—and a letter from George Reed, saying he's proud of her.

CUT TO:

Wide-eyed, she arrives in New Orleans. A wild taxi ride deposits her in front of a dilapidated rooming house on Saint Charles Avenue. When Jane walks into her prearranged room, she's appalled by its squalor. But she has no place else to go. A *montage* of Jane tossing restlessly in her narrow bed in the Louisiana heat. Transforming the room into sparse cheerfulness. Finding respite in the rhythms of the city as she walks the quaint streets of the

Quarter. Stopping to look at the work of the local street artists. Sketching, alone, in her room.

CUT TO:

The conditions in the Art Institute on Decatur Street are spartan. Jane is ridiculed at first for her lack of experienced technique by the school's dean, Mr. Brocklehurst—a petty, foppish tyrant who spends tuition money on his own personal vices. There are two bright moments, however, in Jane's introduction to the Institute: she is impressed by the gracious superintendent, **MISS TEMPLE**, and she makes a dear friend of **HELEN BURNS**, the sickly, almost saintlike New York schoolmate who suffers immensely from the Louisiana heat.

After the New Orleans police arrest Mr. Brocklehurst for embezzlement, life at the Institute becomes more bearable. Jane thrives on academic successes and, after two years, completes her studies. She is selected as a teacher. Although the salary is low, she accepts.

Montage shows her years of teaching: the joys, the frustrations. Jane has found she is an outstanding teacher. Jane has been more and more frustrated by not being able to spend time on her art. Now that she's amassed a modest pension from her ten years of teaching, she decides to pursue her career as an artist. She resigns from the Institute.

CUT TO:

In the Quarter, Jane spots a notice for part-time employment on a French Market bulletin board. It's from a gallery of collectibles and antiques. Jane interviews with the gallery's curator. When the portly, queenish **MR. PERO BEAUCLERC** learns that she speaks French, she's hired. When she inquires about the owner, whose grandfather's portrait dominates the shop's foyer, Mr. Beauclerc tells her she'll meet **MR. ROCHESTER DELICES BROUSSARD** soon enough. Jane's curiosity about the absentee proprietor continues to grow.

One night on her way home from the shop, Jane ducks through an alley to avoid the street roisterers and to take a shortcut to her boarding house. At the end of the alley, a man is slumped on the ground. Jane's first instinct is to call for help, but she sees that the man is bleeding from a head wound. She touches his face, his pulse, and realizes he's unconscious, not dead. She tends to his wound until he comes to. This man is not without charm—in fact, he has a certain mysterious and romantic charisma which Jane finds fascinating. Groggily he tells her he was accosted by thugs, but "got the best of them." She laughs when she compares his statement to his bloody condition. He laughs, too. Then he introduces himself. His name is Rochester Broussard.

Act 2

Rochester, his forehead now showing only a trace of the cut, sits across the dinner table from Jane at Antoine's. It's obvious to both of them that he is as fascinated with her as she is attracted to him. Rochester's personality is a peculiar mixture of brusque refinement, charm, and coldness.

Beauclerc is at first surprised that Mr. Broussard's visits to the shop are becoming more frequent, his trips abroad of shorter duration. But when he sees the look exchanged by Jane and Rochester, he figures he knows what's going on. He's not pleased.

At a late-night, candlelit romantic dinner, Rochester and Jane are holding hands. They take a carriage home. Jane kisses him good-bye, but Rochester wants more. "Let me come up to your room," he says when they reach her boarding house. Jane's confusion vanishes when she looks into Rochester's eyes. She smiles. He dismisses the carriage and follows her up the steps.

When next she sees him, Rochester seems distant—polite, but aloof. Was last night a mistake? She overhears an argument between him and Beauclerc. Then he disappears, and Beauclerc is vague about whether he's gone traveling or returned to his family mansion, The Cypress, in St. Francisville.

One morning Beauclerc calls the shop. He's down with a bad case of the flu and won't be able to deliver the decorations Mr. Broussard needs in St. Francisville. Could Jane please arrange to have a delivery service take them out? She decides to drive to The Cypress herself.

Lightning and thunder, and afternoon rain. As the rain lets up, Jane finds her way to an imposing three-story white-brick plantation, girdled with live oaks laced with majestic moss. She is met by **MARY WABASH**, the African-American housekeeper who looks like she worked for Scarlett O'Hara. Preparations for this evening's party are in full swing, and the decorations have arrived just in time. Jane heads back to her car. From his bedroom window, Rochester sees her—and rushes down the steps and outside just as she is about to drive away.

He insists that she stay for the evening, that it's too dangerous to drive back to New Orleans in the storm that's threatening—that, besides, she might enjoy the party. Rochester removes the keys from the ignition and offers her his arm. He gives her a tour of the grounds, showing her the ancient cypress tree that's all that remains of the mighty grove that once stood where the plantation was built. He insists that she stay for the party. Jane protests that she has nothing to wear. In one of the plantation's guest rooms, he opens an immense closet to reveal spectacular vintage clothes.

Applying makeup at the dressing table, Jane is interrupted by Mary—carrying the emerald dress Jane chose in one hand, a refilled water pitcher in the other. When Jane asks Mary what the occasion of the party is, Mary looks surprised at Jane's innocence. Then something darker comes over her countenance. "Rumor says Mr. Rochester may announce his engagement to Miss Blanche," she says. Jane can hardly contain her emotions as Mary leaves the room.

Act 3

It's all Jane can do to force herself downstairs, and she doesn't enter until the party is in full swing. Rochester sees her entrance and is entranced by her in the vintage dress and makeup. She is quickly the focus of attention. From one of the men, who introduces himself as **RICHARD DUBOIS**, she learns that Blanche Dubois, his cousin, is the daughter of an impoverished plantation owner. The family is delighted that the marriage may reverse Blanche's fortunes.

Rochester asks Jane to dance. She hesitates, but he insists. On the dance floor, they flow together as though they were born to a single rhythm. Rochester, without a word, leads her from the dance floor through the French doors.

Holding her by the hand, and oblivious to his duties as host, he takes her through the dark oaks under the full moon. "But . . . you and Blanche—" she protests. Rochester tells her, "I haven't been seeing anything clearly—until tonight." "What do you mean?" Jane wants to know, not daring to interpret his meaning. He kisses her gently on the lips.

Blanche on the balcony is watching them. As she sees them emerge from the corridor of oaks, she rushes down the stairs. Jane ducks into the shadows toward the side door as Blanche emerges into the light—her face a mask of fury.

In her guest room, Jane is in tears, removing her fancy dress, throwing her day clothes back on and preparing to leave. Suddenly, the lights go out. Jane hears hands groping the walls outside her door and a crazed laugh. The door hurls open, and from the shadows she can barely make out a female form—then she gasps as she realizes that an oil lantern has been hurled on the floor of her room. Before she can react, a match is thrown and the oil bursts into flames. As the flames roar up the lace curtains, Jane rushes toward the door—only to find it locked! She's trapped—and the room is ablaze!

Act 4

Jane rushes through the line of flames to the bureau and reaches for the water pitcher. She flings the water at the lace curtains—just as the door opens and Rochester runs in. As the other men quench the blaze, Rochester demands, "Who did this?!" "I'm not sure. It could have been your fiancée," Jane says. "Blanche is *not* my fiancée," Rochester retorts. "I told her tonight that we were finished."

A Delta Air Lines jet touches down in Kansas City, and Jane takes a shuttle downtown. As she looks out the window at the landscape of her unhappy childhood, all she can see reflected back is her memory of Rochester's darkly troubled face.

Her shuttle pulls into the Alameda Plaza. Standing next to the fountain is George Reed, who greets Jane with an embrace.

At Research Hospital, Jane is with George at the deathbed of her aunt, Sarah Reed. Sarah tells Jane that John Eyre, Jane's uncle in the West Indies, has been trying to locate her. Mrs. Reed admits that she discouraged him. Sarah Reed dies.

On her return to The Cypress, Jane is happy to find Rochester at home. Rochester is even happier to see her and has arranged a regal welcome. That night he proposes to Jane. Jane accepts. A tremendous bolt of lightning strikes. Outside the window, something's on fire. It's the ancient cypress, split in half by the lightning.

Back in New Orleans, Beauclerc tells Jane he objects to the match, noting the difference in their ages. But Jane ignores him in her excitement at a dream coming true. Beauclerc is troubled, wanting to say more but thinking better of it. Instead, he makes a telephone call. "Mr. Briggs?" he asks. "This is Pero Beauclerc, in New Orleans. . . ."

Rochester spends lavishly on his future bride. She is thrilled to see that the darkness of his demeanor has brightened from the powerful love between them. She sends a letter to her Uncle George announcing her upcoming marriage.

On her wedding day, Jane, a picture-book bride, nods her greeting to the smiling George Reed as she follows Rochester beyond the gate at The Cypress to the old white church. They see strangers walking among the raised tombs in the churchyard.

Later, when the priest, **FATHER MANUEL**, begins the ceremony, attorney **BRIGGS** reluctantly halts the wedding—with the announcement that Mr. Rochester is already married. In fact, Briggs says, Rochester's supposedly dead wife may be imprisoned in The Cypress itself.

Act 5

Rochester, mortified, embarrassed, and agitated at the revelation, escorts Jane through the disconcerted guests, followed by the priest, Briggs, and Mason—to the ancient slave cottage on the far side of the plantation yard where he reveals:

Bernice Mason Broussard, a raving madwoman, is locked away and guarded by Mary.

Briggs explains that when Beauclerc learned of Rochester's plan to marry Jane, he couldn't allow her to ruin her life by being party to this bigamy. Rochester is unable, under the Napoleonic Code that governs Louisiana law, to divorce his wife simply because she is insane.

Jane refuses to be Rochester's mistress. What kind of life could they have with his wife alive? They would just be waiting for her to die. She couldn't live that way. His face is troubled, darkly troubled, but he has nothing more to say. That's the way he's been living, and now he's doomed to continue alone. Jane leaves Louisiana.

Arriving in snowbound Kansas City with little money, Jane searches for work and has no luck. She spends her last money on a hotel room in the ghostly K.C. downtown. Her cold has become much worse, yet she forces herself out each morning to look for a job—finally seeing a notice for a guide at the Nelson Gallery of Art.

Three days later, after checking out of the hotel when the hotelkeeper won't allow her to stay on credit, she heads for her interview at the Nelson Gallery. But the cold has turned to full-blown pneumonia. She doesn't realize that today is Saturday, and that the gallery doesn't open until noon. Although the Security Guard sees Jane shivering from the blustering winter weather as she huddles in the portico of the gallery, he doesn't offer to let her in. Finally, Jane collapses on the marble steps of the gallery.

Act 6

The curator of the Nelson Gallery, **JOHN CRAIG**, on his way into work, sees the Security Guard looking down at the collapsed Jane. Quickly taking charge, he hustles her into the warmth of his office fireplace, revives her with tea, and asks her if she wants him to call an ambulance. "I have no insurance." He tells her to wait near the fire, while he makes a phone call. When he returns, he insists that she stay at his house. She can trade giving art lessons to his sister for her lodging, "until you're back on your feet."

At his old brick family home on Rockhill Road, John Craig introduces Jane to his studious invalid sister, **DIANA**.

After recuperating under the Craig family's care, Jane forms a lasting friendship with Diana, and takes a docent's position at the gallery. Insisting that she contribute part of her small income to the upkeep of the house, Jane even gets used to the hot-tempered Craig, whose dedication to his work, in the face of the recession's impact on the gallery and resulting cutbacks, makes him constantly irritable. Only Jane's smile, he says, "makes life bearable." Jane takes a job moonlighting at U.M.K.C. teaching art classes, to compensate for the reduction in her own museum salary.

Craig asks Jane to marry him, but discloses to her that he is on the verge of losing the house to foreclosure. He's been unable to keep up with the second mortgage they took out a few years ago to pay for Diana's last operation. Jane doesn't know what to say. She feels fond of him and of Diana, but . . . Finally she promises to think about his proposal.

A few days later, Craig calls Jane into his office to announce to her that her uncle, John Eyre, has died—and that she, as sole heir, will receive nearly five million dollars from his estate.

Act 7

Jane tells Craig, "I love you and Diana with all my heart, but I can't marry you—and it has nothing to do with this sudden good fortune. I'm still in love with another man."

In the weeks that follow, Jane uses part of her inheritance to refurbish the Craigs' home on Rockhill—and to pay off the second mortgage. When John

Craig protests, she will not hear of it. "You saved my life," she says, "and you and Diana are my family."

Clinging to her loving memories of Rochester, now that her mission to set the Craig family back on firm ground has been accomplished, Jane returns to The Cypress.

When the thirty-six-hour journey finally ends with the Greyhound bus depositing her on the highway, Jane hurries on foot to the ancient manor—and discovers only a burned-out shell.

At the church, Father Manuel, over a hearty breakfast he insists on serving her himself, tells Jane about the events of the past year. He describes in detail Rochester's futile search for her, and the tragic fire that was set by Bernice Broussard, who perished in the flames before Rochester could rescue her. In the fire, Rochester suffered a mangled hand, which was later amputated, and he also was blinded.

Jane borrows Father Manuel's car to drive to New Orleans, to the address in the Garden District that he gave her. A stately river cottage on Saint Charles Avenue is Rochester's current home. She observes him from a distance as he blindly attempts to walk in the gardens. He has obviously been changed by his terrible suffering, but his face still retains its forceful character.

Jane carries a tray to him, reveals her presence, and enjoys a poignant reunion with her love. When Rochester inquires about her year apart from him, Jane describes John Craig and his proposals, but she emphasizes that the kind of love John felt for her and that she felt for him was not the kind of love her spirit requires. Rochester realizes then that Jane is still willing to marry him. Three days later, they marry and settle into the New Orleans river cottage.

Ten years later, Jane is content with her married life. George Reed visits when business takes him to New Orleans, and Rochester has recovered vision in one eye and is able to see their newborn son. Jane continues her friendship with John and Diana, both of whom have married, and she has converted the antiques shop to a studio gallery, where she works on her painting and exhibits her own work and that of others she discovers.

7

Who Are the Buyers?
The Markets for Treatments and What and How to Sell to Them

. . .

It's a fifty-fifty deal. Just make sure we get the best of it.
—Samuel Goldwyn

S ome writers don't care whether their writing sells, or whether it sells *soon*. They have the luxury of writing only what they like, and the freedom to continue doing so without depending on it as a source of income. If time, for you, is not of the essence, you'll simply write what you want to write and let the results find their way onto the screen in their own time. But if you're interested in moving your career along the fastest possible track toward receiving financial rewards in proportion to the effort you're making, it's more than just a good idea to keep your buyers in mind while you're in the process of identifying good dramatic or comedic stories and bringing your treatments of them into focus. By keeping market considerations in mind you'll be able to expedite your career success.

For those who are interested in speeding along, this chapter provides information on who your prospective buyers are and what they're looking for. Of course both buyers and what they're buying change as rapidly as anything else in our accelerating world. The general observations that follow should be supplemented by ongoing research (through phone calls and by checking the most recent directories).

The Television Market

To the casual observer of the industry, the television market's needs seem to be changing constantly. Social trends, such as protests against too much violence, and the evidence of the Nielsen ratings have an impact on the Monday morning meeting that is held at every broadcaster's executive suite to determine that week's acquisitions policy. But to someone who's been around long enough, the overall effect is cyclical. During antiviolence protests, the networks tried nonviolent programming; ratings plummeted, and advertisers were unhappy. Little by little, violence (after all, the stuff of drama) crept back into the programming. By the same token, women-in-jeopardy stories or disease-of-the-week stories go in and out of favor as the audience expresses its preferences through the ratings. Though corporate ownership of television broadcasters continues to change at a dizzying rate, it may be helpful here to list the kinds of television buyers, and generally what they look for.

1. Broadcast television (sometimes referred to as *free TV*) and **basic cable** (advertiser-supported channels that arrive in your home at no extra cost beyond the cost of your antenna or basic cable service) are growing more similar all the time—but they're still not quite the same animal. Broadcast TV is a much more robust market than basic cable. The six broadcast networks buy a lot more programming, of various kinds; cable is divided into many medium- to small-niche networks including TNT, TBS, A&E, and Lifetime. In general, the free networks (and Lifetime) gravitate toward

- stories based on true events
- unique family dramas (whether true or fictional), including "occasional" pieces such as Christmas or Thanksgiving stories
- stories addressing topical female issues, as long as they don't offend broadcast sponsors (a story about breast cancer

that indicts the chemical companies recently could not be sold for fear of offending Dow Chemical). In this respect, the Fox Network is an exception—its market is driven by young men. ABC tries hard to appeal to men as well as women.

• sci-fi/fantasy, as long as it's reality-driven and earth-based, with stories in which today's audience has an identifiable stake (and no more than ten to thirty years into the future!), and sci-fi books by established authors

• heroic stories of any kind, as long as they're contemporary

What's generally *not* marketable to the primary television broadcasters is

• comedy of any kind, romantic or otherwise (unless a major motion picture star is attached). Network movie audiences want serious drama.

• straight romance, unless it's based on a novel by Danielle Steel or Judith Krantz (both of whom already have ongoing network deals)

• movies about minorities. The percentage of non-Caucasian network audiences is small; though there's a developing trend toward expanding minority programming, you'd be better off selling a minority story to a minority broadcaster such as the Black Entertainment Network (though the Fox Network has done wonders in this area of programming).

Advertiser-supported broadcast television networks include ABC, CBS, NBC, WB, UPN, and Fox. *Advertiser-supported cable-delivered networks* are A&E, ABC Family, CNN, Discovery, Disney, FX, Lifetime, TBS, TNN, TNT, and USA.

2. Subscriber cable television (sometimes called *pay TV*) refers to all networks and cable-delivered stations that cost the consumer an extra fee. *Pay-per-view* is a subcategory of pay TV. Subscriber cable television includes HBO, Cinemax, Starz, Encore, and Showtime.

Since the first edition of this book, cable has come of age economically and creatively, to the point that it is almost on a par with broadcast television. The movie-for-television format is a staple for premium pay channels like HBO and Showtime, as well as for a growing number of non-premium cable channels like USA, F/X, TNT, and Disney. The competition has increased so much that pay cable channels are hard-pressed to offer original programming that makes the subscribers feel as though they're getting their monthly money's worth. Cable channels like Sci-Fi, MTV, and Lifetime seem to be most successful when they serve specialized audiences. The same adage applies here as in network television when writing a pitch: "If you can't sell it in a ten-second promo, then you can't sell it."

Who's the Audience?

As we've said, each programmer tends to serve a particular demographic. Although subject matter goes in cycles, the audience profile of a given channel is fairly constant. The most important homework you can do if you're writing for TV is to watch TV yourself! If you watch television regularly, you'll begin to discern what kinds of projects are being bought by which buyers. For instance, a network's evening series lineup is used as a promotional platform leading the same audience into watching that network's movie. So what appeals to the viewers of *Friends* or *Touched by an Angel* is the type of television movie that will ordinarily air following that program.

Keep in mind that competition is forcing constant change among the buyers:

- ABC, which has cut back on its movies, is geared to the young and boomers, gravitating toward adult suspense, strong female appeal, issue pieces.
- ABC Family (formerly Fox Family) repurposes some programming from the ABC network as well as producing original family programming.
- A&E looks for finished scripts, with the exception of

adaptable prestige novels such as *The Great Gatsby*. A&E prefers American subject matter with strong roles for lead actors and entertaining historical drama; series programming concentrates on one-hour dramas of the cop, lawyer, or murder mystery genres, such as *100 Centre Street* and *Nero Wolf*.

- CBS programming traditionally appeals to an older audience (25–55), mature and female. Movies and series tend to be soft, family-oriented dramas with prestige casts, though they are going a bit younger with series such as *CSI* and *Everybody Loves Raymond*.

- Comedy Central does some original programming but is primarily sketch-comedy oriented. They do a lot of stand-up comedy specials since HBO cut back on them.

- Court TV does a few low-budget movies each year based on high visibility cases that are politically acceptable for television.

- Disney Channel, though recently turned to network-style programming, still goes after children and family viewers. *Cadet Kelly*, by Gail Parent and AEI client Michael Walsh, is about a New York girl who gets transplanted.

- Fox, moving away from down-market comedies and quick-hit reality shows, is now going for hip and trendy dramas that appeal to Gen-X viewers. Its focal audience is male, and it will take chances with programming.

- FX has positioned itself as "the HBO of basic cable" but going after men 18 to 34. The series *The Shield* was the first offering along those lines, and FX original movies have issue-oriented themes.

- HBO considers its television films to be lower-budgeted (up to $15 million) theatricals. Presently once again re-evaluating its brand in regard to original movies, HBO has a preference for bios (though *not* cradle-to-grave) and unusual or particular subject matter—all with upscale visibility potential. Since HBO doesn't live and die by the ratings, it will take chances with material that might garner favorable publicity to further enhance the distinguished HBO brand. When it comes to series, HBO likes to take on projects that you'll never see on network television, and that are writer-driven, like Alan Ball's *Six Feet Under* and Tom Fontana's *OZ*. HBO's "limited series" are high-end productions like *From the Earth to the Moon, Band of Brothers,* and *The Wire.* At this writing HBO is considering miniseries that may range over $100 million as well as lower-budget miniseries that deal with big subjects such as the feminist and civil rights movements, difficult issues (example: *The Corner*), and historical figures like John Adams (being developed by Tom Hanks). HBO is not interested in "pure entertainment"; it will acquire finished documentaries as well as license documentaries at the pitch stage. It looks for subjects that nobody else will cover, like *Small Town Ecstasy,* a documentary about a father who takes the drug ecstacy with his children.

- Lifetime features television programming for women and has a preference for finished scripts based on true stories with issue-driven but reliable content, but will consider books with profile or cachet such as *The Pilot's Wife.*
- MTV does inexpensive, music-themed programming, reality and teen to young adult programming; its cousin VH1 does a limited number of original music-themed movies like *Ricky Nelson: Teen Idol.*
- NBC is younger and hipper than CBS, though still programming for boomer-aged female viewers.
- Showtime, known for its sexually charged programming, has managed to step out of HBO's original programming shadow by concentrating on demographically targeted shows. Its projects have been attracting outstanding filmmakers, writers, and actors. Showtime was once known mainly for titillating late-night shows like *Red Shoe Diaries,* but in the past two years has produced a set of hit original

series with its demographically targeted shows. Using these successes as a springboard, Showtime wants to raise the programming ante further by doing fewer—but larger-budgeted—original movies and miniseries.

- UPN is for young men, featuring sci-fi with lots of action.
- Starz and Encore are basically movie channels that commission one to three original movies.
- USA once made genre movies and was male-oriented, but has turned to broadcast network–type programming.
- WB focuses on programming for young women, ages 12 to 25.
- TNT's movie side is well-defined, reflecting Ted Turner's interest in the environment and history (American, Native American, and especially Civil War). TNT will do biographies focusing on one compelling aspect of a subject, but not bios that are "cradle to grave." This network is also star-driven and favors self-promoting material (example: *The Mists of Avalon*).

Because there are so many broadcasters requiring enough programming to fill their channels, and good enough programming to beat the competition's ratings, television is a major, insatiable market for writers. Sometimes identical ideas create a television film simultaneously with a theatrical film, as with TNT's 1995 *Kissinger and Nixon*, which appeared months before Oliver Stone's *Nixon*. Because a sufficient amount of time had passed since the deaths of President and Mrs. Nixon, the examination of his life and presidency at this time made sense. The feature film and the television movie each had a distinct point of view from which to scrutinize Nixon's unique persona.

Good drama tackles a larger-than-life story by focusing on a galvanizing experience or event in the life of the main character. Ideas that aren't strong enough for the theatrical market, or ideas that are similar to theatrical stories that have already been made as feature films, are often perfect for television.

Topical or even political ideas, too "timely" for the long theatrical development process, are often just the thing a harried network programmer needs to "capture the night" against an ordinary film on another channel with an extraordinary cast.

The Market Wants What It Wants

Keep in mind as you write your TV treatment that television is much more market-driven than is the motion picture industry. TV insiders have long considered television an "advertising" or "merchandising" medium, and it's safe to assume that if you can't imagine a mainstream major American sponsor (such as General Mills, Coca-Cola, or Bristol-Myers) backing your idea for a television movie, the idea most likely has no substantial market in the United States of America. When we were giving regular "Writers' Lifeline" lectures at the Beverly Hills Library, one of our faithful attendees kept showing up to tell us, "American TV should take chances. Why don't you mount a production of Rabelais's *Gargantua and Pantagruel* [the classic French comic novel]." We replied, "Simon, we're not in Canada [where the government subsidizes programming simply because of its cultural content]. There's no market in America for Rabelais." You are indeed welcome to become a crusader, and go jousting with network executives to change the face of television. But if your goal is to make money by writing for TV, you'll be more successful thinking like a market analyst instead. Saying your "new idea" is very similar to *ER* or *NYPD Blue* makes every ear perk up; saying, "There's never been anything like this before," is not only an automatic turnoff, but it is probably not even true.

Television is numbers-driven, governed by the Nielsen ratings, which report to the media and the world on a daily basis who's watching which shows when. With forty or more channels for competition, and the consequent slicing up of audiences, the networks have begun to focus on audience demographics rather than on sheer numbers. Rather than shooting for the highest share of the evening, programmers are content with a solid 4 percent share of a particular demographic group such as "Gen Xers" or the "thirtysomethings." Their sponsors, though still interested in high numbers, are intent on the type of consumer they want to reach. Mainstream-TV programmers—the folks who set up the TV schedule by placing programs in time slots— are determined to garner and cultivate a particular audience, making sure to give them what they want to watch. Outlets do exist for those who enjoy cultural programming such as ballets, operas, and documentaries (including the Discovery Channel, the History Channel, Arts & Entertainment, and PBS), but if you choose to write for these "high-brow" broadcasters look forward to having fun in a wonderful creative forum—*but on a shoestring.*

What Can You Sell to TV?

It is a common phenomenon in television that several people come up with the same idea at the same time. So the purchase of ideas can be risky. For this reason, when they buy ideas at all, TV production companies tend to buy them from people they already know and trust.

Yet, although it's relatively rare for a new writer to sell an idea to television, it certainly happens. In the never-ending pursuit of good stories, people in the industry do take risks. "A good story, well outlined," says veteran TV producer Norton Wright, "is as welcome from a new talent as from a known and trusted talent." But it's not enough to say, "I have an idea." Everyone has ideas. The air is filled with them. In a typical week AEI will have nearly the identical idea pitched to us two or three times. What determines whether a story can be sold is your execution of the idea or concept in a treatment (and don't forget to register it with the Writers Guild! See chapter 8). New writers and producers can sell ideas only by creating treatments for them that show the purchaser "where the story is." This explains another problem outsiders face. We hear the following question all the time: "I have a great idea for TV. Can you find me a writer to collaborate with so I can sell it and break in?"

Writers who've already broken in have done so because they know how to execute their ideas in an effective manner. When they work on other people's ideas, including those given by experienced producers to executives, they're paid to do so. For an inexperienced writer or producer to approach an experienced writer and ask him to write "on spec" (that is, without guarantee of payment) makes no career sense for the writer. If one of our experienced writers has time, we'll arrange for him to be paid by the inexperienced "idea person" so that the idea can be brought to a salable level. But if you can find a writer on your own to collaborate with you, chances are that writer will be of no use in making the sale—on the premise that if he were successful, he wouldn't have time to take a chance on your idea. And if he has a chance of being successful, he usually has so many good ideas of his own that he doesn't want to distract himself with someone else's—over which he has no control—unless he's paid as he writes.

Everything we've just said applies primarily to original, fictional ideas. Things are easier for the inexperienced writer or producer when it comes to nonfiction. If what you're trying to sell is a true story the rights to which you control (and, as we discuss in chapter 5, if you don't control them, find out how to secure them before you take the next step), you may indeed attract a cowriter to work with you on spec. In this case, some of the same precautions apply. If the cowriter has no credits, he or she may be a detriment to your potential deal. If he has credits, he'll probably want money up front; or, if he thinks the idea is eminently salable, he may agree to act as a writer-producer in exchange for the right to pursue the sale.

If you have the rights to a powerful true story, another approach is to go directly to a producer like AEI (our phone number and e-mail address are printed at the end of the book) after registering your story with the Writers Guild (as described in chapter 8). If we think your story is salable, we help you secure the rights, make a deal with you, and, often, assist you in preparing a treatment in order to justify a "story by" credit for you. As the story evolves toward production, you may end up sharing this credit with an experienced writer, but it is still a major step forward in the business.

A TV Buyer's Checklist

Subject matter aside, all television buyers determine a particular story's attractiveness by considering the following elements:

- **Concept.** Does this story provide a fresh new angle on a subject important to our audience?
- **Castability.** Is the protagonist a character one of today's TV stars—or, even better, motion picture stars—will want to play?
- **Setting.** Does it fit TV? Setting should be scaled down to limited locations. If your true story actually took place in three cities, try to set it in one or two (keeping in mind, of course, that Peoria, New York City, Paris, and Spokane can all be shot in Montreal).
- **Budget.** Can the story be done for a price? Movies for television have licensing fees ranging from $2 million (Court TV and Lifetime) to $6 to $15 million (HBO, Hallmark), with the networks averaging around $2.9 million. This contrasts with up to $100 million for feature film budgets. The more expensive it is to film this story, and the longer time needed to shoot it (TV movies are generally shot in eighteen to twenty-one days), the

more likely it will be considered a feature film rather than a television film.

You can see how important it is to determine your career goals before you set out to sell to TV. If what you want to accomplish is a one-time sale of a family story, you should probably go directly to someone in the business after registering the story. Tell them what you've got. If your goal is to establish a career in writing for TV, you should attempt a treatment before going to that same source, or work with a collaborator, but only if you're absolutely certain that your collaborator is, in every sense, an asset to the deal—and that you have a clear written agreement with him before you begin your work.

Obviously, the first skill needed to sell to television is to be able to recognize what a good story idea is. To train this instinct, we repeat: *Nothing can take the place of actually watching TV*—and with Tivo available, there's no excuse at all.

TREATING YOURSELF

Because I rarely pitch for a studio deal and prefer to take a finished product into the marketplace—whether it's a screenplay or a novel—I'm inclined to say the treatment is more a part of my process than it is a sales tool.

I'm inclined to say it, but it's not entirely true. The three- to eight-page documents I write are indeed designed to sell the project . . . to myself. Well, mostly to myself, but also to the people whose opinions matter to me, like my agent, a handful of readers, and often a producing partner (like Ken Atchity, my partner in Warp & Weft Productions, or another production company we've decided to work with).

What I've learned in the last several years is that the best creative decisions you make are the projects you choose to write and, maybe more important, the ones you choose *not* to write. You simply can't write yourself out of a bad idea, no matter how hard you sweat. On several occasions, what sounded cool and interesting to me as a loose notion, one-liner, theme, or "area" became less interesting when I tried to tell it as a three-act story.

I write fast. I write in a zone. I can't get "sort of" wet once I've dived into a story, mind and soul. So it's become a matter of sanity preservation to take the time up-front to be sure this is what I want to devote the next several months of my life to. It's a decision based not just on whether it will sell or not, but whether it will be a fulfilling creative experience for me, one that won't make me wish I could turn back the clock and take a moment to dip my toe in the pool.

For more verbal thinkers, that process is "talking out" the story, telling it to their family and confidants. I really need to see it on the page, fleshed out, and written to provoke, excite . . . and sell.

Even if it's an audience of one: myself.

—John Scott Shepherd, author *Henry's List of Wrongs*,
screenwriter *Sherman's March*, *Joe Somebody*,
Life or Something Like It, *The Prince of Pools*

The Feature Film Market

Because of the studio's fear of litigation, it's virtually impossible for an unknown writer to sell a first treatment directly to a major studio. Your best bet is to hunt down a production company and try to entice them first. Production companies come in two primary flavors:

1. In-house production companies. Successful writers, producers, and directors are given *housekeeping deals* at the major studios in exchange for the studios' *right of first refusal* for the products they develop. Because an in-house production company has a close relationship to a studio that finances and distributes films, generally speaking its interest in your treatment puts you in a good position for a sale. The problem is that once an in-house company has one, two, or three projects in development (depending on the principal's clout in the marketplace and at the studio), the studio is loath to put yet another story into the works until it sees the outcome of the others.

The key question to ask an in-house producer who's interested in your treatment is, What do you have in development? If the answer is, "We just set up house with MGM, and we have yet to place something in development," you're in good shape. If the answer is, "We have ten projects in development," proceed with caution. Too often the in-house producer is forced to sit on projects until the outcome of other development deals is known.

Technically, most *first look* or *right of first refusal* housekeeping deals allow the producer to go to another studio if the host studio has passed on a project offered by him. But, in practice, shopping that project outside the host studio can be dangerous for the producer, primarily because he doesn't want to jeopardize the status of his projects already in development. Both in-house and independent producers are listed in *The Hollywood Creative Directory* (see Sources and Recommended Reading for ordering information). In any directory you can tell which producers are which flavors because an in-house producer's address is most often, though not always, identical to a studio's address (Richard Donner's company, for example, lists its address at the Warner Bros. lot). *The Hollywood Creative Directory* actually tells you whether the production company has an in-house deal. Under *Zide-Perry Entertainment*, for example, it lists: "DEAL: MGM" (at this writing).

2. Independent production companies. An independent producer, like AEI, pays its own overhead and does its best to deal with the everyday vagaries of cash flow in a notoriously volatile industry—in exchange for the freedom to sell to anyone without restriction. AEI, in partnership with Zide-Perry Entertainment, sold Rick Lynch's *180 Seconds at Willow Park* to New Line Cinema for Renny Harlin (*Cliffhanger*) to direct. Also in partnership with Zide-Perry, but represented by International Creative Management, we sold Brett Bartlett's *Sign of the Watcher* to Propaganda Films, Steve Alten's *Meg* to Walt Disney Pictures, and, with Paradigm, *Henry's List of Wrongs* to New Line. We've also made deals with Fox 2000 (*Joe Somebody*), New Regency Pictures (*Life or Something Like It*), Paramount Pictures (*Ripley's Believe-It-or-Not!®*), Warner Brothers (*The Kill Martin Club, Eulogy for Joseph Way*), and so on.

Observe caution in working through an independent producer, making sure you check the company's credits and reputation in the industry. In the rough-and-tumble world of entertainment, these companies come and go like restaurants in Los Angeles or New York. Asking an independent producer what he has in development will help you judge his future stability. The producer who answers with the names of several projects is a better bet for you than one who tells you only what he's already done. If he has no credits, and little or nothing in development, keep shopping! Getting an option payment for your treatment isn't as important as getting the film made. Don't judge a company's effectiveness by how much it's willing to pay you up front or promise you. Some of the most successful independent producers in town pay almost nothing for options; they figure you're lucky to have them as partners because their chances of getting the film made are better than anyone else's.

The in-house producer has the studio's "deep pockets," as does the inexperienced independent producer who enters the industry with a bankroll. But keep your eyes focused on the production money, not just an option payment, and you'll do a better job of sorting out who's the best ally in getting your treatment sold.

Using a Spec Script to Sell Future Treatments

In order to sell yourself as a screenwriter, you should have a completed screenplay. You may be able to find an independent producer to take your treatment to the buyers. Even if they pass on the project, if you've already written a spec script that has impressed people in the industry, you may be asked what other ideas you have. Working with the independent producer to write these in treatment form, you may be able to make a development deal with the studio that will pay you to write a script based on that treatment.

How to Sell the Feature Treatment

Both in-house and independent producers are constantly on the lookout for good stories to make into films. When you're ready to approach a producer, call or e-mail the producer's company and ask for the name of the *head of development*, who is responsible for acquiring and developing new screenplays and projects. In most cases he or she is the person to approach first, not the principal of the company—unless of course an introduction, chance encounter, or recommendation gets you directly to the principal.

Once you've determined the appropriate individual at the production company, your approach will be the same as with an agent or manager. The in-house producer may tell you that you need an agent to submit your work to them. Their relationship with the studio makes them particularly vulnerable targets for nuisance suits. The independent producer is more likely to listen to your story and to read your treatment even if you are without representation; you'll know his intentions are honorable if he tells you to register it with the Writers Guild first.

Selling Book-Film Treatments

Developing your idea into a book is, in fact, an excellent strategy for piquing the interest of the feature film community. Treatments based on novels or nonfiction books, whether published or unpublished, are sold every month in Hollywood. And, of course, if your story sells as a book first, your chances of selling it as a film are greatly enhanced. You may sell your story as a film and not as a book at all, nonetheless launching your career in show business. The ideal scenario, which we focus on at AEI, is, of course, to sell a story in both the publishing and film worlds.

WRITING TREATMENTS TOOTH BY BLOODY TOOTH

Let me preface this by saying I hate writing treatments. To me, writing treatments is like having to floss before brushing—it's painful, it makes you bleed a little, but you know you have to do it.

I use treatments in two different ways: first, to lay out a story for a yet-to-be-written novel or screenplay; second, to create a "selling tool" describing an already written novel or screenplay.

As a guide for a yet-to-be-written project, treatments can be an invaluable road map in outlining the steps that move the plot and characters from start to finish. The more detailed the character descriptions, the easier it is to create character conflicts and flesh out the story later on. Flaws in characters and story lines are also easier to remedy at this level, before you become too emotionally attached to either.

The pain comes in writing a treatment that describes an already completed project. How do you condense a 500-page novel into a two- to three-page selling document and still create the excitement and tension to inspire filmmakers to turn the story into a motion picture? Maybe the secret lies in flossing those teeth—one painful gum line (action beat) at a time, keeping it short and sweet—as your wounded writer's ego spits bloodied saliva into the sink.

—Steve Alten, *New York Times* bestselling author whose novels include *Meg; The Trench; Domain; and Goliath,* and whose treatments for *Meg* and *Journey to the Center of the Earth* were sold by AEI to Walt Disney Pictures

A Motion Picture Buyer's Checklist

The feature-film buyer, though he has much wider latitude for selection than does the television buyer, still considers the following elements in a story offered for production:

- **Concept.** Does this story provide subject matter and/or a theme broad enough to attract a film-going audience? Will the concept appeal to a top director? Is it a *high concept*, one that translates in a very few words to word-of-mouth and one-line advertising campaigns?
- **Castability.** Is the protagonist a character one or more of today's stars would want to play?
- **Production values.** Does the setting or the concept lend itself to highly visual, compelling film images—as in the opening scenes of *Arachnophobia* or *The Perfect Storm* or the in-flight covert boarding of a 747 in *Executive Decision*? Because feature filmmakers seek the remarkable production values today's audiences demand, they are less concerned with budget than are TV filmmakers. Recently, an industry report stated that the average price of a feature film was now $60 million—more than the entire annual budget of some TV networks.

Now that you understand the relationship between your product and its market, it's time for some practical advice on how to register and protect your ideas—the subject matter of chapter 8.

8

Protecting Your Work

. . .

Accounting terms used herein shall be defined by the
Twentieth Century Fox accounting department at such
time, if any, that litigation shall be entered into among the
parties.

—from a Twentieth Century Fox
boilerplate distribution contract

It's difficult to protect an idea from being stolen. Generally
speaking, ideas are not themselves protected by copyright
laws, and other legal claims involving the theft of ideas are difficult to prove. Novelist John Gardner (*October Light, The Sun-
light Dialogues, Grendel*) once remarked that he was always
relieved when someone stole an idea from him: "Then I don't
have to live with the damned thing the rest of my life!" He told
us about a film that he had snuck into a theater to see many
years before. It was about a giant alligator haunting a swamp in
Louisiana. "When I walked out of that theater," he said, "I
thanked God that someone had stolen my idea. It was so bad, I
knew I had been spared the humiliation. God had been protecting my career." Gardner claimed that his chief protection
against theft was his own speed and ambition. He was so pro-
lific he could afford to be generous. Like the little old lady who
lived in the shoe, he had so many creative children he didn't
know what to do with them and didn't mind having one or
another of them "adopted"—or even kidnapped.

Caution is always a good idea in the entertainment business, but paranoia and obsessiveness can be counterproductive and generally don't make for wholesome long-term relationships. After all, if you're that worried about having your ideas stolen, you shouldn't be communicating them. *Communication always brings risk.* Major studios and production companies aren't in business to steal your idea. They have plenty of money and make more by paying for stories—which they do gladly and readily when they find one they like. No one, except attorneys, likes litigation. If you worry about having your work stolen during a pitch, you announce yourself as being a "litigious" person—to be placed on your buyer's life-is-too-short list—and you limit getting your work out there to be read.

Most entertainment professionals recognize that there are no truly original ideas. All of us are stimulated by the same events (world and local news, social issues and trends, popular culture, consumer disenchantment, weather), and it's par for the course to see similar story ideas in development at the same time in *The Hollywood Reporter's* regular "Films in Development" and "Films in Production" sections.

Theft does occur—most of it, in our experience, inadvertent. Ideas are so common that people forget where they first heard them. The writer who's taken reasonable precautions can best defend against stolen work.

First Line of Defense: Register!

Ideas, in themselves, can't be copyrighted any more than can titles; both ideas and titles are in the public domain (though under the trademark laws, you can't use the title of an already successful work; this protects the consumer from being deceived into buying your work believing it to be the successful work). Ideas written down in the form of a treatment or synopsis *can* be registered, however, and we recommend registering everything you write with the Writers Guild of America (WGA), if for no other reason than that it makes you and inexperienced others who see the registration number take your work more seriously (see instructions at the end of this chapter).

Just because you've registered your treatment with the WGA doesn't mean someone won't steal it. But if someone you've sent your work to attempts to use all or a substantial part of it without your permission, the registration is invaluable. If you bring suit against the alleged thief, the court will open the envelope in which the WGA sealed your story at the date of registration. If someone registered the same story at an earlier date, whether that someone is the alleged thief or not, your claim is diminished. Separate creation of similar ideas *does* vest both parties with rights to their own work, which can be defended.

When you register something with the Writers Guild, be sure it is as detailed and specific as possible. All the treatments used as samples in this book have been registered with the WGA and can be used as models. If what you register is written with strokes that are too broad, your legal protection will be minimal. "Two opposites on a river" can apply as easily to *Huckleberry Finn* as to *A River Runs through It*, or *The African Queen*. The more general the idea, the more it belongs to the public domain.

Once a writer called to accuse us of showing an idea of his to Universal Studios (which we had not done) simply because he read that Universal was now in development with an almost identical idea. We were very upset by the accusation. A few days later, we read an article in the *Los Angeles Times* about the background of the Universal story. The journalist reported that the story had been based on a 1920s novel—which the writer who made the accusation claimed not to have read or even heard of.

Follow Your Instincts about People

Ultimately, your best protection is to follow your instincts about who to do business with. If you don't feel comfortable with the person you've contacted, remember the folk wisdom often offered about first dates: "It ain't gonna get better." Govern yourself accordingly and find someone else to sell your treatment to. In the network of relationships that forms the entertainment business, people continue to deal with those with whom they feel comfortable and to weed out work that doesn't first attract the attention of a quality manager or agent. Begin your entertainment career with this attitude. There are plenty of decent people in the business, as in any other business; don't deal with the flakes, who may indeed be more numerous in entertainment's carnival atmosphere than in many other businesses.

"Please Resubmit through an Agent"

The receipt of thousands of unsolicited properties (for the most part unusable), coupled with the occasional crank lawsuit, has made entertainment companies cautious to the point of preferring to lose the outside chance of finding a gem than to spend the time, energy, and risk with strangers. For one thing, their Errors and Omissions (E & O) insurance policies require that they take every precaution. The larger the company, the more likely that they will insist you submit your treatment or script through an agent, manager, or attorney.

Indeed the general industry feeling is that if someone else has found something worthwhile, then it might be worth the time and effort. At the end of the day no one knows whether this is a good policy or a stupid one, but it's a policy dictated by the very real need of getting insurance to protect the company in this highly litigious society—and by the lack of time to cover everything. The fear of litigation and the surfeit of inexperienced people trying to find a deal make it extremely difficult for the unrepresented writer to have his work read by the studios and production companies.

Should I Sign a Release?

Some production companies will read unrepresented work, but require a standard release form that both documents the submission of your idea and provides permission for the recipient to consider the idea.

A release, generally used by the smaller companies (the larger companies refuse to deal with anyone but authorized agents or managers), is meant to assure the producer that the writer is fully aware there may be ideas and scripts similar in concept and design to the one he is himself submitting. Should a disagreement arise about the authorship, the writer, in a typical release, pledges not to litigate but to seek instead some sort of arbitration.

SUBMISSION RELEASE

Regarding a <u>SCREENPLAY</u> currently titled <u>GOING FOR BROKE</u>
          type of work   *title of work*
written by <u>Phyllis Adashek</u> which is being submitted on <u>11/19/96</u>
          name of author   *submission date*
to <u>AEI-Atchity Entertainment</u> for the RECIPIENT'S evaluation
      recipient
for possible exclusive purchase or option, the following conditions
apply:

The AUTHOR and/or his representatives WARRANT that the work
described is an original screenplay which he has written and is
submitting to the RECIPIENT freely and without any obligation in
order for the RECIPIENT to evaluate the work for possible purchase,
option or representation, and that the RECIPIENT shall not be liable or
accountable for the condition or return of the work and assumes no
legal liability whatsoever either now or in the future in connection
with this work which has been duly registered with the Writers Guild
of America, Registration No. 101500.

This work is being submitted in the following format(s):

☑ a printed and bound screenplay.

☐ a 3.5-inch IBM compatible disk, or IBM compatible CD, with
synopsis & screenplay.

☐ an IBM compatible e-mail attachment.

                                           ————————————
                                        signature of author

Contact information: Phyllis Adashek
                              5000 Prosperity Farms Road
                              Boca Raton, FL 33410
                              (561) 851-9940

Are Pitches Safe?

According to the WGA, even the act of hearing a pitch on the part of a producer or financier may imply a contract that you will be paid if your material is used, but this may be difficult for you to prove. Because of the general nature of pitches, very little of what you present is actually protectable. Conversely, from the buyer's viewpoint, listening to a pitch is fraught with legal risk. For this reason, many buyers have two executives listen to a pitch to serve as witnesses in case of possible litigation. Or the recipient may take notes during the pitch to serve as a written record.

From the writer's viewpoint, telling a story to a producer is not the same as assigning it to him. Find a way of establishing ownership before you make the pitch, which can be done simply by mentioning that you've registered your story with the WGA. Responsible producers may ask you whether your story has been registered before they listen to a pitch, even by telephone. Scrupulous producers prefer not to deal with an unprotected new writer.

Before pitching your idea, do whatever you can to leave a "paper trail" behind you. This means having your treatment on paper beforehand and documenting, perhaps in your daybook, who heard the pitch, when, where, and what developments occurred. Then ask the person you're pitching to if she'd like a *leave-behind* (see the sample at the end of this chapter). If she's at all interested, she'll say yes. Of course your leave-behind should indicate on its cover page that your story's been registered with the WGA ("WGAw Registration #111111"). If yours is a phone pitch, follow it up with correspondence including the registered treatment you pitched by phone.

TREATMENTS ARE GREAT WHEN YOU CONSIDER THE ALTERNATIVE

Treatments. Blecchhh. I despise the very concept, for two reasons: (1) no treatment of reasonable length can possibly do justice to an outstanding script, and (2) treatments give away the plot twists before the reader has so much as glanced at page one. The cold, hard truth of the matter, however, is this: few people in Hollywood are going to read your treatment, regardless of quality. Fewer still will read your script. BUT: Some of those who would not otherwise read your script will read it if they like the treatment. Therefore, you should probably write a treatment.

—John Robert Marlow, Nicholls finalist, author of *Nano*

Copyright

Copyright is a form of protection provided, since the original Copyright Act of 1790, by the laws of the United States (Title 17, U.S. Code) to the creators of "original works of authorship" including literary, dramatic, musical, artistic, and certain other intellectual works. Additionally, the concept of *common law copyright* still exists in certain states, alongside the federal copyright statute. This protection is available to both published and unpublished works. The following copyright information has been provided by the copyright office of the Library of Congress and the Writers Guild of America:

Copyright includes five exclusive rights related to an original work. These are the right to:

- reproduce copies of it
- distribute copies of it
- perform the work
- publicly display the work
- prepare derivative works from it

Only the owner of the copyright of an original work or those he authorizes are entitled to pursue each of these activities.

Copyright automatically comes into existence the moment an original work is tangibly expressed; that is, put onto paper or computer memory in any form. As a general rule, the term of copyright continues for seventy years beyond the death of the author, at which time the copyright falls into the public domain. The publisher or producer of your words should place the copyright notice on published or produced versions in order to publicize the ownership of your copyright. But unpublished and unproduced works are automatically and absolutely protected by copyright whether or not the copyright notice appears on them.

However, although the copyright exists the moment your words appear on paper, there are certain legal advantages to registering your copyright claim with the U.S. Copyright Office. In an infringement suit you might bring to court, the law allows the copyright claimant to recover statutory (pre-set) damages and attorneys' fees if the copyright was registered before the date on which the infringement took place or within three months of publication. However, even if the registration takes place after the date of infringement, you may make a claim for actual damages, profits, and even an injunction. So, even though registering for copyright is not a precondition to copyright protection, it can be helpful in the event you sue for infringement. As we'll see at the end of this chapter, registering a copyright is easy.

We get so many questions on this subject that it's worth reviewing it in more detail.

Who Can Claim Copyright?
Copyright protection exists from the moment the work is created in fixed form; that is, it is an "incident of the process of authorship." The copyright in the work of authorship *immediately* becomes the property of the author who freely created it.

Only the author or those deriving their rights through the author can rightfully claim copyright. The authors of a joint work are co-owners of the copyright in the work, unless there is an agreement to the contrary.

Work for Hire

When you're hired to write or rewrite something, the copyright will most probably reside with your employer and your writing may be considered a *work for hire*. Make sure you are clear about the relationship and the copyright arrangements before you undertake a paid writing assignment—and ask for a reversion of copyright in the event the motion picture is not produced within a certain time period (say, three years). Don't be surprised if you can't get it, however; it's quite normal for writers to be hired to produce work that will be copyrighted by the employer and not subject to reversion. When the motion picture rights to a screenplay or book are sold to a producer, the copyright is generally assigned to the producer or distributor. That's what they're buying: control over the copyright—and corporations get that for ninety-five years under the current law.

Published Copyright

When a book is sold to a publisher, the publisher prints a copyright notice in the name of the author in the book, and files for its registration with the Copyright Office of the Library of Congress. In negotiating your publishing contract, you or your agent should make sure that the copyright (a) will be registered and (b) will be registered in your name. If the copyright is printed in the name of the publisher, any future deal related to that particular work will require that the publisher sign off on it, or be included in the contract. Publishing your work with the proper copyright notice (© 1997 Kenneth Atchity and Chi-Li Wong) serves as an advertisement to the world that you own the copyright.

What Works Are Protected?

Copyright protects "original works of authorship" that are fixed in a tangible form of expression—in other words, the *written expression* of your story. Works that can be copyrighted include the following categories:

- literary works
- musical works, including any accompanying words
- dramatic works, including any accompanying music
- pantomimes and choreographic works
- pictorial, graphic, and sculptural works
- motion pictures and other audiovisual works
- sound recordings
- architectural works

Can Characters Be Copyrighted?

Yes and No. To be copyrighted, characters must be described in enough detail to distinguish them from any other character ever created; they must have special or peculiar physical or personality characteristics, and/or unique relationships. Walt Disney copyrighted his characters—Mickey and Minnie Mouse, Goofy, and the Seven Dwarfs. As long as the copyright lasts, no one can write a new story about Doc, Dopey, and Happy without the permission of the Walt Disney company. The character George Bailey, the protagonist in *It's a Wonderful Life*, can't be used in a story without permission of that movie's copyright holder. Nothing stops you from using the *name* George Bailey, however, unless it is separately trademarked.

Can Locations Be Copyrighted?

Yes and No. You can't copyright Chicago, but you can copyright a location to the extent that it is fixed in a tangible medium (such as paper or film) if it's fictional and unusual, such as most all the locations in George Lucas's *Star Wars*. Real locations, such as the bridge on the River Kwai, may be protected from "unfair competition" by state law. An example of unfair competition would be for someone other than the producers of *The Bridge on the River Kwai* to make a film that suggests a connection with the previous film by using the same bridge. The operant principle is whether the new use may mislead the marketplace into believing it's a continuation of the old use—when the old use has been successful at the box office. Using *Tara* as the name of your plantation may lead to trademark and fair-use problems since *Gone with the Wind* established the commercial success of that plantation name (recently an African-American parody, *The Wind Done Gone*, was judged to be an infringement of copyright).

Can Dialogue Be Copyrighted?

Yes. Fictional dialogue is a protectable element, though it's difficult to prove infringement unless a substantial amount of dialogue is stolen. Dirty Harry's "Make my day!" may belong to the copyright holder, but the doctrine of fair use allows the words to be used in parody. Each of the following wonderful lines of dialogue is hard to protect, though a writer who steals them without adapting them to his own story's needs betrays nothing so much as his lack of originality:

from the film *Cobb*:
COBB: I'm really not myself.
STUMPF: Who is?

from the film *Clueless*:
RODNEY: Do you have any idea what you're talking about?
CHER: No, why? Does it sound like I do?

from John Patrick Shanley's script *Moonglow* (which became the film *Moonstruck*):
ROSE: Do you love him, Loretta?
LORETTA: Yeah, Ma, I love him awful.
ROSE: Oh God, that's too bad.

from the film *Mrs. Doubtfire*:

KIDS: Who did this to you?

MRS. DOUBTFIRE: Your Uncle Charlie and Aunt Jack.

What you want to do instead is to create memorable dialogue like this so that you can sell the copyright to it for big bucks.

Are Sequels Automatically Copyrighted?

Yes. Automatically. But by registering the copyright to the protectable material in one script, one does not get "blanket" protection for future scripts or series derived from it. Under copyright laws, a sequel must be registered *separately*, once it's ready for release, to ensure its published copyright protection.

One of the enumerated rights held by the copyright holder is the right to prepare and publish *derivative works* (sequels, TV programs, merchandising, etc.). This is almost always assigned to the producer. The writer should negotiate to have the first opportunity to write the screenplay or teleplay for each derivative work if he receives sole credit on the first production. If you don't end up rendering your services on the sequel or sequels to your work, you should get a royalty of one-half of all moneys paid you on the first picture; on remakes, you should get a royalty of one-third; and on television, minimum royalties dictated by the Writers Guild Agreement.

What Is *Not* Protected by Copyright

Several categories of material are generally not eligible for statutory copyright protection. These include among others:

- works or ideas that have *not* been fixed in a tangible form of expression (committing your words to paper is a must!);
- titles, names, short phrases, and slogans;
- familiar symbols or designs, such as the octagon or the Greek key design;

- mere variations of typographic ornamentation, lettering, or coloring;
- mere listings of ingredients or contents;
- ideas, procedures, methods, systems, processes, concepts, principles, discoveries, or devices, as distinguished from description, explanation, or illustration;
- works consisting *entirely* of information that is common property and containing no original authorship. The phone book is a good example.

How to Secure and Register Copyright

The way in which copyright protection is secured under the present law is frequently misunderstood. No publication or registration or other action in the Copyright Office is required to secure copyright. Copyright is secured *automatically* when the work is created, and a work is "created" when it is fixed in a tangible medium for the first time. Again, a *tangible medium* is a material object from which work can be read or visually perceived either directly or with the aid of a machine or device, such as books, manuscripts, sheet music, film, videotape, computer discs, or microfilm.

Copyright registration occurs when the Copyright Office forms are filled out and filed at the U.S. Copyright Office of the Library of Congress. Whether or not this is done, your copyright still exists. If you're concerned about the possibility of theft, register your copyright so that you have the benefit of statutory damages and attorneys' fees discussed earlier. Although registration may be done after an infringement takes place, it is far better to register the work immediately. In any event, registration is a prerequisite for suing for infringement. To register your copyright with the Library of Congress, fill out Form PA, obtained by writing to:

Copyright Office
Library of Congress
Washington, DC 20559-6000

Or by calling the Copyright Hotline, available twenty-four hours a day, at:

(202) 707-9100

To order registration forms or General Information Packet No. 118, which contains general information on copyright protection and registration, call:

(202) 707-3000

Information by fax is available from FAX-ON-DEMAND at:

(202) 707-2600

Frequently requested copyright circulars, announcements, regulations, and other related materials—and all copyright applications—are available on the Internet. You may access them via the Copyright Office home page at:

www.loc.gov/copyright

Or the Library of Congress home page at:

www.loc.gov

The cost to register copyright is currently $30 per work. A copy of your material must be returned with the completed application form. Different drafts or scripts in a series should be differentiated by a number or issue date. The application instructions are simple, but must be followed step-by-step in order for the registration to be effective.

To preserve your copyright registration, type © or "C" or "Copyright" on the cover of your work, followed by the year, your name, and your copyright registration number, which will be returned to you from the Copyright Office when your application has been accepted and processed. Note that it is unnecessary to include the number, and that if you have not yet registered, the rest of the notice is still effective. A sample copyright application form appears on pages 190 and 191.

Frequently Asked Questions about Copyright

Although we recommend that you take your copyright questions to an experienced attorney, here are some general answers to questions we're frequently asked by writers:

How Can I Protect Myself in Cases Involving Authorship?
Legally, nothing beats having an agreement in writing signed by the producer, affirming that you'll be paid if the producer decides to go forward with your story. Because you can only grant rights under copyright law by signing a written instrument, or working within a work-for-hire relationship, if a producer moves forward without your consent, you may have a claim for copyright infringement.

Under present law, following the copyright notice requirements described previously and registering your work for copyright will make enforcing your rights under copyright easier in the event of infringement.

COPYRIGHT APPLICATION FORM

FEE CHANGES
Fees are effective through June 30, 2002. After that date, check the Copyright Office Website at www.loc.gov/copyright or call (202) 707-3000 for current fee information.

FORM PA
For a Work of the Performing Arts
UNITED STATES COPYRIGHT OFFICE

REGISTRATION NUMBER

PA   PAU

EFFECTIVE DATE OF REGISTRATION

Month   Day   Year

DO NOT WRITE ABOVE THIS LINE. IF YOU NEED MORE SPACE, USE A SEPARATE CONTINUATION SHEET.

1

TITLE OF THIS WORK ▼

PREVIOUS OR ALTERNATIVE TITLES ▼

NATURE OF THIS WORK ▼ See instructions

2   a

NAME OF AUTHOR ▼

DATES OF BIRTH AND DEATH
Year Born ▼   Year Died ▼

Was this contribution to the work a "work made for hire"?
☐ Yes
☐ No

AUTHOR'S NATIONALITY OR DOMICILE
Name of Country
OR { Citizen of ▶_____
Domiciled in ▶_____

WAS THIS AUTHOR'S CONTRIBUTION TO THE WORK
Anonymous? ☐ Yes ☐ No
Pseudonymous? ☐ Yes ☐ No
If the answer to either of these questions is "Yes," see detailed instructions.

NATURE OF AUTHORSHIP Briefly describe nature of material created by this author in which copyright is claimed. ▼

NOTE

Under the law, the "author" of a "work made for hire" is generally the employer, not the employee (see instructions). For any part of this work that was "made for hire" check "Yes" in the space provided, give the employer (or other person for whom the work was prepared) as "Author" of that part, and leave the space for dates of birth and death blank.

b

NAME OF AUTHOR ▼

DATES OF BIRTH AND DEATH
Year Born ▼   Year Died ▼

Was this contribution to the work a "work made for hire"?
☐ Yes
☐ No

AUTHOR'S NATIONALITY OR DOMICILE
Name of Country
OR { Citizen of ▶_____
Domiciled in ▶_____

WAS THIS AUTHOR'S CONTRIBUTION TO THE WORK
Anonymous? ☐ Yes ☐ No
Pseudonymous? ☐ Yes ☐ No
If the answer to either of these questions is "Yes," see detailed instructions.

NATURE OF AUTHORSHIP Briefly describe nature of material created by this author in which copyright is claimed. ▼

c

NAME OF AUTHOR ▼

DATES OF BIRTH AND DEATH
Year Born ▼   Year Died ▼

Was this contribution to the work a "work made for hire"?
☐ Yes
☐ No

AUTHOR'S NATIONALITY OR DOMICILE
Name of Country
OR { Citizen of ▶_____
Domiciled in ▶_____

WAS THIS AUTHOR'S CONTRIBUTION TO THE WORK
Anonymous? ☐ Yes ☐ No
Pseudonymous? ☐ Yes ☐ No
If the answer to either of these questions is "Yes," see detailed instructions.

NATURE OF AUTHORSHIP Briefly describe nature of material created by this author in which copyright is claimed. ▼

3   a

YEAR IN WHICH CREATION OF THIS WORK WAS COMPLETED
This information must be given ◀ Year in all cases.

b

DATE AND NATION OF FIRST PUBLICATION OF THIS PARTICULAR WORK
Complete this information ONLY if this work has been published.
Month ▶_____ Day ▶_____ Year ▶_____
◀ Nation

4

See instructions before completing this space.

COPYRIGHT CLAIMANT(S) Name and address must be given even if the claimant is the same as the author given in space 2. ▼

TRANSFER If the claimant(s) named here in space 4 is (are) different from the author(s) named in space 2, give a brief statement of how the claimant(s) obtained ownership of the copyright. ▼

APPLICATION RECEIVED

ONE DEPOSIT RECEIVED

TWO DEPOSITS RECEIVED

FUNDS RECEIVED

DO NOT WRITE HERE   OFFICE USE ONLY

MORE ON BACK ▶
• Complete all applicable spaces (numbers 5-9) on the reverse side of this page.
• See detailed instructions.
• Sign the form at line 8.

DO NOT WRITE HERE
Page 1 of _____ pages

DO NOT WRITE ABOVE THIS LINE. IF YOU NEED MORE SPACE, USE A SEPARATE CONTINUATION SHEET.

PREVIOUS REGISTRATION Has registration for this work, or for an earlier version of this work, already been made in the Copyright Office?

☐ Yes ☐ No If your answer is "Yes," why is another registration being sought? (Check appropriate box.) ▼ If your answer is "no," go to space 7.

a. ☐ This is the first published edition of a work previously registered in unpublished form.

b. ☐ This is the first application submitted by this author as copyright claimant.

c. ☐ This is a changed version of the work, as shown by space 6 on this application.

If your answer is "Yes," give: **Previous Registration Number** ▼   **Year of Registration** ▼

5

DERIVATIVE WORK OR COMPILATION Complete both space 6a and 6b for a derivative work; complete only 6b for a compilation.

Preexisting Material Identify any preexisting work or works that this work is based on or incorporates. ▼

a

6

See instructions before completing this space.

Material Added to This Work Give a brief, general statement of the material that has been added to this work and in which copyright is claimed. ▼

b

DEPOSIT ACCOUNT If the registration fee is to be charged to a Deposit Account established in the Copyright Office, give name and number of Account.

Name ▼   **Account Number** ▼

a

7

CORRESPONDENCE Give name and address to which correspondence about this application should be sent.   Name/Address/Apt/City/State/ZIP ▼

b

Area code and daytime telephone number ▶ (   )   Fax number ▶ (   )

Email ▶

CERTIFICATION* I, the undersigned, hereby certify that I am the

Check only one ▶
☐ author
☐ other copyright claimant
☐ owner of exclusive right(s)
☐ authorized agent of _____

Name of author or other copyright claimant, or owner of exclusive right(s) ▲

of the work identified in this application and that the statements made by me in this application are correct to the best of my knowledge.

8

Typed or printed name and date ▼ If this application gives a date of publication in space 3, do not sign and submit it before that date.

Date ▶

Handwritten signature (X) ▼

☞   X _____

Certificate will be mailed in window envelope to this address:	Name ▼	**YOU MUST:** • Complete all necessary spaces • Sign your application in space 8
	Number/Street/Apt ▼	**SEND ALL 3 ELEMENTS IN THE SAME PACKAGE:** 1. Application form 2. Nonrefundable filing fee in check or money order payable to *Register of Copyrights* 3. Deposit material
	City/State/ZIP ▼	**MAIL TO** Library of Congress Copyright Office 101 Independence Avenue, S.E. Washington, D.C. 20559-6000

As of July 1, 1999, the filing fee for Form PA is $30.

9

What's Copyright Infringement?

Unless excused as "fair use," infringement occurs when a person copies, distributes, performs, publicly displays, or prepares a work derived from a literary or artistic property without the permission of the owner of the copyright.

What Can I Do about Infringement?

Unless you think the offender is willingly going to remedy the situation, you need to register the work for copyright, then go to federal court. Copyright infringement is an unpredictable area of the law that actually leans toward protecting the copier. This may sound ridiculous, but part of the law's purpose is to encourage creativity, not stifle it. Thomas Jefferson felt that the entry of material into public domain after a reasonable period of protection for the author (originally fourteen years plus one fourteen-year renewal) was one of the fundamentals of a free society. Therefore, copiers enjoy the benefit of the doubt; they're innocent until proven guilty.

You begin to fight infringement by:

1. **Making sure you own the copyright.** Was what you created your own to copyright, or was it created as a work for hire? Have you previously granted these rights in a contract? Who owns any portion of the rights you've sold, including underlying material owned by a third party? Or did you sell them?

2. **Ascertaining substantial similarity.** The law recognizes two kinds of substantial similarities: literal and comprehensive. Literal is word for word: "Go ahead, make my day!" Or, for example, someone lifted a portion of or the entire script. Similar: "Go on, make my afternoon!" Without literal similarities, the court will look for comprehensive similarities in the overall work: character relationships, dialogue, plot elements, theme, and point of view.

3. Determining access. Did the person you're accusing have "reasonable opportunity" to view your work?

4. Defining damages. The amount of money you lost as a result of the infringement plus the amount of money the infringer made. Simply put, how much did you get hurt?

With a jury and a good case you have a fair chance of winning, but remember, this is an unpredictable area of the law. Copyright infringement cases are tricky, and without too much concrete precedent, judges have been known to throw out even the most obvious cases. Just to give you an idea of how the issues sound in legal terms, here's an example (from *Entertainment Law Digest*) of a Hollywood lawsuit filed in U.S. District Court (case CV 96-7621 GHK) by plaintiffs' attorney Michael Blaha on behalf of screenwriters Steven Patrick and William Patrick against Eddie Murphy Productions and Universal Studios.

The Patricks' suit claimed that the hit film *The Nutty Professor* was derived from a script entitled *Brand New Me*, which they submitted to Universal in 1991. *Brand New Me* is about an overweight geneticist who discovers a formula that would allow her to lose weight instantly, but would also cause her to regain it unexpectedly in successively shorter intervals. The protagonist's motivation is her love for a man who doesn't like fat girls. Universal rejected the Patricks' script, saying it was too similar to *Death Becomes Her*, which they were about to release; they didn't return the script to the Patrick brothers. (Scripts are only sometimes returned, partly because scriptwriters don't enclose stamped return envelopes and partly because the prospective buyer wants to hold onto a script in case "something changes"—an actor or director, for example, becomes attached to the project.)

Universal then released what they presented as a remake of the 1963 Jerry Lewis classic, *The Nutty Professor*. In the Jerry Lewis film, the protagonist is a nerdy professor who discovers a formula that turns him into a suave and self-confident seducer.

But in the new *The Nutty Professor* the overweight geneticist, played by Eddie Murphy, invents a formula that enables him to lose weight instantly—only to regain it unexpectedly in successively shorter intervals.

The plaintiffs claimed:

> In both the Screenplay and the Picture, the protagonists' thin alter-ego (Amelia in the Screenplay, Buddy Love in the Picture) becomes a separate and distinct character who begins to disdain the "host" protagonists. The alter-ego characters try to "take over" the protagonists' persona, and temporarily succeed in doing so;
>
> In both the Screenplay and the Picture, the protagonists have a dream wherein they are gigantically obese, looming over large crowds of people;
>
> In both the Screenplay and the Picture, an evil colleague (Steve in the Screenplay; the Dean in the Picture) conspires to mass-market the formula against the protagonists' wishes;
>
> In both the Screenplay and the Picture, the formula begins wearing off on the very first date, which occurs in a night club, that the alter-ego has with the object of the protagonists' affection;
>
> In both the Screenplay and the Picture, the protagonists unintentionally utter double entendres of a sexual nature to their love interest.

The plaintiffs' attorney listed among other *causes of action:* breach of implied contract, breach of confidential relationship, interference with prospective economic advantage, unfair competition, and unfair trade practices.

That's an overview of the legalities of copyright. In practice, we recommend simply registering your treatment or screenplay with the Writers Guild of America.

How the Writers Guild of America Protects Writers

The Writers Guild of America is the trade union organized to protect the rights of screenwriters and to negotiate the standard Guild Agreement by which compensation and credits are negotiated in the entertainment industry. When dealing with a prospective buyer, it's important to know that they are either a *signatory* to the Guild Agreement, or that they allow their writers' deals to be governed by the Guild Agreement.

The Writers Guild operates an invaluable registration service to help screenwriters protect their rights to their material against plagiarism or copyright infringement. Writers can file treatments, outlines, synopses, and scripts intended for the fields of radio, theatrical and television motion pictures, as well as video cassettes/discs, including interactive media—before they circulate them to prospective representatives or buyers. Here's where you can find, or write to, the WGA registration service:

WGAw Intellectual Property Registry
7000 West Third Street
Los Angeles, CA 90048-4329

Registration hours are between 9:30 A.M. and 5:30 P.M., Monday through Friday. For your added convenience, a 24-hour drop box is available in the main lobby of the Writers Guild.

Telephone Numbers:
(323) 782-4540
(323) 782-4803 (fax)
(323) 782-4500 Recorded Information

WGAe, Inc.
555 West 57th Street, Suite 1230
New York, NY 10019
ATT: Registrations

Registration hours are between 9:30 A.M. and 4:30 P.M.,
Monday through Friday.

Telephone Numbers:
(212) 767-7800
(212) 757-4360 Registration Hotline

The Guild will also register written ideas and concepts. Be aware, however, that registration of ideas and concepts may be of limited utility because it is difficult to lay claim to an idea or concept as such, since they can't be copyrighted. Nonetheless registering your pitch notes based on your idea or concept for a film creates a valuable paper trail that gives you credible evidence should you run into a problem down the road. The Guild's registration office also accepts novels and other books, stage plays, short stories, poems, commercials, lyrics, and drawings. *Registration with the WGA is not a substitute for filing with the U.S. Copyright Office.* But WGA registration is, in everyday industry practice, sufficient to let your reader know that you're serious about protecting your work.

The Writers Guild's legal department does not provide legal advice on copyright infringement or plagiarism issues. The WGA has long maintained a policy of remaining neutral in copyright disputes, primarily because the violation is not subject to the agreements the Guild has effective legal mechanisms to enforce. If you need legal advice, obtain the help of an experienced copyright attorney. If you can't afford to do this, call Advocates for the Arts, a group of attorneys who volunteer their help (*pro bono*) to artists (they're usually listed in your local phone book; if not, call your local bar association for help in finding them).

WGA Registration Service

Purpose and Coverage

The Writers Guild's Registration Service has been set up to assist members and nonmembers in establishing the completion dates of particular pieces of literary property written for the fields of radio, theatrical and television motion pictures, and video cassettes/discs, including interactive media.

- Registration provides a dated record of the writer's claim to authorship of a particular literary material. If necessary, a Guild employee may produce the material at a hearing or deposition.
- The Registration Office does not make comparisons of registration deposits, nor does it give legal opinions or advice or confer any statutory protection.
- Registration with the Guild doesn't protect titles.

Registering in Person or by Mail

The Registration Office must receive:

1. one unbound copy of the material (no brads, staples, or folders), on standard 8 1/2 × 11 paper.
2. cover sheet with title of material and author's(s') full legal name(s);
3. Author's or authors' social security number(s) [or foreign equivalent(s)], return address(es), and phone number(s).
4. registration fee (currently $10 for members and $20 for nonmembers).

The received material is sealed in an envelope, with the time and date recorded. A numbered certificate is returned that serves as the official documentation of registration and that should be kept in a safe place.

Notice of registration should be placed on the title page and should consist of the following wording: Registered WGAw (or WGAe) No. XXXXX.

Registering Online

www.WGA.org

www.WGAeast.org

Preferred file formats are ASCII, PDF (Adobe Acrobat), Word, and Final Draft; however, all file formats will be accepted. You will be prompted to select the file on your hard drive that you wish to register. Please note that only *one file* for each online register request will be accepted. Currently the file size limit is 10MB. Zip files are prohibited.

Since all registrations are final upon submission, make certain you are sending the correct file and version of your material.

Browser Requirements

To access the WGA Online Registry at www.wga.org, you must have at least IE 5.0 or Netscape Navigator 4.8 or higher. If the website does not work properly with your current browser version, you can follow the links provided on the WGA website to update your browser.

Procedures for Online Registration

- Fill in material details and registrant's(s')/author's(s') information.
- Fill out the credit card information.
- Select on your hard drive the file to be submitted.
- Submit your registration request.

Some special characters in file names may impede your ability to upload. If this occurs you should rename and save your file.

Your registration request is processed immediately; you will receive your registration number once your transaction is completed. A registration certificate will also be mailed to you within two weeks. Your registration is not complete until you receive the registration number.

Online registration fees are $20 (U.S.) for the general public, $10 for WGA members in good standing. The Intellectual Property Online Registry system accepts only Visa or Master-Card as a form of payment. You will be billed in your local currency outside of the United States.

Note that only the writers listed on the registration receipt may request confirmation of registration, the registration number, date of deposit, or any other information.

The WGA will honor such written requests from writers regarding the registration of their own work(s) only if accompanied by a photo identification. All verification or confirmation requests from a writer should contain as much specific information as possible, such as registration number, title of material, effective date, and social security number of writer, and may be submitted by facsimile, mail, or in person.

Access to Copies of Deposited Material

Because the deposited material cannot be returned to the writer without defeating the purpose of registration, registered material may not be withdrawn. That's why it's important to always retain a separate copy of the material being registered.

If a writer finds it necessary to obtain a copy of deposited material, duplicates may be purchased for the price of registration upon written request by one or more of the listed authors, identity verified by photo identification. In the event an author is deceased, proof of death and consent of the representative of the heirs and/or estate must be presented in order to obtain a copy of the material.

Requests for duplication of deposited material must be submitted by 5:00 P.M. Thursday of any week. Duplicates will be available Wednesday of the following week.

Duration and Expiration

Writers Guild registration is valid for a term of five years and may be renewed for an additional five years at the registration rate in effect at the time of the renewal(s). Renewals will be accepted up to three months prior to the expiration of the registration. A grace period will be extended, allowing late renewals up to three months following the expiration of the registration.

At the time of registration or renewal, you authorize the Guild to destroy the material without further notice to you on the expiration of the first term of registration or any renewal period.

The Bottom Line on Protection

If all this sounds intimidating, perhaps overpowering, think of it as a great sign: you're involved in a serious business, the production and sale of intellectual property. Serious business requires serious attention to details, legal and otherwise. You wouldn't buy or sell real property without checking into the pitfalls and fully understanding your rights. Your writing is extremely valuable. Take the business seriously, and your success will come sooner!

Sample Leave-Behind

<u>TREATMENT FOR A MOTION PICTURE</u>

JOE SOMEBODY
by
John Scott Shepherd
[starring Tim Allen and Jim Belushi; directed by Jon Pasquin]

Theme

Fear is the barrier that keeps the ordinary from becoming the extraordinary. Joe Somebody is about fear—living with it . . . conquering it . . . and the perils of both. Seen through the eyes of an everyman, Joe, as he breaks through his fear for the first time to achieve a goal and to answer the question, "What do I want?"

Story Treatment

JOE SCHEFFER, 30s, is the manager of internal communications at Phitzer Pharmaceuticals, a massive Fortune 500 company that makes drugs nobody has ever heard of. That means he edits an insipid company magazine and oversees production of training videos and "internal product introduction." He's had this job for ten years.

Joe's wife, **CALLIE MOWTON-SCHEFFER**, left him just over a year ago. The reasons were hazy and vague, as if they came from cue cards. She loved him but she wasn't in love with him. It was wrong for both of them just to keep going in a marriage that had faded into little more than a habit.

They have a ten-year-old daughter, **NATALIE SCHEFFER**. She's preternaturally wise, like Natalie Portman in *The Professional* and *Some Girls*. She sees things others don't and we don't have to hear her speak to know that.

Callie is a famous entrepreneur in a midsize city—she owns a chain of upscale "bakeries" in town. She's regularly on the cover of the city magazine and thinks of herself as a superstar, a person of power, and position.

But back to Joe. He honestly doesn't know why Callie left him. It was a bolt out of the blue. He's got "a good job," a nice house, a beautiful daughter, a reasonable number of friends (all from work).

By title **MEG HARPER** is a Wellness Counselor in the Phitzer Pharmaceuticals "Synergy!" program, complete with exclamation point. Synergy! is hailed as a progressive employee assistance program, but its real purpose is to guide employees back into line with company objectives. True, they try to help "associates" quit smoking or drinking, get into fitness programs, play company sports, etc., but it's not out of kindness. Synergy! looks to minimize missed workdays and further "enculture" associates into the company to reduce turnover.

One of Meg's goals is to replace personal objectives—"What do I want?"—with corporate objectives—"What's best for the company is what's best for each of us."

When Joe talks to Meg it reflects his total lack of self-awareness. He doesn't know he's living in fear . . . but we catch on through bits and pieces.

And so, when he gets bitch-slapped in front of his daughter and coworkers during an argument with a seven-year employee who takes the last parking spot in the ten-year lot that Joe's entitled to, it sends him into a dramatic, sudden spiral down. He has a nervous breakdown. He locks his doors, closes his windows, and drinks.

Meg finally gets him to let her into the apartment. Joe can't explain why the event has affected him so profoundly. When Meg asks Joe what he wants, it's a mistake, said out of frustration. But in asking it, she opens an unexpected door not only for Joe but for herself. What Joe wants is to kick **MARK RIDDICK**'s ass! And when Joe says he wants to stop being afraid, Meg is forced to acknowledge her own fears in her efforts to make Joe realize the bravest thing to do would be NOT to fight.

Glossary of Entertainment
Industry Terms

■ ■ ■

act break: Free TV term describing the end of each of the seven acts of a film, marking the place where a commercial or station break will be inserted.

action: A sequence of character-related visual events linked to plot development that move a story toward its dramatic conclusion. Dramatic action normally consists of physical action (fights, chases, gestures) and dialogue.

act, three- or seven- (act) structure: Classical dramatic story structure containing a beginning, middle, and end. Television may impose artificial (commercial) breaks that divide up an act, but the three-act structure remains the backbone.

adaptation: The process of transforming a story already written in another medium (novel, stage play, short story) into a motion picture treatment or screenplay.

advertiser-supported networks: Free-broadcast networks, including ABC, CBS, Fox, and NBC, whose revenues come from sponsors who buy commercial time.

advertiser-supported cable-delivered networks: Include A&E, CNN, Discovery, Lifetime, TNT, and USA.

agent: A broker, paid on commission (generally 10 percent), who sells stories and talent to the production companies.

angle: The approach or viewpoint that makes a story new, provocative, or timely. *See* **take**.

antagonist: The force or forces that stand in the protagonist's way. *Antagonist* is the dramatist's term for the protagonist's opponent in a story, sometimes confused with the term *villain*. Although the antagonist may not be a villain, he (or it) always opposes the protagonist. In *Scarface*, Al Pacino's character is the protagonist; the *law* is the antagonist.

arbitration: The formal process by which the Writers Guild of America determines screenplay credit when it is under contention. The arbitration board consists entirely of writers.

ASCII (file): Acronym for American Standard Code for Interchange Exchange. An ASCII file, also called a text file, can be read by most computer word processors.

associate producer: Entry-level production title given to a member of the producing team for a variety of reasons, including bringing in the story, participating in financing, and/or actually working on the preproduction, production, and postproduction of the film.

attachment: "Is there anything attached?" is an industry question meaning, positively, "Is there a star or director interested in the project?" and negatively, "Are there so many producers or writers attached to the deal that it becomes unmanageable from a budgetary or administrative viewpoint?" *See* **baggage**.

baggage: Industry term for the people "attached" to a motion picture script or treatment, adding to the film's budget and sometimes "killing" the deal. *Star baggage* means executive producers, family members, and others whom the star considers necessary to his or her participation in a film.

based on a true story: Refers to a story involving no fictionalization or an insignificant amount of fictionalization.

beat: An important moment in a drama's development where conflict produces change.

bible: A treatment for a proposed dramatic television series, including various elements outlined in chapter 4.

bidding war: What happens when two or more buyers make a bid on the same story.

broadcast television: Includes advertiser-supported broadcast networks and cable-delivered advertiser-supported channels. Also known as "free TV."

buzz: Industry term for gossip, "grapevine," rumor, all with positive connotation. The manager's goal is to create a buzz around his client's new work.

cable: Television programming available for a fee to a subscriber and delivered to his household via cable.

castable: Adjective describing the appeal of a character to a major star.

characters: The various real or fictitious individuals who take part in a dramatic story. The first time a character is introduced in the treatment, the entire name is capitalized.

cliffhanger: A dramatic turn of events in a story that prompts the audience to continue watching to find out what happens next. In TV, the suspenseful beat at the end of an act that keeps the viewer tuned in through the station break.

climax: High point of dramatic action, where all its elements come to focus as the protagonist faces the antagonist in the ultimate confrontation.

collaboration: Any creative partnership, formalized by a collaboration agreement that spells out the responsibilities and rights of each party to the collaboration.

conflict: Dramatic opposition, forces aligned against each other, is the heart of drama. Conflict should characterize not only every act but also every scene and every line of dialogue.

continuing characters: Characters in a dramatic television series who continue from episode to episode, as opposed to *recurring characters* who show up from time to time.

co-producer: Production title used in film and television to designate a position above associate producer and beneath producer.

copyright: Legal protection of intellectual property through due processes administered by the Copyright Office of the Library of Congress.

coverage: Descriptive and diagnostic document of a treatment, book, or script provided by story department readers for executives making acquisition decisions in theatrical film and television. Includes synopsis as well as the reader's opinion of the material.

created by: WGA designation for the originator of a program for television, entitling the recipient to payment for residuals.

creative elements: Refers to the director, star or stars, or major writer who may be "attached" to a property being offered for sale.

credits: Designation used for the list of individuals and their functions involved in a production when it appears at the end of the program, as opposed to *titles*, the term used when the list appears at the beginning.

crisis: Maximum point of accumulating obstacles faced by the protagonist in a drama, leading to the **climax**, which occurs when he deals with the crisis.

CUT/CUT TO: Instantaneous transition (change) from one scene (or shot, or person) to another. Always typed in capital letters.

deal: Term that describes the decision to move ahead with a project toward production, and the paperwork that legally memorializes the decision.

defamation of character: Causing damage to a person's reputation by saying untrue things about him.

deficit financing: Source of revenue covering the shortfall between production costs and network licensing fees. A television film generally is sold to a network for a licensing fee that does not cover the entire budget (NBC, for example, may pay $2.8 million to license a film that costs $3 million to make). The difference, or deficit, must be covered by a *deficit financier* who the network knows can deliver the film within the budget and at the level of quality it demands. In exchange for taking this risk, the deficit financier retains the non-network rights to the film, including syndication rights, foreign rights, DVD, and video rights, etc.

demographic: Statistics defining a particular focal audience, as in "the twenty- to twenty-five-year-old white female demographic."

development: Production cycle that begins with acquisition of a literary property and ends with preproduction of the film, during which a story's elements, including script, director, and cast, are finalized.

development deal: An agreement in which a writer is hired to develop a screenplay from idea or treatment through completion of a first draft and usually two sets of revisions and a polish. Development deals are harder to get than ever. As one executive puts it, "I'd rather pass on my feet than develop on my knees."

development hell: Because relatively few films make it to production, "I have six films in development" may translate, in Hollywood jargon, to "I'm broke and may never see the light at the end of the tunnel." In other words, "I'm in development hell."

development meeting: Brainstorming session when the writer and his production executives discuss or develop various story elements.

dialogue: A character's speech; a conversation between two or more people.

dissolve: Transition from one scene, which fades out, as another simultaneously fades in. Dissolves are also used to indicate a lapse of time and/or change of place.

docudrama: The depiction of an actual event in dramatic form, using actors, actresses, and a screenplay. Not to be confused with a **documentary**, which see.

documentary: A filmed account of an actual event, without dramatization by actors or actresses. *See* **docudrama**.

drama: A story of adventure or conflict told through a series of related events.

dramatic rights: The right to adapt a nondramatic work, such as a novel, book of nonfiction, or newspaper or magazine article, for the screen or stage.

dramatis personae: "Characters of the drama," classical Latin term for the list of major characters in a play.

elements: shorthand for **creative elements**, which see.

E & O coverage: Insurance that protects the policy owner (usually a production company) from nonmalicious "errors and omissions," like losing a title credit in the editing machine or failing to register a copyright claim in a timely manner.

episode: An installment in a dramatic television series, or the teleplay of that installment.

episodic: Term used, generally with a negative connotation, to describe a story that has no structural unity, whose parts do not unfold inevitably toward a focused climax.

episodic series: A dramatic television show with one or more continuing characters whose various adventures or emotional entanglements appear on television each week at the same time slot. Also known as "dramatic series."

exclusive deal: Industry term referring to a producer, star, or director's company able to set up films only with the provider of its housekeeping deal. For a number of years Kopelson Entertainment had an exclusive deal with Twentieth Century Fox and was unable to produce a film for any other studio.

executive producer: (1) In television, the producer with maximum creative authority, usually the originator of the project and very often its writer. (2) In feature films, the title given to one of the producers for contributing an important element to the deal, and who generally is involved more in the deal making than in the actual production.

FADE IN/FADE OUT: Smooth, gradual transition from complete blackness to a scene (fade in); gradual transition from a scene to complete blackness (fade out). Always typed in capital letters.

fair use: Legal doctrine that allows for quotation of a limited amount of copyrighted material for academic or review purposes. The precise number of words is not specified by law and is subject to the court's judgment about the fairness of use.

FCC: Federal Communications Commission, the government agency in charge of administering the public airwaves.

feature film: A film made for release in motion picture theaters.

film: *See* **motion picture**.

financier: Source of production funding.

first-look deal: Loosely defined industry term referring to a company's right to see a producer's or writer's dramatic properties before anyone else in town. Sometimes combined with **right of first refusal**.

first refusal, right of: Legal term defining a company's right to have the first opportunity to accept or refuse a dramatic property.

franchise: Term used to describe the setting of a dramatic series, such as the Golden Girls' ranch house, Archie Bunker's brownstone, the emergency room in *ER*, or the radio station in *Northern Exposure*. Also refers to a protagonist's unique skill or character that justifies his or her involvement in the lives of the other characters.

free TV: *See* **broadcast television**.

green light: The final go-ahead from the powers that be that puts a project into production.

hierarchy of rights: Rights pursued when turning a true crime into a film. In order of importance, and depending on the exact situation, these are:

- the victim's rights
- the perpetrator's rights
- the investigator's rights, the rights of the families of both the victim and the perpetrator
- friends' and neighbors' rights, etc.

high concept: Hollywood term that describes a literary property or idea that can be pitched in six words or less. For example, *Under Siege* was sold as "*Die Hard* on a boat" ("in a tunnel": *Daylight;* "on a bus": *Speed*). AEI-Zide Films sold *Meg* to Disney and Doubleday-Bantam as "Jurassic Shark." One of the jokes going around Hollywood, reported by Thomas Taylor in *ScreenWriter Quarterly*, tells of a young agent saying to his new client, "Why don't you go write '*Die Hard* in a building!'" A story that takes an entire paragraph to pitch is *not* high concept.

hook: An inciting incident, scene, or image that captures the interest of the audience.

housekeeping deal: An arrangement in which an independent production company (headed by a producer, star, or director) is attached to a financier, who, in return for funding the company's overhead, has the exclusive right or a "first look" at, or a "first refusal" of, any story acquisitions.

inciting incident: An event occurring early in a drama that cranks the primary story line into action.

independent producer/production company: Producer who pays his own housekeeping overhead in exchange for the freedom to "set up" his stories with any studio or financier.

infringement: Legal term used to describe the unauthorized use of written material, a violation of the copyright laws.

in-house producer/production company: Producer with a housekeeping deal that pays his overhead in exchange for giving his host an exclusive or at least a "first look" at any story he wishes to produce.

inspired by a true story: Descriptive label given to a story that, although derived from the truth, has been significantly fictionalized.

interior (INT.): Scene intro indicating that a scene takes place, or is supposed to take place, indoors: a set representing an indoor scene. Always abbreviated in capital letters.

leave-behind: A brief treatment of a story being pitched as a motion picture that is left with the person to whom the pitch is being made as an aid to memory and, if he has registered it with the Writers Guild of America, to establish the writer's legal right to the story.

legs: General industry term for "potential," or "longevity," as in, "Recent Nielsen reports prove that this series continues to have legs"; or, "The writer's outstanding bible makes it clear that the proposed series has legs."

libel: Legal term designating the crime of saying untruthful negative things about a person's character.

license fee: The amount of money negotiated between seller and buyer to grant the buyer the right to air a television project for a limited number of showings. For example, NBC might pay the production company a $2.8 million license fee to show a movie twice within a twelve-month period.

life rights: The right given to a writer or producer to make a film from a living person's life story.

line-up: A television broadcaster's programming, time slot by time slot, for an entire week.

literary manager: *See* **manager**.

location: The actual (physical) setting for a production; the part of a scene heading that describes where the scene takes place.

log line: One-line description of a story, like those that appear regularly in *TV Guide*, aimed at making someone want to watch it.

long form: Term used in television to designate movies and miniseries, as opposed to "short form," referring to series.

manager: Industry representative who works with writers (as talent managers work with directors, actors, and actresses) to develop their careers, both creatively (through consulting on story development, time-management, and prioritizing) and financially (through marketing the client's products). Managers perform many of the same services as do agents, but aren't allowed to secure employment for their clients. Managers are, however, allowed to produce films (Eric Gold and Jimmy Miller, for example, produce films starring their client

Jim Carrey), whereas agents until recently were not. Managers often work in tandem with agents, and, in general, provide writers with an array of consulting, advising, and marketing services that few agents have time for.

miniseries: A movie for television that is longer than the usual two-hour time slot, ordinarily broadcast over a period of two or three days.

mission: In dramatic writing, the term used to describe the protagonist's quest.

montage: Scene heading that indicates a rapid succession of shots.

motion picture: A sequence of still pictures, usually including sound, in a specified order, showing objects at successive intervals of time, which gives the illusion of motion.

motivation: The protagonist's psychological makeup, which determines the dramatic pattern of his actions.

narration: Off-screen commentary that is heard over the action. Also referred to as a voice-over.

network: A group of television stations located throughout the United States that are interconnected by satellite and are programmed primarily from a single corporate headquarters.

network executive: Individual employed by a network to supervise programming and/or to meet with writers and producers to acquire and develop stories.

Nielsen ratings: Ratings reported daily by the Nielsen Company, indicating statistical realities of audience viewing behavior.

obligatory scene: Dramatic term for a scene without which the story makes no sense. In a murder mystery, for example, the discovery of the body and the revelation of the killer are obligatory scenes.

obstacle: A dramatic hurdle the protagonist must confront in order to accomplish his mission.

Off Screen (O.S.): A character extension. Dialogue or sounds heard while the camera is on another subject. Always abbreviated in all capital letters and enclosed in parentheses.

open market: Term used to describe a free-for-all offering of a property unencumbered by a right of first refusal, often after refusing, or ignoring, a preemptive bid.

option: Legal term for the document by which a producer acquires control of a story, equivalent to an "option to buy" in real estate.

original: Industry term used to describe a new take on a familiar subject.

outline: Unlike the narrative form of the treatment, the outline is a skeletal list of the scenes in a cinematic story.

packaging: Attaching the elements of talent (actors, director, rewriter, name producer) to a project to make it a more attractive property.

pan: Camera shot (from the word *panorama*) in which the camera moves gradually from right to left or left to right, without stopping; to slowly move to another subject or setting without cutting the action.

pay-per-view: Subcategory of pay television in which individual events, instead of monthly service, are sold separately at premium prices.

pay TV: Another name for **subscriber cable television**.

pilot: Sample episode of a proposed series that introduces the leading continuing characters and sets up the franchise or setting, and the series style.

pitch: The act of orally relating a project to a prospective representative or buyer for the purpose of marketing an idea, adaptation, or true story for eventual production as a film. A treatment is a written pitch; a pitch is an oral treatment.

plagiarism: The act of using someone else's intellectual property without obtaining rights or permission to do so.

player: Industry term for a person who is regularly making high-visibility deals in either television or film.

plot: Pattern of elements that make up the action line of a story; the situation that brings a story into focus.

Point of View (POV): Camera position that views a scene

from the viewpoint of a particular character. Always abbreviated in capital letters.

postproduction: The period after the shooting of a film during which the film, music, and sound track are edited.

preemptive bid: A bid made by a prospective buyer, giving a short deadline before its withdrawal. The preemptive bid keeps the agent/manager from taking the property into the open market.

premise: A dramatic story's focus or moral.

preproduction: The period following development during which a film is officially prepared for production. During preproduction, the art department is set up, locations scouted, casting completed, transportation and craft services lined up, etc.

pre-sold: Industry term referring to a concept that already enjoys high public awareness, as in, *"Ripley's Believe-It-or-Not!*® was a pre-sold franchise" (same as self-promoting).

principal photography: The filming of the primary script, as opposed to "second unit" shooting with a secondary director of photography and crew that might, for example, film location shots from distant cities to provide ambience. Payments for the screenwriter and the owner of the underlying literary material are generally fully payable and due no later than the first day of principal photography.

producer (production company): The person (company) with overall responsibility for a project from its initiation to its final distribution.

production: The period during which a film is actually shot; and/or the act of shooting the film.

property: Literary material—whether treatment, script, book, or article—that forms the basis for a film project.

protagonist: The "primary actor" or initiator of the action in a story, sometimes loosely termed "the hero," even though the protagonist can be villainous or unheroic.

psychology of the audience: Term used by the British drama critic Kenneth Burke to describe the audience's expectations when they arrive at the theater (the audience may come to be edified, or terrified, or moved to tears). Burke used the term to distinguish the psychology of the audience from (a) the psychology of the author (who writes to seek revenge on his ex-wife) or (b) the psychology of the character (is Hamlet being consistent when he tells Ophelia he loves her and orders her to get herself to a nunnery?). The greatest script writers and directors are masters of the psychology of the audience, always seeming to give us exactly what we want at precisely the most dramatic moment.

public domain: Term used to describe the availability to the public of an intellectual property that is not protected under copyright, trademark, or other private claims.

recurring characters: Characters in a dramatic television series who appear frequently, as opposed to continuing characters, who appear in each episode.

registration: The act of filing claim to ownership of an intellectual property, either with the U.S. Copyright Office or with the Writers Guild of America.

relatable or **relatability:** The need for characters to involve the interest or sympathies of the audience.

release form: A legal document stating that, if a producer agrees to read a script, its writer will not subsequently sue for plagiarism. Usually required if a writer has no agent.

residual: Money paid by production companies for each airing of a program after the initial license period has expired, or for airing each episode of a dramatic series. Similar to the publishing industry's concept of royalties.

resolution: The last act or scene of a story, in which all dramatic elements are tied up to a satisfying conclusion.

reveal: The moment in a story when a previously hidden element is made known to the audience, as when, in *The Crying Game*, the hero discovers, in bed, that his sweetheart is a man. Now that's a reveal!

right of first refusal: *See* **first refusal, right of.**

scene: The basic building block or unit of drama, involving a protagonist in a situation of conflict. Like the entire treatment itself, the well-made scene has an involving beginning, a well-developed middle, and a conclusive and compelling ending.

scene cards: File or index cards used in the process of storyboarding.

screenplay: A script for a feature film that is (or could and hopefully will be) made into a motion picture. Generally 90 to 120 pages in length.

script: Text of a screenplay, including dialogue and action. In the director's form (a production script), scene numbers and sometimes camera shots and moves are added.

self-promoting: A project is termed *self-promoting* when it involves a topic that is already a household word to theatergoing or television-viewing audiences. *See* **pre-sold.**

sequence: A group of connected scenes that move a story forward. A feature script usually has between seven and ten sequences.

series: Dramatic television programming that airs weekly on an ongoing basis. Also known as "episodic series."

setting: The place in which a drama occurs.

set up: An industry term for making a deal with a financier for a literary property.

seven-act structure: Format used by network television movies, allowing for commercial breaks after each act.

share: Nielsen ratings' term for the percentage of the viewing audience captured by a particular program on a particular night, as in "NBC's *Shadow of Obsession* garnered a 21 share."

shooting schedule: A schedule for shooting a film with the scenes grouped together and ordered with production considerations in mind.

shop: Verb used to describe the offering for sale of a dramatic property to the various buyers, as in "The minute we began to shop the treatment around town . . ."

short form: Term used in television to designate a series, as opposed to movies and miniseries (long form).

shot: The basic unit of a motion picture. A moving image of objects, persons, buildings, and/or landscapes.

show runner: Term designating a TV writer-producer with enough clout, talent, or experience to run an entire series.

sitcom (situational comedy): Usually refers to a television comedy in which humor is derived from situations or predicaments of the characters, rather than from incidents or gags.

slot: The time available for a TV program; for example, "CBS's 8 P.M. slot is weak because the ratings are dropping."

sound effects (SFX): Special effects that require some type of technical sound reproduction or manipulation.

soundstage: Enclosed studio environment where shooting can be done under optimum controlled conditions.

spec: Short for *speculation*, the industry term for work done without a contract, "on the come," and therefore solely owned by the writer. A spec script, if the buzz around it is hot enough, is often auctioned.

special effects (EFX, FX): Altering or manipulating images digitally, optically, or chemically to produce a scene that differs from what was originally shot.

stakes: What the protagonist risks if he fails.

standards and practices: Broadcasters' need to comply with the regulations set by the FCC regarding violence, explicit sex, language, etc.

story by: Credit indicating that a film is based on a story originating with the writer credited.

story editor: Writing supervisor on a series who is responsible for its consistency and style; or a development executive in charge of readers.

subplot, or **secondary action line:** A minor plot that serves the main plot by reflecting, or contrasting, with it.

subscriber cable television: Networks and cable-delivered stations—including Cinemax, Disney, HBO, and Showtime—that cost the consumer an extra fee.

suggested by: Indicates a story that is predominantly fiction, although somewhat related to a true event.

SUPER (superimpose): The effect of showing one image over another. Always typed in capital letters.

syndication: Free television outlets, apart from the major networks, formed by a special syndication of independent stations (known as a *syndicated network*) specifically for the purpose of airing or producing particular programming. An episodic series might be syndicated, as might a sports event or a movie.

synopsis: Matter-of-fact summation of a story's plotline; a shorter version of the screenplay. A synopsis is distinguished from a treatment primarily by its writing: whereas a treatment is written in a compelling, dramatic style, a synopsis tends to be bare-bones, dry, and analytical.

T & A: Short for "tits and ass," insider slang for shows or movies that exploit female flesh (for example, *Baywatch* on television, or the feature film *Coyote Ugly*).

tag: Descriptive characteristic used to make a character memorable, like those given to distinguish each of the Seven Dwarfs: Dopey, Sneezy, Grumpy, etc.

take: Industry term for what journalists call the "angle," as in, "What's the new take on the O. J. Simpson case that would justify doing another movie?"

tangible medium: Legal term describing a material object from which written work can be read or visually perceived either directly or with the aid of a machine or device, such as books, manuscripts, sheet music, film, videotape, computer discs, or microfilm.

teleplay: Alternate term for a screenplay written for television.

theme: What a story is *about*.

three-camera format: A script format used in television production.

through line: The movie's backbone, its main story line that continues through to the climax.

title page: Includes the title, centered in the upper third of the page, the writer's name, contact information (address, phone), and WGA registration number (optional).

titles: Term used for the names of individuals involved in a film and their respective functions when these appear at the beginning of a program. *See also* **credits**.

trackers: Production company assistants and industry scouts whose job it is to track down stories as they are happening, or to pursue novels they "get wind of" at early stages in the publishing process.

trades: Industry periodicals such as *The Hollywood Reporter*, *Weekly Variety*, screentalk.org, and *Daily Variety*.

TRANSITION: Indicates the end of a scene. Always typed in capital letters.

treatment: Summary of a story, integrating all its elements, detailing the plot, and providing a sense of who the characters are, including their motivations. A relatively brief and loosely narrative written pitch of a story intended for production as a film for theater or television broadcast. Written in user-friendly, dramatic, but straightforward and highly visual prose in the present tense, the treatment highlights in broad strokes your story's hook, primary characters, acts and action line, setting, point of view, and most dramatic scenes and turning points.

turnaround: When a studio fails to produce a literary property it has purchased outright within a stipulated amount of time, the project goes into turnaround—which means that it becomes free for resale, but that the new buyer must pay a turnaround fee, usually equivalent to the old purchase price, plus whatever moneys the original buyer has spent on development and the interest thereon, before he can proceed to make the movie.

twist: Unexpected turning point in the story when the characters move in dramatically unpredictable directions under the impulse of previous events and their character makeup.

TWO-SHOT: Camera shot of two people, usually from the waist up. Always typed in capital letters.

vehicle: Industry term for a script that offers a potential star his or her breakthrough role, as *Clueless* did for Alicia Silverstone.

viewpoint: Perspective through which a story is told, usually associated with that of the protagonist.

voice-over (V.O.): A character extension in which a character's voice is heard over a scene, as in narration; a tape-recorded voice; a voice heard over the phone. Always abbreviated in capital letters and enclosed in parentheses next to the name of the character whose voice is featured in the voice-over.

WGA: The Writers Guild of America.

work for hire: Term used in copyright law to describe the situation in which an employer hires a writer to write a property for which the employer will hold the copyright.

Writers Guild of America: Professional association of writers for television, motion pictures, and radio with offices in Los Angeles (WGAw) and New York (WGAe).

written by: Credit meaning that the writer or writers whose names appear wrote the entire original script, including the "story," from their own idea or concept.

ZOOM IN/ZOOM OUT: A quick transition from a long shot to a close shot or the reverse, usually achieved by manipulating the camera's lens. Always typed in capital letters.

Appendix

■ ■ ■

Striking Oil

An Interview with Ken Atchity and Chi-Li Wong, Atchity
Editorial/Entertainment International, Inc.
by
P. J. McIlvaine

What do Minnesota governor, bestselling author (*I Ain't Got Time to Bleed*), and former pro wrestler Jesse "The Body" Ventura, *Ripley's Believe-It-Or-Not!*®, and novelist/screenwriter John Scott Shepherd (who made an astounding six film sales and one TV series sale in little over a year) have in common?

If you guessed a body slam, sorry. They're all represented by the burgeoning AEI firm (www.aeionline.com), a self-described "one-stop full service management machine for screenwriters, novelists, and nonfiction writers."

AEI's recent features include "Life or Something Like It" (Angelina Jolie, Ed Burns, Stockard Channing; directed by Stephen Herek) and *Joe Somebody* (Tim Allen, Jim Belushi, Julie Bowen; directed by John Pasquin), as well as nearly twenty films for television including *Amityville: The Evil Escapes* and *Shadow of Obsession* for NBC.

Chairman and chief executive officer Ken Atchity is a veteran producer, teacher (Occidental College, UCLA's Writing Program, and Fulbright Professor), literary manager, entrepreneur, and author of the multi-editioned *A Writer's Time* and coauthor with AEI partner and president Chi-Li Wong of *Los Angeles Times* bestseller *Writing Treatments That Sell: How to Create and Market Your Story Ideas to the Motion Picture and TV Industry*. Ken is also chairman of www.thewriterslifeline.com, which helps writers with stories to find a way of telling them and writers who want to perfect their craft to find mentors and coaches.

The interview was done by www.screentalk.org, for which Atchity and Wong write a regular Q & A column on treatments.

PJ: First of all, let me say that I liked the book [*Writing Treatments That Sell*] a lot. It works for the beginner, the intermediate, and the more experienced screenwriter.

KJA: Thank you. That's what we were trying to accomplish.

PJ: How did the book evolve?

KJA: Chi-Li and I gave talks around the country on selling to television. The questions we were asked the most often were about treatments: How do you write one, and what do you do with one? So, basically, we answered the question so many times that we got tired, and looked around and realized there were no books on treatments. We also started talking to people in the industry and realized there wasn't a clear kind of agreement on what a treatment was. We find now that almost every studio uses our book as a kind of handbook—when somebody says, "We need to do a treatment," they hand them our book. It's very exciting that a lot of creative writing classes have also adopted it as the first book on treatments. We based it [the book] partly on a survey we did of development executives in television and film to find out what they consider to be a treatment.

PJ: What do you receive more of at AEI, completed scripts or treatments?

KJA: It's a mixture of both, but we get more treatments than we do scripts, partly because we want them. You know, it's much harder to sell a script unless the script is outstanding. But somebody can write a pretty good treatment when their goal is just to sell the story and get started, so that's when a treatment can be very, very useful. We can sell the treatment and have a great script writer attached to it.

PJ: This is the opposite of what people have told me—write the script and then try to sell that. You, on the other hand, seem to be saying, no, write the treatment and then try to set that up. Am I correct?

CLW: It's not that simple. It depends on what your goal is as a writer. If your goal is money and/or just getting a credit, then writing a treatment is a faster way to go and get you into the business—and get you some money. And it also gives the buyer maximum flexibility. Let's say you come up with a great idea for a story but you're not a known writer yet. Rather than invest a year in writing a script, write a treatment. We sell it, they attach an A-list writer to it, and you have a movie up there that's based on your story. But if your goal is to be known as a screenwriter, then yes, that advice is the right advice—which is to write a spec script first, and let us go out with it—because studios pay more money for spec scripts than almost anything else in the business, other than novels by famous novelists.

KJA: The two important reasons for writing a treatment are to sell and to diagnose your story. It's not always easy to write a treatment of the whole story before you've tried to write at least part of the script. Sometimes you start writing it and it flows along nicely until page twenty, when suddenly you pause. Generally that's a good time to stop and write a treatment of the whole thing because it will help you structure the rest of the screenplay. To me, it's a complete waste of time for a screenwriter to write a screenplay for six months, then we look at it and say, "This is never going to work because what's happening in Act 3 means I can't sell it to today's buyers." If the writer sent us twenty great pages of a screenplay with a treatment of the rest of it, and if we were excited by the writing and the treatment, then we could say, "This is great, but you need a new Act 3"—and the writer wouldn't mind because "it's only a treatment." He hasn't yet committed all that time to writing the screenplay, which to me is the most challenging kind of writing there is. A screenplay is highly precise, technical writing, and you've really got be very, very good by that time and know your story inside out. So many people drill right through a screenplay and turn it in, and it's just no good at all. So what good does that do when instead you should take the time to work out the story? In my earlier book, *A Writer's Time*, I talk about how you should never sit down to write until you know what you're going to write. And that's what a treatment lets you do. It lets you know what the story is, and you just put it down in broad beats, as though you're writing a letter to a close friend and just telling her what happened to you the other day. That letter's free form is similar to that of a treatment—anything goes. The point is to get the story across, and do whatever you have to do to get the story across. A good joke teller can tell a fully elaborated ten-minute version of a joke if he's got the audience's attention, or he can tell a two-minute version if he has to. The same beats are there to make the joke work either way.

PJ: Maybe this is a misconception, but a lot of my screenwriting friends would really love to set up treatments. That's their goal. They go to websites where you can pitch for free, send in a log line or a synopsis, and want somebody to pay them to write the script.

CLW: Yes, that is a misconception. Unless you're already an established screenwriter who has sold projects, it's rare. I'm not saying it never happens, but it's extremely rare that someone would buy a treatment and ask a writer to write it without having some kind of track record.

PJ: What do you think are the most common mistakes screen-writers will make in writing a treatment?

KJA: Somebody that should know better sent me a thirty-four-page treatment yesterday. I said, "I'm not even going to read that—you've got to be joking. After we've been doing this for four years! Send it back to me at eight to twelve pages at the most." The most common mistake is to put everything in the treatment, try to get everything into it when the truth is you don't need to put everything into it—just put enough. It's a selling tool. But also the purpose of it is to put in the skeleton of the story so that the bones show clearly, so you can see what the story structure is. You don't need to go into so much detail; it's the flavor of the story that's important. The mistake people make is trying to make it into a synopsis, which is something that tries to cover every detail in the story.

CLW: They write them too long, put too much dialogue in, are not concise, that kind of thing, when they don't realize that it needs to be very short and the action and the characters need to be presented very quickly. That's probably the biggest mistake when writers are first starting, but that's okay, because writing a treatment is like making chicken soup, you have to have that big huge pot of water and throw everything in it and then just reduce it down. So start that way and teach yourself.

PJ: Can a treatment be less than eight to twelve pages, or is that pretty much the standard?

KJA: We say in parts of the book that the ideal thing is to have a battery of treatments of different sizes starting with the longest one, which might be at the most twenty pages, and then a shorter one that might be five to eight pages, and then an even shorter one that might be two or three pages, and then, ideally, a one-pager, and then one that's a paragraph, and then finally you get down to the log line, which is the shortest treatment of all and just gives you, for example, *"Under Siege* is *Die Hard* on a boat."

PJ: It sounds like a Chinese menu.

KJA: The writers should do it backwards, because it's easier for writers to write long than short. Mark Twain said, "If I had more time I would have written a shorter letter." Writers tend to write long, but the discipline is to keep shortening it, and sometimes you have to write the long one first to know what you have to cut out.

PJ: In my own work, I feel that since writing a treatment is almost as hard as writing the script itself, why not just write the script first and the treatment will come later?

KJA: The second purpose of a treatment is diagnostic. If you write a treatment first it's easier to spot the flaws in the story structure. When you do it that way, you're less invested in what's in the treatment than you are with the script. I know it sounds like a lot of hard work to write the treatment as compared to the script, but the truth is, I think once you have a version of your script, then you generally end up, realistically, having to do five or six versions of the script before it's really presentable. So you count all of that time and before you know it the script has taken you six or nine months or a year at least to write. At least with a treatment, if you really got serious about putting down your story beats, you could actually do that in a couple of days. Chi-Li is really the best one in the company at writing treatments and helping writers write treatments. Her treatments are very, very strong.

CLW: I think that every writer has her own process, so if that's what works for you or another writer, then that's the way you should do it. Some writers need to first have everything in there, and know their characters and what they're saying and how they're reacting before they can go back and figure out how to tell the story in treatment form—although I do know a lot of writers, both novelists and screenwriters, who can't write a treatment. That's it. It's just something they cannot do. I suppose it's a different kind of writing. I don't know. I've done it for so long. I started in a business where I was immediately asked for treatments of books, so I learned to write them short and quick right off the bat.

PJ: What do you think of Internet websites cropping up like mushrooms where writers can pitch an idea or a treatment? At some of these websites, they don't even require that the idea be registered [with the Writers Guild].

CLW: If I knew that our clients were putting up stuff on the Internet without protecting it, I'd be very upset with them. It's so easy to have things go off in different directions that way. I think it's very, very alarming for writers. And I doubt that professional writers—those who are actually making sales—make this mistake. They know better.

PJ: So newer writers should be more careful, which is hard when it seems like everyone from Canada to Peoria is trying to get a leg up. It's very enticing when you see websites offering access, whether it be free or fee-based.

KJA: I've never seen much evidence of those websites really working. I mean, if a major studio like Disney or Warner Brothers was saying put your treatment up on our website and we'll look at it, and you have to sign a release, maybe I'd believe it. But I've never seen anything other than what appears to be a vanity press situation. We all get e-mails every day saying put your short stories, poetry, and screenplays up on our website—but what does that invitation have to do directly with the business of buying and selling stories? It's only a few people in town who know how to sell, and only a few people in town who have the money to buy, so they're the only ones you want to be dealing with as far as I'm concerned. I guess the answer depends on exactly what the situation is on the particular website. I'd be very, very cautious.

PJ: I see this all the time on my screenwriting boards. Someone will post that they have an idea that will make a lot of money and if you help me write it, we'll split the profits fifty-fifty. I mean, you can have an idea, but that doesn't mean you have a marketable idea or that it will even make a good script.

KJA: Yes, and one of the problems is that when people come to us wanting us to find a writer to work on their idea—a writer who will do it on spec—it doesn't make sense. The good writers don't have to do it on spec. We refer such inquiries to thewriterslifeline.com, where we have writer clients who are very promising and working on their own projects. We put these writers together with people who need somebody to write for them and are prepared to pay for it. Our writers would otherwise be working on something of their own, so they need to be paid one way or the other. I have a rule of thumb about collaboration—you should collaborate only with someone who's better than you, never someone who's worse than you or who's at the same level, because you can't profit from that. It's called "value added." Nobody's adding value to the situation if you get somebody who's at your own level.

PJ: Is it easier to sell a treatment to television or to a studio or production company, or does it take a different type of treatment?

CLW: In general TV uses treatments as a way of buying much more often than the feature world does. Many, many shows and movies start from a treatment. In effect, the way a series starts—we went into preproduction today on client John Scott Shepherd's series *Sherman's March*, that started with him writing a bible which was based on what he read in our book [chapter 4: Treatments for Television Series], which he'd never done before. He began with the short treatment, then a bible. Television is used to operating this way because the experienced execs can then guide the project in more successful directions. Let's say they don't like the mix of the characters, they prefer a diversified group of characters. A treatment will tell them that easily, before you've invested yourself in creating characters in a script. Feature film producers tend to buy treatments when they're extremely high concept and/or when they're from well-known writers they've already dealt with. But it's very hard for an unknown writer to sell a treatment to feature films; they like to deal with people they know. An exception—and Hollywood is filled with "exceptions" to every rule—is if you've got a truly great story. We can then take your treatment and attach a writer to it who's already a known entity. We get calls every day from attorneys and managers and agents who say they have clients looking for stories—Columbia owes them a deal, Disney owes them a deal—do you have any stories that we can attach one of our writers to?

PJ: But you'd think their writers would have their own ideas.

KJA: Just because you're a well-known writer in demand doesn't mean you always have ideas. A lot of writers are good in terms of writing structure and dialogue, but they don't always have great ideas. About a third of the scripts we see are very well written and completely unsalable because of the concept.

PJ: I'm an unofficial, unpaid reader for an entertainment company, which has given me a good sense of what's selling in the industry right now, and I have to admit, the one thing that most surprised me is the quality of the scripts. Most of them are dreadful.

CLW: We find the same thing. I don't know what that means about the industry, or what it even means about writers today. One of the things I find interesting is that I don't think people read much anymore. People trying to write a script have not bothered reading professional scripts. I also don't think people have literary backgrounds or foundations as they had in the past, and it really shows. One of the things I think is brilliant about Ken in development—and which makes me feel fortunate to be his partner—is his literary background and his knowledge foundation in mythology. That's why the scripts we develop end up having so much flesh on the bone, because Ken has all that background. When you meet people who don't know any of that stuff, who don't know the basics, or haven't read basic literature, you're confused how they can write at all. But it's the same thing in the publishing world.

Nobody reads, and it's tough to sell literary projects to publishers for that reason. We have the same problem in this industry. People don't read, and there's so little time to get someone's attention. That's why writers shouldn't look at a treatment as something that's going to deter the sale of their script. If you can blow somebody away in three great pages, a buyer's going to read that script—and he's going to take on that script. The business has changed today because we all move almost faster than the eye can see.

PJ: Between cable, television, movies . . .

CLW: Yes. And that's why the treatment is so valuable and why it's valuable to learn the treatment process and get very good at it.

PJ: Given the current state of the industry, is it easier to break into television and still a little bit harder to break into features without an agent?

CLW: It's difficult to break into either without an agent or manager. Period. Young writers, new writers—they're going to have difficulty no matter what, so they just have to be tenacious and figure out a way to get to people. They should research who's taking on new writers.

PJ: Do you think newer writers tend to have unrealistic expectations, shooting for the top agencies rather than a midsize or a boutique agency?

CLW: I don't know if it's unrealistic, because I always say you should set your sights high and then work your way down if you have to. So I would say sure, go to the big agencies first, why not? But where new writers become unrealistic is when they want to be paid to write a script. I went to a pitch festival that was sponsored by *Fade In:* magazine—and some very wonderful agencies and production companies show up for this; it's a great pitch festival—and actually had someone argue with me about the fact that he had pitched something to me and I had asked, "Is this written?" I don't know what made me ask the question, something must have told me, and he replied, "Oh no, I expect to be paid to write this." I was trying to explain to him, "You're going to have to write it first, and I'd love to see it because it's a great idea," and this guy got really annoyed with me. I mean, angry, telling me off. Geez, get a life! Find out how people actually break in!

PJ: Because you weren't telling him what he wanted to hear.

CLW: Yes. And he was saying, "I should be paid, I'm a writer," and I was saying, "But it doesn't work this way." The unfortunate reality is that you have to be entrepreneurial or you have to have another job, a day job, as a writer. The clients we love to work with are the ones who keep plugging away at improving their writing no matter how much financial hardship they have to endure until they break through.

PJ: One problem is that it takes the average screenwriter a couple of months to write something; they're working on something that was hot six months ago, and by the time they turn in the draft, it's not so hot.

CLW: Exactly. We've had writers who have developed something and we got it at the right time and said, "Okay, we know we can sell this," but then the writer couldn't finish it in time and we lost the window. We've had that happen to us a couple of times, and it's unfortunate. But you can't make writers hurry up and come out with a good product. They have to do it in their own time, and sometimes if we miss the window, we miss it. So we just wait. And certain things never change. They always want romantic comedies, even though they're hard to sell, but if you can find a unique concept for a romantic comedy and write it, you'll always sell it. Or a unique angle in an old story. If you can find a new hook for anything that was a winner; for instance, when *Dangerous Liaisons* came out, they made *10 Things I Hate about You*, *The Taming of the Shrew*. We ended up with three or four romantic comedies over a two-year period. I thought that was really smart. The idea is to make anything old new again and you can sell it.

PJ: Concerning a newbie breaking in, would it be easier to slant their writing toward television rather than features? Or would you be fearful of them getting pegged in one particular genre? Or can you be both?

CLW: It all depends on who your manager is, frankly. We like to develop our writers in every area, and some are novelists as well as screenwriters and TV writers. And that all depends on the vision of your coaches. Agents tend to want to pigeonhole writers because many of the agencies themselves are organized as pigeonholes, with each agent specializing. But it's up to the writer to avoid that. Some writers are very happy working in only one medium and other writers want to write in many different media, so there isn't a simple answer—it's really a matter of your individual character and vision about yourself and your career.

PJ: For someone starting out, it's hard to get a manager or an agent to look at your work.

KJA: It's very true, but because managers are generally more entrepreneurial by nature—the very idea of "management" evolved to fill a niche in the industry that was more or less becoming a vacuum—they tend to be more open. I look at my writers as creating assets—for themselves and for us. Obviously, if you're creating diversified assets, you have a bigger chance to succeed. It's like the oil business. If you don't drill new holes, you don't advance. If you drill fourteen holes, you have a much better chance of striking oil than if you just drill one or two. Literary properties are that way both generally and particularly. The more an individual writer can write in different media, the better chance she's going to have financial freedom—and freedom to me is the key to creativity.

PJ: Do you think writing can be taught or is it an innate talent? For example, anyone could pick up your book—maybe somebody who doesn't have any writing talent, but maybe has an idea—and it's possible that they could write a decent treatment.

KJA: I think storytellers are born, not made. Talent is something you're almost born to, that you nurture from an early age. But I think the difference is craft and skills. Every writer who's really great has some degree of talent. The industry gets so many scripts that show promise, but no one has the time to develop them anymore—which is why we started thewriterslifeline.com, as an extension of my former teaching career, so we could develop promising talent. Now, after our first years in the management business, everyone refers writers to us—studios, publishers, agencies, and production companies—because they don't have the time to develop a writer who has plenty of potential but just isn't there yet. Thewriterslifeline.com is focused on teaching the craft and the skill and reminding people of the main important points about storytelling. But you have to be born a storyteller. It's like a joke. Some people can tell a joke, some people can't— and if you can tell a joke, that's a different thing from somebody who tells a joke and nobody laughs because his timing's so bad.

PJ: In my own writing, I've discovered that it's useful to write the treatment first rather than the script to find out if your idea is already out there. You've written a fine treatment and then somebody tells you that your great idea is already being developed by Dreamworks. I've had that happen to me.

KJA: And you saved all that time! Imagine how you'd feel if you spend six months on it dying to get it right, and you turn it in and somebody tells you within ten minutes, "I'm sorry, we can't read it, there are already three movies like this in development." You've wasted all that time. So you see, the marketing value of a treatment is to let you know what the market is much sooner, which is why we urge people we think are talented to send us short e-mails just saying, "Here are some things I'm thinking of writing, which ones do you like?"—and we can instantly pick out the ones that are more commercial. Don't waste your time on ideas 4, 5, and 6; ideas 2 and 3 are great, these could be commercial. Then you're motivated to write a longer treatment and we can work out the story details with you.

PJ: One aspect a lot of screenwriters tend to forget is that when we write our treatment or script, we don't think of the marketing end of it or the selling part of it.

CLW: I have a writer who's become very good at writing treatments, though when we first started, it drove him crazy when I'd tell him I want a three-page treatment, I want a one-pager, I want a teaser—I want a little bit of everything because all my buyers are different. Some buyers prefer just a teaser, a log line, just a paragraph, and they may say, yup, I like that, and take it into their meetings—it kind of depends on how they work. They have their meetings, let's say every Monday, and they'll do a teaser or a one-page pitch of scripts that they're going to consider for a read or a purchase. This is where we use the treatment a lot. These executives aren't actually going to bring in the script for everybody to read but they want everybody to see what it contains and why they like it, why they should be buying.

PJ: Now let's say a writer pitches you an idea or a treatment that you like, and perhaps you don't like the treatment they hand in, then what would you do? You like the concept, but you don't like the writer's take on it.

CLW: I'd develop it with them just like I do everything else. As a matter of fact, I just did that with a young woman. Brandy [the singer-actress] was looking for a project for herself. The writer had a script and I asked her to change it to accommodate a twenty-year-old rather than this older ballerina, the character she had written. I wanted to make the character younger and in college. With the treatment form, I can tell her you need more of this, or less of that, or have your character do this or have her do that. Because this writer already has a script that exists—even though it's not the same script and she's a new writer—I might be able to sell her project based on the revised treatment. Since it's a project she's already working on, a buyer might say, "Okay, I like the way the treatment reads, I like the way you write, now write the new script for Brandy"—that could happen. That's why I told the writer to put the time in and do it. They'll see that you can change the treatment for them, and if they like the way your original script reads, they may say go ahead and readapt it for Brandy. This is an example of the ways we try to get people to read treatments.

PJ: Now what if you have a writer whose writing you like but just hasn't come up with a concept that you think can sell or is marketable?

CLW: We might give them ideas that are running through our heads, or ideas based on something we read that might be commercial, and might be more to their taste. We have matched up novelists and screenwriters, and people who have good concepts but aren't great writers. We're sort of an odd company in that way; we match up a lot of writers with different kinds of writers, so if a writer has a certain weakness, maybe we can match him up and still get the project sold. So everybody's happy and everybody gets involved. But it's a lot of work, too, because you really have to know your writers and who's going to do what, figure out all the credits—it can get a little crazy.

PJ: But you would advise a writer breaking in to write the script first rather than try to set up the treatment.

CLW: I would never say do this or do that because anything can happen. If you can get to a buyer and get them to read a treatment and it blows them away, and you have a spec script—you have to have some kind of script written, let's put it that way—I say go for it. The whole idea is that buyers want to know if you can write. So if you have a really good treatment and a really good spec script, you could get hired to write the script based on that treatment. Why not? Stranger things have happened in this town. So I would say to a writer it's probably better if you write the script. It's not impossible.

PJ: It's not impossible, but not probable.

CLW: Nothing's impossible, I've learned that. I tell people all the time, even if it's something I don't like or I turn it down, don't ever give up. Go somewhere else, never stop trying, you have to get to that "yes." My taste is only one aspect; with treatments, I have a certain style I like and maybe somebody else likes another style. I've heard people say that there shouldn't be any dialogue in treatments. Well, I guess that's a rule for some people. But because dialogue is action, you can sometimes give information fast in a piece of dialogue. Sometimes it fits in a treatment.

PJ: I think one concern that screenwriters have in treatments is that they don't want to give too much information, they want the producer or the manager or the agent to read the entire script, so they try to leave it a little bit tantalizing at the end to make them want to read more.

CLW: The idea of the treatment is to get the story across, so they're doing themselves a disservice if they don't prove that they can tell the story fully. A teaser is another thing. When someone sends me a query and it just has a paragraph or two about a script, that to me is a teaser—it's not a synopsis and it's not a treatment. So I might call back and say you've intrigued me, send me the synopsis and the script, and I often hear that they don't want me to read the shorter form because they're afraid I'm not going to read the script. That's not the case at all. The reason we ask for a treatment is to save time, to make sure we don't have projects that are similar. This is also why we require a release. You can register treatments and synopses—and don't send it to me until it's registered. We used to read submissions without releases, but now, because we're selling so much product, we take our lawyers' advice and require releases, just as a safety net. Also, if I read the treatment, I usually know in the first act whether I like the writer. I can then save more time by calling that person up and saying, "Look, I read the first act, I think you're a really good writer—good dialogue, everything is there for me, the treatment tells me the whole story, come in and talk to me about developing this." I can get through more scripts that way.

PJ: Because based on your years of experience, you've developed your sense of what you like so you can do that.

CLW: I guess that's true. I can tell pretty quickly if I like something.

PJ: AEI seems to be very accessible to new writers.

CLW: Definitely. We love new writers—that's really what we're known for. We're known as developers. If something isn't even quite there, or it's 99 percent there but the buyers want to change something, they'll probably take the chance on our property because they know we're going to guide the writer through the development process they require. That's because we're producers, not just managers; Ken and I were producing before we went into the management business. Management just gave us a wider reach. We will go in and say, okay, tell us what you want and we can redevelop it and sell it. Because there's so little development money out there now, few do this anymore, so we're unique in this way. For that reason we really like new writers. They tend to have the excitement, enthusiasm, and willingness to develop and work on their stories. A lot of writers who achieve success too fast are unwilling to go through that process. They think everything they write, every word, is golden, and they want it sold, or they want it sold and then, "Pay me to rewrite it." If you're in that place in your head, we don't want you as a client. If you're willing to do anything you need to do to succeed—no matter how long it takes—give us a call when you've got a great treatment ready!

Sources and
Recommended Reading

. . .

Amer, Alan A. *Writing the Screenplay: TV and Film*. 2d ed. Belmont, Calif.: Waveland Press, 2002.

Atchity, Kenneth. *A Writer's Time*. 2d ed. New York: W. W. Norton, 1995. Includes, in addition to step-by-step instructions on creating stories, chapters covering "Breaking into Show Business," "Myth and Story," and "Pitching to the Movies."

Blum, Richard A. *Television Writing from Concept to Contract*. New York: Hastings House, 1980. Contains an interesting 19-page chapter on "Developing a Story or Treatment."

Brenner, Alfred. *The T.V. Scriptwriter's Handbook: Dramatic Writing for Television and Film*. Los Angeles: Silman James Press, 1992. Leads the reader through the step-by-step process of creating a script for television.

Cooper, Dona. *Writing Great Screenplays for Film and TV*. 2d ed. New York: Arco Publishers, 1997. Contains information regarding typical structure of a script for television.

Crawford, Tad, and Tony Lyons. *The Writer's Legal Guide*. New York: Allworth Press, 1997. Tells writers what to do to protect their literary properties. Copyright law is carefully and cogently explained, as are contractual details, income tax requirements and exemptions, estate planning, and other topics.

Field, Syd. *Selling a Screenplay*. New York: Delacorte Press, 1989. How to pitch, sell, and market your screenplay.

———. *Screenplay: The Foundations of Screenwriting*. Exp. ed. New York: Delacorte Press, 1982. The foundations of screenwriting: a step-by-step guide from concept through typed script.

Gianakos, Larry James. *Television Drama Series Programming: A Comprehensive Chronicle*. Vols. 1947–59, 1959–75, 1975–80, 1980–82,

1982–84. Metuchen, N.J.: Scarecrow Press. Featured programming arranged in chronological sequence with a list of series regulars and episodes and overview of the years indicated.

Goldberg, Lee. *Unsold Television Plots, 1955 through 1988.* Jefferson, N.C.: McFarland, 1990. Flopped pilots for prime-time network TV with emphasis on the concepts, the continuing characters, and the stars.

Goldman, William. *Adventures in the Screen Trade.* New York: Warner, 1984; paperback, 1989. A major screenwriter's inspiring look at the typical turbulence and irrationality of the most challenging of all industries, beginning with the now-legendary observation, "No one knows anything."

———. *Which Lie Did I Tell? More Adventures in the Screen Trade.* New York: Vintage Books, 2001. *Which Lie* follows the structure of the original. Both Goldman books have three parts: stories about his movies, a deconstruction of Hollywood (here the focus is on great movie scenes), and a workshop for screenwriters.

Hauge, Michael. *Writing Screenplays That Sell.* New York: Harper Perennial, 1991. Practical guide for writing and selling to movies and TV, from story concept to development deal.

Hollywood Agents and Managers Directory. Santa Monica, Calif.: An insider's industry listing of talent and literary agencies (indexed by type) published tri-annually: "1,300 agents and their titles, addresses, phone numbers, and faxes." To order a copy, call 1(800) 815-0503 or (310) 315-4815.

Hollywood Creative Directory. Santa Monica, Calif.: The tri-annually published insider's industry listing of producers and production companies, with credits, addresses, phone numbers, and fax numbers for the major creative personnel in each company (by title). To order a copy, e-mail them at hcd@hollyvision.com, or call 1(800) 815-0503 or (310) 315-4815.

McKee, Robert. *Story: Substance, Structure, Style and the Principles of Screenwriting.* New York: HarperCollins, 1997. McKee puts into book form what he has been teaching screenwriters for years on story structure; his seminar is considered by many to be a prerequisite to the film biz.

Noble, June and William. *Steal This Plot: A Writer's Guide to Story, Structure, and Plagiarism.* Middlebury, Vt.: Paul S. Eriksson Publishers, 1985.

Obst, Lynda. *Hello, He Lied, and Other Truths from the Hollywood Trenches.* Boston: Little, Brown and Company, 1996. An insider's overview of the daily ups and downs of feature film producers.

Resnik, Gail, and Scott Trost. *All You Need to Know about the Movie and TV Business.* New York: Fireside, 1996. Leads the reader topic by topic through job descriptions, kinds of deals, how to protect and sell creative work, the nuts and bolts of a boilerplate contract, and an explanation of profit participation.

Russin, Robert U., and William Missouri Downs. *Screenplay: Writing the Picture*. Belmont, Calif.: Wadsworth Publishing Co., 1998. Down-to-earth, practical guide to the craft of screenwriting intended to help writers choose, develop, and perfect their stories while avoiding common mistakes, with practical examples and exercises designed to avoid a formulaic approach.

Safir, William, and Leonard Safir. *Good Advice on Writing*. New York: Random House Value Publishing, 1993.

Seger, Linda. *Making a Good Script Great*. Hollywood, Calif.: Samuel French Trade, 1987. An entertainment industry inside view by a noted script consultant.

———. *The Art of Adaptation*. New York: Henry Holt, 1992. A handbook for transforming factual or fictional material into film.

———. *From Script to Screen*. New York: Henry Holt, 1994. Complete with exclusive interviews with some of Hollywood's best-known artists, this book offers rare insight into the process of making a feature film.

Studio Directory, Pacific Coast. Published semiannually on January 1 and July 1. Each issue consists of a wall chart and index and a supplement with more than 6,000 companies pertaining to the motion picture and television industries. See www.studio-directory.com.

Terrace, Vincent. *The Complete Encyclopedia of Television Programs: 1947–1979*. 2 vols. New York: Barnes, 1979. Complete information on 3,500 network and syndicated programs, story lines, cast lists, credits, and running dates and times.

———. *Fifty Years of Television: A Guide to Series and Pilots: 1937–1988*. New York: Cornwall Books, 1991. Network, syndicated, and cable programming story lines, dates, running times, and extensive cast listing.

Vogler, Christopher. *The Writer's Journey: Mythic Structure for Writers*. 2d ed. Studio City, Calif.: Michael Wiese Productions. *The Writer's Journey* sets forth archetypes common in what Vogler calls "the hero's journey," the mythic structure that he claims all stories follow. In the book's first section, he lists the typological characters who appear in stories. In the second, he discusses the stages of the journey through which the hero generally passes. The final, supplementary portion of the book explains in detail how films like *Titanic* and *The Full Monty* follow the patterns he has outlined.

Whitcomb, Cynthia. *Selling Your Screenplay*. New York: Crown, 1988. An outstanding, though now dated, inspirational guide to selling to television by a successful and respected movie-for-television writer.

Writers Guild of America West. *Written By* is the official publication of the WGAw—the premiere magazine written by and for TV and film writers. *Written By* provides a unique look into the art, craft, and business of writing in Hollywood. For information about subscriptions, visit thewriterslifeline.com/resources.

The authors welcome inquiries, correspondence, and registered "perfected" treatments:

> Atchity Editorial/Entertainment International, Inc.
> Motion Picture Production & Literary Management
> 9601 Wilshire Blvd., Box 1202
> Beverly Hills, CA 90210
> (323) 932-0407
> e-mail: jp@aeionline.com
> website: www.aeionline.com

For those who seek mentoring for their screen career or "perfecting" for their treatments:

> The Writers' Lifeline, Inc.
> 501 South Fairfax Ave.
> Los Angeles, CA 90036
> (323) 932-0905
> e-mail: amc@thewriterslifeline.com
> website: www.thewriterslifeline.com
> or subscribe free to our daily "inspiration-information newsletter"
> inspire@thewriterslifeline.com

Index

. . .

About the Authors

Kenneth Atchity, chairman of Atchity Editorial/Entertainment International, Inc. (AEI), a motion picture production and literary management company, and of The Writers' Lifeline, Inc., a company specializing in coaching writers, is the author of a dozen books, including *A Writer's Time: A Guide to the Creative Process, from Vision through Revision* and *The Mercury Transition: Career Change Empowerment through Entrepreneurship.* After teaching comparative literature and creative writing at Occidental College and UCLA's Writers Program from 1970 to 1987, and serving as Fulbright Professor of American Literature at the University of Bologna, he left the academic world to develop, publish, and produce literary properties. Atchity has produced films for television, video, and theater, including *Joe Somebody, Life or Something Like It, Amityville: The Evil Escapes, Champagne for Two, Falling Over Backwards,* and *Shadow of Obsession.*

Chi-Li Wong, after serving as associate administrator of the Fort Lauderdale Film Festival, began her television career as a reader and story analyst and worked her way up to president and partner of AEI. As head of AEI's television and film acquisitions, development, and production she has edited, rewritten, and created treatments that have led to dozens of development deals; and she has served as co-producer of NBC's *Shadow of Obsession,* executive producer of Fox 2000/New Regency's *Joe Somebody,* and producer of New Regency's *Life or Something Like It.*